Understanding Local Area Networks

Written by: Dr. Stan Schatt

HOWARD W. SAMS & COMPANY

A Division of Macmillan, Inc.

4300 West 62nd Street

Indianapolis, Indiana 46268 USA

©1987 by Howard W. Sams & Company
A Division of Macmillan Inc.

This book is dedicated to Jane, who understands why all of my books are dedicated to her.

FIRST EDITION
SECOND PRINTING — 1988

International Standard Book Number: 0-672-27063-3
Library of Congress Catalog Card Number: 87-62168

Acquisitions Editor: Greg Michael
Manuscript Editor: Don MacLaren
Illustrator: Wm. D. Basham
Cover Art: Diebold Glascock Advertising Inc.
Cover Photography: Castle Productions, Inc.
Components Courtesy of: Applied Instruments, Inc., and Belden Electronic Wire and Cable
Compositor: Shepard Poorman Communications Corp.

Printed in the United States of America

Table of Contents

Preface

Since the birth of the IBM PC, the microcomputer has become a common sight. Until recently we lacked the technology to connect these units so that companies could share expensive resources and ensure data integrity. The release of MS-DOS 3.1 with its network features and the development of faster microprocessors, such as the Intel 80286 and 80386, to serve as the workhorses of network file servers means that we now have the necessary software and hardware to implement cost effective, efficient local area networks (LANs). We use companies in our examples for convenience. The use of LANs is certainly not limited to them, and such organizations as universities and hospitals are increasingly LAN-filled.

In order to understand the benefits of a local area network and what greater connectivity can mean for a company, we need to understand the basic building blocks of a LAN. The first three chapters of this book cover the hardware and software fundamentals of a LAN and the requirements for a network to communicate with other networks and with mainframe computers and minicomputers. This micro-mainframe connection is increasingly important since we now have the software to transfer mainframe data to a LAN and to manipulate this data within the programs. Because the telecommunications industry now has the ability to transmit voice and data simultaneously, we will examine how some companies are using their telephone system as LANs.

The next five chapters apply this network theory to major LANs from IBM, Novell, 3Com, AT&T, and Corvus, as well as to other networks and pseudo-networks offered by smaller vendors. In many cases, we have provided sample screens and detailed descriptions of routine network procedures required by these LANS in order to give you a feeling for differences among various network software and hardware. Some vendors now offer multiuser systems that combine the advantages of inexpensive terminal workstations with the ability to use the great quantity of DOS Version 3.1 network software. We will examine how this approach works and why it might be a viable solution for many small companies. Finally, since a network is only as effective as its software and network management, the final two chapters cover these critical areas and offer suggestions for the development of a request for proposal and the implementation of a local area network.

This book is arranged somewhat like a textbook with quizzes following each chapter. Each chapter builds on the previous chapter's information. Try to master a chapter before moving on. If you wish to explore the data communications topics in even more depth, a companion book in this series titled *Understanding Data Communications* should prove helpful. We hope this book will help you understand why local area networks are destined to become an important part of our lives. We hope it will also prove valuable if you are considering the purchase of a local area network.

S.S.

Acknowledgments

I wish to acknowledge the technical expertise and generous help of Marc Covitt of Hewlett-Packard; Steven Fox, David Gerrero, and Randy Sprinkle of AT&T; Orval Luckey of IBM; and Bob Schulte of 3Com. I also want to acknowledge the support of Dean Ramalcant Gayakwad and Learning Resource Director Linda McKinney of the DeVry Institute of Technology.

Trademark Acknowledgments

All terms mentioned in this book that are known to be trademarks or service marks are listed below. In addition, terms suspected of being trademarks or service marks have been appropriately capitalized. Howard W. Sams & Co. cannot attest to the accuracy of this information. Use of a term in this book should not be regarded as affecting the validity of any trademark or service mark.

COMPAQ is a registered trademark of COMPAQ Computer Corporation.
dBASE III and dBASE Plus are registered tradmarks of Ashton-Tate.
Ethernet is a registered trademark of the Xerox Corporation.
IBM is a registered trademark and IBM PC AT, PC XT, and PC jr. are
    trademarks of International Business Machines Corporation.
Intel is a registered trademark of the Intel Corporation.
IRMA is a registered trademark of Digital Communications Associates, Inc.
KnowledgeMan is a trademark of Micro Data Base Systems, Inc.
LANLink is a trademark of The Software Link.
LOTUS 1-2-3 is a trademark of the Lotus Development Corporation.
Microsoft is a registered trademark and WORD and Multiplan are
    trademarks of the Microsoft Corporation.
Multimate is a trademark of Multimate International Corporation.
Novell and NetWare are registered trademarks of Novell, Inc.
Omninet and Omnishare are trademarks of Corvus Systems, Inc.
PROLOGIC is a trademark of PROLOGIC Management Systems, Inc.
StarHub, StarHub 8, StarHub 16, TurboStar, and StarPort are trademarks
    of AST Research.
TYMNET is a trademark of Tymshare, Inc.
UNIX is a registered trademark of AT&T laboratories.
WordPerfect is a registered trademark of WordPerfect Corporation.

An Overview of the IBM PC and Local Area Networks

ABOUT THIS BOOK

This book is intended to explain how local area networks and their various hardware and software components work. It will provide you with an understanding of the theory behind the various kinds of network architecture (the different forms networks take) and data transmission methods (how information is sent through a network). It will also provide you with an understanding of the major local area networks on the market and the degree of compatibility among these networks. Finally, the book should help a potential network user determine whether a local area network is a viable solution for his or her particular office.

Because local area networks do not exist in a vacuum, we will examine the ways that they communicate with mainframe computers. We will also look at some of the innovative approaches to integrating voice and data over a network. And we will consider several of the major issues facing local area network users today, including network security, compatibility between network software and already existing application software written under DOS, and bridges between local area networks.

ABOUT THIS CHAPTER

Before studying the theory behind contemporary local area networks, it is important to understand the personal computer that serves as a network workstation. We will see how an IBM Personal Computer processes information. If you are already familiar with this subject, you may wish to skip to the second half of the chapter, where we review the history of local area networks and observe a typical company's use of network technology to handle a wide range of office functions.

THE IBM PERSONAL COMPUTER: A TUTORIAL

Because so many businesses have selected IBM Personal computers (PCs) or computers designed to run IBM PC programs (compatibles), these machines have become the building blocks of local area networks. We will see how dozens and in some cases hundreds of these computers can be linked together by network software, hardware, and cabling so that information and resources such as printers can be shared by a number of users. Since each network user has a microcomputer, often an IBM PC or compatible, we need to understand how information is processed by a microcomputer such as the IBM PC. *Figure 1-1* shows an AT&T PC 6300, a popular IBM compatible.

**Figure 1-1.
An AT&T 6300 PC
Offers IBM PC
Compatibility** *(Courtesy
of AT&T)*

Bits and Bytes

Computers are capable of keeping track of whether a wire has current flowing through it (1) or no current flowing through it (0). We refer to each of these binary digits of information as a "bit." The American Standard Code for Information Interchange (abbreviated ASCII) specifies that each character of the alphabet requires 7 bits of information with an eighth, *parity*, bit as insurance that the information has not been garbled. To the IBM PC, the binary combination of 10000010 represents the letter "A." This 8-bit unit of information is known as a "byte."

The Central Processing Unit

The IBM PC contains an Intel 8088 microprocessor, a microcomputer chip that serves as the central processing unit (CPU) or "brains" of the computer. It is capable of processing 16 bits (2 bytes) of information at a time. The CPU has a clock speed of 4.77 Megahertz (MHz). This means that the microprocessor produces 4.77 million pulses each second. It schedules its work based on these pulses. Some microprocessors have faster clock speeds and thus can perform tasks faster. The IBM AT

(Advanced Technology), for example, uses an Intel 80286 microprocessor and has a clock speed of 8.0 MHz. The Compaq 386 Computer uses an Intel 80386 microprocessor that is capable of a clock speed of 16 MHz. Since a local area network generally will use its fastest, most powerful computer to service network workstations, clock speed becomes a significant factor in a local area network's overall efficiency.

In addition to performing routine mathematical operations, the CPU also processes information that comes to it from a variety of sources, including the keyboard. It needs a workspace area in which to store some of its calculations temporarily; this need for temporary workspace is satisfied by using some of the computer's memory.

RAM and ROM

Two types of memory are associated with the IBM PC and compatibles—random-access memory (RAM) and read-only memory (ROM). ROM is permanent; it retains information even when the computer is turned off. The IBM PC stores its most critical programs in ROM, including a program that diagnoses the computer when it is turned on to ensure that all components are working properly. It also stores a program in ROM that provides the computer with enough knowledge to load information from a disk. Finally, the IBM PC keeps its BASIC language in ROM so that when the machine is turned on the language is ready to use.

Unlike ROM, RAM is temporary; it only retains information while the computer is on. It is measured in *kilobytes* (thousands of bytes of storage). The IBM PC generally comes standard with 256 kilobytes (256K) of RAM on its system board (called the "motherboard"), but this can be expanded to 640K by adding a memory circuit card to one of the expansion slots located on the motherboard. *Figure 1-2* illustrates the location of both ROM and RAM on the motherboard.

Expansion Slots

The expansion slots illustrated in *Figure 1-2* are sometimes known as "peripheral slots" since they serve as the way to link the computer's CPU with external devices, or peripherals. One slot might be used for a disk-controller card, which links the computer to a disk drive capable of reading information on disks. A second slot might contain a printer interface card, which connects the computer to a printer. A third slot might hold a card containing a built-in modem, which can transmit information from one computer to another over a telephone line.

Monitors and Video Adapters

One of the IBM PC's expansion slots will be used for a video adapter, a circuit card that sends video signals to a computer monitor. A monochrome monitor is capable of displaying one color in addition to black. Amber, green, and white are the types of monochrome monitors generally used with an IBM PC. A monochrome monitor is ideal for word processing, spreadsheet analysis, and database management—tasks that

Figure 1-2.
An IBM PC Motherboard

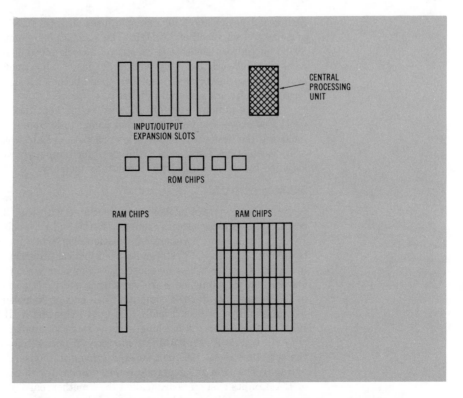

do not require color. A monitor's screen contains a number of small block-like picture elements (called "pixels"), which form characters by being either lit or unlit. The number of pixels that can be displayed horizontally and vertically is a function of both the monitor and its video adapter card. The IBM Monochrome Display Adapter can display 720 horizontal pixels × 350 vertical pixels, which is considered very high resolution.

A monochrome monitor requires a monochrome adapter card in one of the PC's expansion slots and a cable connecting the card to the monitor. Many computer users with monochrome monitors want to see graphs displayed on their screens; this is possible only if the monochrome adapter card is also capable of displaying graphics. While IBM's own monochrome adapter card does not permit graphics to be displayed, several companies offer video adapters that can display graphics while still providing the same high resolution. Hercules Technology's Hercules Monochrome Graphics Card is an example.

IBM PC users who wish to display color graphics usually select a color graphics adapter (CGA) or an enhanced graphics adapter (EGA) along with a monitor capable of displaying the appropriate level of resolution. CGA cards are capable of providing a monitor with 640×200 resolution and of displaying sixteen colors, only four of which can be displayed at a time. EGA cards, on the other hand, are capable of 640×350 resolution and can display sixty-four colors, sixteen of which can be displayed at a time. *Table 1-1* summarizes the standards for monochrome, CGA, and EGA cards.

Table 1-1.
PC Video Adapter Card
Standards

Protocol	Resolution (Pixels)	Total Colors	Colors/Screen
CGA	640×200	16	4
EGA	640×350	64	16
PGA	640×480	4096	256

Most programs require a user to indicate specifically which type of video adapter card will be used so that the program will send the proper signal to the card. We'll see later in the book that this can present some problems when a program is used on a local area network since different workstations may contain differing video adapter cards.

Floppy Disk Drives and Disk Storage

Since RAM only retains information while the computer is turned on, a disk drive serves as the standard storage device. A floppy disk, shown in *Figure 1-3*, must be prepared to handle information sent from the IBM PC; we call this procedure "formatting." A disk that has been formatted to handle IBM PC information can hold approximately 360,000 bytes of data. A formatted disk contains 40 concentric circles, or tracks, each of which contains a number of 512-byte sectors, or blocks, where data can be stored. The computer maps these sectors so it can keep track of precisely where specific information is stored. The IBM PC and compatibles format a disk so that it is double-sided double-density (DSDD). There are 9 sectors on each track and 40 tracks on each side of the disk. So each formatted DSDD disk can hold 40 tracks/side $\times$ 9 sectors/track $\times$ 512 bytes/sector $\times$ 2 sides/disk or a total of 368,640 bytes/disk. Since ASCII requires 7 bits to represent a character with the additional parity bit to check for errors, a DSDD disk can hold 368,640 characters.

**Figure 1-3.
Floppy Disk for IBM PC
or Compatible**

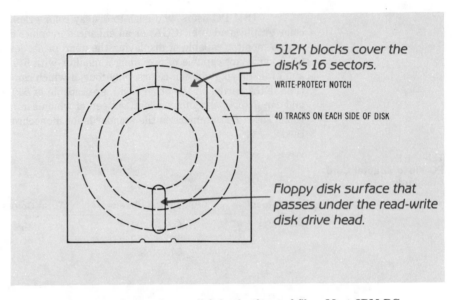

512K blocks cover the disk's 16 sectors.

WRITE-PROTECT NOTCH

40 TRACKS ON EACH SIDE OF DISK

Floppy disk surface that passes under the read-write disk drive head.

Information is saved on a disk in the form of files. Most IBM PCs and compatibles have two disk drives (labeled A and B) so that information can be copied from a disk in one drive to a disk in the second drive. In much the same way that a record player functions, a read-write head on a disk drive moves across the tracks of a spinning disk until it locates a particular file of information. Then it stops the disk from spinning and copies the pattern of bits to RAM locations within the computer. The time it takes to accomplish this task, called the "access time," is measured in milliseconds (thousandths of a second) while tasks performed by the CPU are generally measured in nanoseconds (millionths of a second). If several computers need information stored on a particular disk and this disk access procedure must be repeated several times, there will be a measurable slowdown in computer operations. We will discuss this problem in later chapters and examine the methods several local area network manufacturers have developed for speeding up this procedure.

Hard Disk Drives

Loading all programs and data files onto one hard disk drive is much faster and more efficient than using floppy disks. Where several dozen floppies might be necessary, a computer user can place all information on a single hard disk drive unit, which is capable of holding anywhere from 10 megabytes (10 million bytes) to several hundred megabytes of information. A hard disk, shown in *Figure 1-4*, is actually a rigid platter coated with a metal oxide material. It looks very much like a record. In the sealed hard disk unit, the read-write head travels rapidly (around 3600 revolutions/minute) on a very thin cushion of air that separates it from the magnetic surface of the hard disk. The distance between the read-write heads and the magnetic surface of the hard disk varies from 1 millionth of an inch to ½-millionth of an inch depending upon the brand of hard disk. It might take approximately 30 milliseconds access time for the hard disk to locate and load a file compared to 90 milliseconds with a floppy disk drive. You will learn in the next chapter how hard disk drives can serve several different personal computers in a network environment.

Figure 1-4.
A Hard Disk *(Courtesy of Seagate Technology)*

The Disk Operating System (DOS)

With the IBM PC and compatibles, a series of programs handle such "housekeeping" tasks as loading programs into the computer from a disk, saving information to disk, and translating keyboard characters that have been typed into a number language the computer can understand. Collectively, these programs make up the Disk Operating System (DOS). The IBM PC version licensed from Microsoft Corporation is known as PC-DOS; the identical program used by IBM PC compatibles is known as MS-DOS (Microsoft Disk Operating System). Among the routine tasks that DOS helps users perform are the formatting of a blank disk, the copying of a file from one disk to a second disk, and the deletion of a file from a disk.

Among the most significant routines of the Disk Operating System are the Supervisor, the Input/Output Manager, the File Manager, and the Command Processor. The Supervisor coordinates the activities of the other programs. If certain programs must be run sequentially, the Supervisor ensures that they do. The Input/Output Manager ensures that the computer is able to communicate effectively with a wide range of peripherals, including disk drives and printers. These programs, for example, must be able to translate data into a form that a particular printer can accept and utilize. The File Manager keeps track of all information stored on disk. It must know exactly where this information is stored so that it can be retrieved quickly. The Command Processor provides for communication between the user and the computer; the characters the user types are converted into a language the machine can understand.

Microsoft has published several versions of PC-DOS and MS-DOS which, for the most part, are upwardly compatible. Under most conditions it is not possible to mix different DOS versions of programs on the same disk, although later in this book you will learn how some local area networks divide a hard disk into various sections, each of which can contain programs running under a different version of DOS.

While DOS is designed specifically to coordinate the communication between a computer and the rest of its world, including disk drives, printers, and keyboard input, some local area network programs superimpose a "shell" around the DOS programs and intercept commands normally handled by DOS. When we examine the Novell NetWare software later in this book, we'll see how this provides a number of advantages, among them enabling several users to utilize a program designed for only one user without ruining the program or its data files.

Parallel and Serial Transmission

As we saw earlier, an IBM's expansion slots serve as the computer's means of communicating with peripherals such as disk drives and printers. A Parallel Printer Adapter, also known as a "printer interface," fits in an expansion slot and is connected by cable with a printer. Eight bits of data travel in parallel along eight separate wires from a PC to a printer. This method of transmission is relatively fast, but its range is limited to about 25 feet (ft) or 8 meters (m) before data is lost.

Some printers and virtually all modems require an asynchronous communications adapter, usually known as a "serial port." This circuit card converts data from the parallel form found within the PC to serial form in which the bits travel in single file along the same wire. While serial transmission often is not as fast as parallel transmission, it is capable of transmitting data for longer distances. A serial cable contains twenty-five different wires. Normally, the data is transmitted along one of the wires while other information is sent along the other wires. Printers, both parallel and serial, and serial modems are critical elements of most local area networks.

We turn now to the evolution of the PC before examining our hypothetical company that has linked its PCs together to form a local area network. We'll explore the applications described in this example in greater detail in subsequent chapters dealing with specific brands of local area networks.

A BRIEF HISTORY OF DISTRIBUTED PROCESSING AND NETWORKS

In three decades we have seen the computer industry evolve. Initially, all processing was performed on mainframe computers using a batch approach. Time sharing using public telephone lines was an improvement, but the concept of distributed processing using minicomputers provided a quantum leap in computer affordability and convenience. Many companies gradually replaced their minicomputers with microcomputers and a local area network.

While it is only with the arrival of the microcomputer that companies have been able to implement local area networks, the concept itself is not new. It represents a logical development and evolution of computer technology. The first computers in the 1950s were mainframes.

Large, expensive, and reserved for a very few select users, mainframes often occupied entire buildings. They were not designed for on-line response to a user's commands. They used a *batch approach*, in which users submitted coded cards containing their data and program commands. Computer professionals fed these cards into the computer and usually sent the printed results to the users the next day. A miscoded card often meant that the user would have to resubmit the entire program the following day.

At this time there was little need to share computer resources such as printers and modems because there were so few computers that the average office couldn't afford one. The solution to this expense problem was the concept of time-sharing. During the 1960s it became possible for an office to use a "dumb" terminal to connect through a telephone line with a mainframe. By leasing (or "sharing") time on this computer, the user was able to enjoy the benefits of computerization without massive capital expenditure.

The major problem with time-sharing was the slowness of sending information over telephone lines. The production during the early 1970s of the minicomputer avoided this problem; because of the dramatic drop in prices, departments were able to have their own computers. A new user simply needed a terminal and the cabling between it and the minicomputer to become operational. As *Figure 1-5* illustrates, several users were able to use the same computer, and much higher speeds were possible than under time-sharing.

**Figure 1-5.
Distributed Processing
with a Minicomputer**

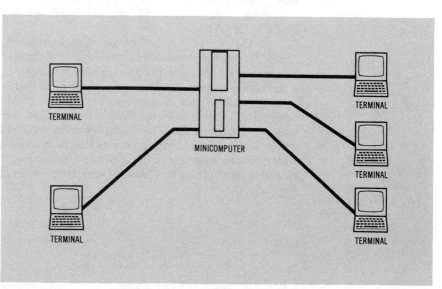

The concept of distributing the computer resources through a company by providing different departments with their own computers rather than using a central computer for everybody became known as "distributed processing." But even though several departments within a company might have their own minicomputers, there was still a problem in providing communications among these computers. So, companies began cabling the computers together and writing the software necessary for the different units to communicate.

As microcomputers became more and more powerful and less and less expensive during the 1980s, companies began to take a second look at their minicomputers. Costing hundreds of thousands of dollars, these larger computers were not able to run the newer, more sophisticated business programs that were coming out for IBM PCs and compatibles.

By the mid-1980s, thousands of office workers were bringing their own personal computers to work in order to use the office-productivity software available for microcomputers. Companies began to experience serious problems maintaining the integrity of data as employees began exchanging floppy disks and keeping their own databases. The answer to these problems was the local area network.

WHAT IS A LOCAL AREA NETWORK?

A local area network covers a limited distance and facilitates the sharing of information and resources.

We'll define a local area network (LAN) in the broadest sense. It is a communication network used by a single organization over a limited distance that permits users to share information and resources. In the next chapter we will survey the different physical configurations possible for a LAN. Whether PCs are arranged in the form of a star, a ring, or even a straight line, the speed of the network will depend to a great extent on the type of media used to connect all units together. In the next chapter we will return to this subject and examine the different types of cabling available for LANs.

Distributed processing taken to its logical conclusion means the linking together of microcomputers to share information and peripherals. The first local area networks were relatively primitive, and were faced with a serious shortage of software designed for more than one user. At best, these first LANs used *file locking*; only one user could work with a single program at a time. Gradually, though, the software industry has become more sophisticated. Today local area networks are able to use sophisticated accounting and productivity programs that permit several users to work with the same programs at the same time (*record locking*). Let's take a close look at an actual local area network in operation at the Widget Company.

HOWARD W. SAMS & COMPANY

Bookmark

DEAR VALUED CUSTOMER:

Howard W. Sams & Company is dedicated to bringing you timely and authoritative books for your personal and professional library. Our goal is to provide you with excellent technical books written by the most qualified authors. You can assist us in this endeavor by checking the box next to your particular areas of interest.

We appreciate your comments and will use the information to provide you with a more comprehensive selection of titles.

Thank you,

Vice President, Book Publishing
Howard W. Sams & Company

COMPUTER TITLES:

Hardware
- ☐ Apple 140
- ☐ Macintosh 101
- ☐ Commodore 110
- ☐ IBM & Compatibles 114

Business Applications
- ☐ Word Processing J01
- ☐ Data Base J04
- ☐ Spreadsheets J02

Operating Systems
- ☐ MS-DOS K05
- ☐ OS/2 K10
- ☐ CP/M K01
- ☐ UNIX K03

Programming Languages
- ☐ C L03
- ☐ Pascal L05
- ☐ Prolog L12
- ☐ Assembly L01
- ☐ BASIC L02
- ☐ HyperTalk L14

Troubleshooting & Repair
- ☐ Computers S05
- ☐ Peripherals S10

Other
- ☐ Communications/Networking M03
- ☐ AI/Expert Systems T18

ELECTRONICS TITLES:

- ☐ Amateur Radio T01
- ☐ Audio T03
- ☐ Basic Electronics T20
- ☐ Basic Electricity T21
- ☐ Electronics Design T12
- ☐ Electronics Projects T04
- ☐ Satellites T09

- ☐ Instrumentation T05
- ☐ Digital Electronics T11

Troubleshooting & Repair
- ☐ Audio S11
- ☐ Television S04
- ☐ VCR S01
- ☐ Compact Disc S02
- ☐ Automotive S06
- ☐ Microwave Oven S03

Other interests or comments: _____

_____

Name_____

Title _____

Company _____

Address _____

City _____

State/Zip _____

Daytime Telephone No. _____

A Division of Macmillan, Inc.

4300 West 62nd Street Indianapolis, Indiana 46268

27063

Bookmark

HOWARD W. SAMS & COMPANY

BUSINESS REPLY CARD

FIRST CLASS   PERMIT NO. 1076   INDIANAPOLIS, IND.

POSTAGE WILL BE PAID BY ADDRESSEE

HOWARD W. SAMS & CO.
ATTN: Public Relations Department
P.O. BOX 7092
Indianapolis, IN 46209-9921

HOWARD W. SAMS & COMPANY
HAYDEN BOOKS

Understanding Expert Systems
Louis E. Frenzel, Jr.
ISBN: 0-672-27065-X, $17.95

Understanding Advanced Solid State Electronics
Don L. Cannon
ISBN: 0-672-27058-7, $17.95

Understanding Artificial Intelligence, Second Edition
Dan Shafer
ISBN: 0-672-27271-7, $17.95

Understanding Automation Systems, Second Edition
Robert F. Farwell and Neil M. Schmitt
ISBN: 0-672-27014-5, $17.95

Understanding Automotive Electronics, Third Edition
William B. Ribbens
ISBN: 0-672-27064-6, $17.95

Understanding C
Carl Townsend
ISBN: 0-672-27278-4, $17.95

Understanding Communications Systems, Second Edition
Don L. Cannon and Gerald Luecke
ISBN: 0-672-27016-1, $17.95

Understanding CAD/CAM
Daniel J. Bowman and Annette C. Bowman
ISBN: 0-672-27068-4, $17.95

Understanding Computer Science, Second Edition
Roger S. Walker
ISBN: 0-672-27011-0, $17.95

Understanding Computer Science Applications
Roger S. Walker
ISBN: 0-672-27020-X, $17.95

Understanding Data Communications, Second Edition
Revised by Gil Held
ISBN: 0-672-27270-9, $17.95

(more titles on the back)

To order, return the card below, or call 1-800-428-SAMS. In Indiana call (317) 298-5699.

- -

Please send me the books listed below.

Title	Quantity	ISBN #	Price

☐ Please add my name to your mailing list to receive more information on related titles.

Name (please print) ⎯⎯⎯⎯⎯⎯⎯⎯⎯⎯⎯⎯

Company ⎯⎯⎯⎯⎯⎯⎯⎯⎯⎯⎯⎯⎯⎯

City ⎯⎯⎯⎯⎯⎯⎯⎯⎯⎯⎯⎯⎯⎯

State/Zip ⎯⎯⎯⎯⎯⎯⎯⎯⎯⎯⎯⎯

Signature ⎯⎯⎯⎯⎯⎯⎯⎯⎯⎯⎯⎯
(required for credit card purchase)

Telephone # ⎯⎯⎯⎯⎯⎯⎯⎯⎯⎯⎯⎯

Subtotal ⎯⎯⎯⎯⎯⎯
Standard Postage and Handling **$2.50**
All States Add Appropriate Sales Tax ⎯⎯⎯⎯⎯
TOTAL ⎯⎯⎯⎯

Enclosed is My Check or Money Order for $⎯⎯⎯⎯⎯⎯

Charge my Credit Card: ☐ VISA   ☐ MC   ☐ AE
Account No.   Expiration Date ⎯⎯⎯⎯

☐☐☐☐ ☐☐☐☐ ☐☐☐☐ ☐☐☐☐

27063

**Understanding Digital
Electronics, Second Edition**
Gene W. McWhorter
ISBN: 0-672-27013-7, $17.95

**Understanding Digital
Troubleshooting,
Second Edition**
Don L. Cannon
ISBN: 0-672-27015-3, $17.95

**Understanding Electricity
and Electronics Circuits**
David L. Heiserman
ISBN: 0-672-27062-5, $17.95

**Understanding Electricity
and Electronics Principles**
David L. Heiserman
ISBN: 0-672-27061-7, $17.95

Understanding Fiber Optics
Jeff Hecht
ISBN: 0-672-27066-8, $17.95

**Understanding
Microprocessors,
Second Edition**
Don L. Cannon and Gerald Luecke
ISBN: 0-672-27010-2, $17.95

Understanding MS-DOS®
*Kate O'Day and John Angermeyer,
The Waite Group*
ISBN: 0-672-27067-6, $17.95

**Understanding Security
Electronics**
Joseph J. Carr
ISBN: 0-672-27069-2, $17.95

**Understanding Solid State
Electronics, Fourth Edition**
*William E. Hafford and
Gene W. McWhorter*
ISBN: 0-672-27012-9, $17.95

**Understanding Telephone
Electronics, Second Edition**
John L. Fike and George E. Friend
ISBN: 0-672-27018-8, $17.95

Place
Postage
Here

HOWARD W. SAMS & COMPANY

Dept. DM
4300 West 62nd Street
Indianapolis, IN 46268-2589

WIDGET'S LOCAL AREA NETWORK

The savings a company can realize by sharing hardware and software resources are staggering. Equally important, though, is the increase in productivity as the company runs more efficiently.

Its local area network enables Widget employees to share peripherals (hard disk drives, printers, plotters, etc.), software application programs (databases, spreadsheets, word processing programs, accounting programs, etc.), and data. So instead of each personal computer workstation having its own dot matrix printer, the Widget network enables dozens of workstations to share a variety of printers, including laser, daisy wheel (letter quality), and dot matrix. Instead of buying dozens of copies of a word processing program, Widget buys a special network version of the program that enables dozens of network users to share the program and, even more important, share each other's documents. A single computer's hard disk functions as a network file server, acting very much like a waiter in a busy restaurant, serving up the items requested by the customers. With its local area network, Widget can keep dozens of varying standard contracts on its network disk server so that individual workstations can load these documents, make whatever changes are necessary to individualize the contracts, and then save them under appropriate names. The cost savings from these and other communal uses are staggering.

Using Word Processing, Graphics, and Electronic Mail on a LAN

A task such as producing an annual report requires that several people write different portions and then make revisions to the material. Since its electronic mail facilitates communication, speeding up the revisions, Widget's LAN makes this process quite efficient.

Every year Widget is required to produce an annual report that is printed and sent to stockholders. Since the company connected all departments with its LAN, the job has become much easier. The Accounting department's audited balance sheet is already available through the network since its general ledger, accounts payable, accounts receivable, inventory, purchase order and receiving, and payroll programs are already installed on the network. The corporate Controller prints a copy of the balance sheet to disk (rather than send it to the printer) and then uses a word processing program to comment on several aspects of Widget's financial position before also saving the document on the company's file server.

Since many stockholders prefer to view financial information in graphic format, the President asks two graphic artists in the Marketing department to develop appropriate pie and bar charts to show the company's growth over the past few years. The artists use a graphics program designed for the IBM PC to develop their charts and then send the information to a plotter that is part of the local area network. After they receive the President's comments by electronic mail over the network, the artists revise the charts and then save the files on the file server.

Everyone at Widget with an IBM PC or compatible that is connected to the LAN can receive and send mail electronically. The network informs users as they are entering the network ("logging on") that they have mail, so Widget employees find that they no longer can use the excuse that they never saw a memo because it was lost in the mail. The electronic mail program lets the sender know when a message has been read. It even permits the sending of blind copies (bcc) to other network users as well as the sending of letters and even reports to distribution lists.

Secretaries who used to spend hours photocopying reports for distribution to managers now simply use the electronic mail to send a copy of each report to each manager's workstation.

Since Widget manufactures four very different products designed for four very different markets, the President asked each of the four product managers to write a description of their products' current status and plans for the future. Each product manager saved his or her comments in a word processing file on the file server.

Meanwhile the President is busy writing a letter to the stockholders analyzing Widget's performance and indicating the direction the company would take for the following year. After the staff prints the requested material from the Marketing and Accounting departments, the President reads the documents and then sends electronic mail to other employees requesting material to fill in remaining gaps in the corporate report. After another round of revisions, the annual report is finished, printed with a laser printer that provides letter quality text and crisp graphics, and sent to the print shop for reproduction. The whole process is fast and efficient because the company's LAN permits almost instant sharing of information.

Connecting a LAN to the Rest of the World

The ability to share information is particularly valuable in a competitive sales environment. Each of Widget's outside salespeople has a portable computer with a built-in modem to access the LAN over a phone line. Widgets come in an assortment of colors and configurations, and the company used to lose several thousand dollars worth of orders each year through cancellations. A salesperson would take a large order, drive to Widget headquarters, and submit the order to the sales manager. Only after the order was input into Widget's mainframe computer would the salesperson learn that several of the ordered items were backordered. When customers were informed that there would be a delay before delivery, they often canceled the entire order.

Now the situation has changed dramatically. Widget's LAN contains a *gateway*, a bridge that connects the network to an outside computer. The salespeople use their portable computers, which contain built-in modems and communications programs, to connect to the network using their customers' regular telephone lines. They enter an order while with the customer. If an item is backordered, the computer indicates a possible alternative: "The yellow widgets are backordered two weeks, but green is very popular this time of year and it is available immediately." Since the customer is in a buying mood and the salesperson is present and very persuasive, it is not surprising that many customers choose an alternative or agree to wait for a backordered item.

As a customer's order is entered into the computer, a file is established for the customer. Salespeople find this information invaluable since they are able to determine buying trends and preferences. Frequently they will mail individualized form letters announcing new product releases or suggesting that the old widget might need an overhaul.

By using a gateway to connect the local area network to the outside world, Widget salespeople are able to enter orders from remote customer locations and update inventory levels on-line. Another major tool utilized by the entire company is the customer database. Salespeople can utilize the gateway and the LAN to generate personalized sales letters.

Because the customer list is integrated with the company's accounting programs, including accounts receivable, the Accounting department occasionally might ask a salesperson to contact a delinquent customer about an overdue account. The receivables clerk sends the account information by electronic mail to the salesperson. (Widget's accounting program on the LAN contains a useful safeguard to keep its receivables low. If a customer has an overdue account, when a salesperson inputs an order from that customer site, the order-entry program flashes a message on the screen. Frequently, the salesperson can collect a check and then override the message to enter the new order.)

Sharing Database Information on a LAN

A common database is particularly valuable for marketing functions. Researchers are able to download network information into Lotus 1-2-3 spreadsheets, analyze the data, and then save these spreadsheets on the network file server for consolidation into one report.

While Widget's salespeople are busy transmitting orders from customer locations, the Marketing department's researchers and analysts are busy sifting through sales reports to discover trends and develop market forecasts. The department's personnel share their data on the LAN. The analysts, for example, have used a Lotus 1-2-3 spreadsheet program to analyze the buying patterns of the company's major distributors. Traditionally, Widget has offered volume discounts to encourage large purchases, but now it is considering offering monthly sales specials to help balance its inventory. By identifying specific items and the month when major customers purchase them, the marketing analysts will develop a twelve-month sales plan.

Because the analysts are using the same Lotus 1-2-3 program and then saving their spreadsheet data on the network file server, the information can be shared among them. This means that after the researchers develop an item-by-item sales analysis, one researcher can access all three spreadsheets to develop a composite report summarizing information by product group. Using the Lotus 1-2-3 spreadsheet, the researcher sends a command over the LAN to the six-pen plotter in the sales office to print a series of detailed graphs.

Accounting on a LAN

The Accounting department's use of the local area network reflects the major advantage of flexibility that a LAN provides. Since programs contain record locking, it is possible to utilize several employees running the same program during peak periods.

The Widget Company's accounting information is on the LAN, but many of the programs have password security beyond the usual network level of security. Only a few employees in the Accounting and Personnel departments, for example, have access to payroll records. The information on customer orders and inventory usage is only available to certain employees in Marketing, Sales, and Manufacturing. The marketing analysts were able to use a special interface program to take sales order and customer information from the accounting programs and convert this data into a form that could be used in a Lotus 1-2-3 program. Note that while a copy of this valuable accounting information can be moved to another program, the original accounting data is protected from tampering. This is necessary to ensure that the Accounting department maintains a clear *audit trail*, which means that all changes to accounting program data must be done from the Accounting department by a journal entry. This method leaves a permanent record that can be traced to answer future questions.

The Controller has been delighted with the advantages of having all accounting programs available on the company LAN. During peak periods, accounting clerks can be shifted from doing payables to doing receivables. Any workstation in the department may access any accounting program if the user has the proper level of password security. Most of the clerks only have a security level that permits them to perform routine tasks. Payroll clerks, for example, cannot change employee salaries although they can prepare the monthly salary check printing.

The Controller must consult with the LAN administrator before providing newly hired accounting clerks with new workstations. Every LAN requires a network administrator, who is responsible for the network's overall management. Among the administrator's tasks are adding new users and providing them with new passwords. If a department wants to add a new program to the LAN, the network administrator will analyze the effect of the program on the network as a whole to ensure that the program will integrate completely with the other programs already present.

Using Printers on a LAN

Word processing on a LAN provides the user with a number of advantages, including print spooling and the choice of several different kinds of printers.

Perhaps the major use of the LAN requires the least amount of the network administrator's time. Every day secretaries, administrative assistants, and managers use the network's powerful word processing program. All of Widget's form letters, including direct sales solicitations, requests for additional warranty information, notification that service contracts are about to expire, and the actual service contracts themselves, are word processed. The LAN contains a couple of laser printers with triple-bin cut sheet feeders, making it possible to automatically print a cover letter on Widget Corporation stationery, a second sheet on plain bond paper, and the corresponding envelope.

The company LAN has what is known as "print-spooling" software, which enables a user to specify a specific printer for a job and then "spool" the file to a storage area where it will be held until its turn to be printed. The President can specify that a job requiring immediate attention exchange places with another file in the spooler in order to be printed immediately. The LAN is able to print several documents simultaneously on its various letter quality and dot matrix printers without slowing down the network performance.

The most sophisticated word processing is handled by the Technical Publications department, which supports Sales, Marketing, and Service and works on special projects for the President's office. Four technical writers use many of the advanced features of the word processing program, such as the ability to create multiple columns and the ability to create indexes and tables of contents automatically. These materials require feedback from engineers, programmers, and trainers. The technical writers use the LAN's electronic mail to send their rough drafts to appropriate departments for comments before beginning the revision stage. Because they no longer have to take the time to mail copies of the manuscript and then wait for their return, the technical writers have increased their productivity substantially. Now when the writers receive electronic mail informing them that a section has been read and revised for technical accuracy by an engineer, they just load the revised section and proofread for grammatical and spelling problems.

A technical writer and illustrator are assigned to support the Marketing department. They develop brochures and other sales materials. Since it is absolutely necessary that all sales materials reflect the products accurately, the two send manuscript sections and illustration files to appropriate technical personnel for comments and corrections before moving on to the finished product.

Communications Between a LAN and a Mainframe Computer

The Manufacturing department's use of the LAN illustrates how local area networks can communicate with mainframe computers to share information.

The Manufacturing department was the only department not to leave its mainframe environment. Located at the manufacturing facility, the mainframe runs a sophisticated manufacturing resource planning program. This program controls manufacturing costs by making sure that the plant runs at maximum efficiency. The computer makes sure that the assembly line will not run out of key raw materials so that all standing orders can be filled on time.

Since the Accounting department now runs all its programs on microcomputers as part of the LAN, Manufacturing needs to have access to all sales order data now at the company headquarters. It needs to know what has been sold in order to update its inventory file and revise its forecasts. This communication is accomplished using the same gateway to the local area network that salespeople use when communicating from customer sites.

There is one critical difference, however. While the salespeople were using microcomputers to communicate with the company's microcomputer local area network, the Manufacturing department needs to establish communications between microcomputer and mainframe, two machines that don't even speak the same language. Widget Company's network administrator uses the LAN software interface to the accounting programs to convert the data into a form that can be sent over a telephone line. The administrator uses another program to emulate the mainframe and convert the information into the synchronous form that the mainframe can understand.

Every evening the LAN sends the day's sales information over a telephone line to the company's mainframe which digests the data and produces a revised schedule for the next day's assembly line work. When supervisory personnel arrive in the morning, they use their terminals to read this information from the mainframe.

All the LAN activities of Widget Company described here are available today. In the next few chapters you will learn how a LAN's hardware and software work together to produce this level of integration of information. You will also survey the leading LANs and the differences among them that could prove significant in helping you determine which kind of local area network is in your future.

WHAT HAVE WE LEARNED?

1. A local area network is a communications network used by a single organization over a limited distance that permits users to share information and resources.
2. Time-sharing with terminals and modems enabled companies to share the resources.
3. Minicomputers were the first computers to permit distributive processing in a cost-effective way.
4. A dedicated file server is not used as a workstation.
5. Electronic mail is a major feature of many local area Networks.
6. Outside computers can use a gateway to communicate with computers within the local area network.
7. Print-spooling software permits users to designate which printer they wish to use to print their files.
8. Record-locking software permits more than one user to use the same program at the same time.

Quiz for Chapter 1

1. Handing in program cards and receiving the results the next day is characteristic of:
   a. batch processing.
   b. on-line processing.
   c. distributed processing.
   d. remote processing.

2. Time-sharing was not a very effective way for a company to do its data processing because:
   a. it required a computer at every station.
   b. communication over a phone line with a modem was too slow.
   c. computers were constantly breaking down.
   d. computers do not like to share.

3. Distributed processing means:
   a. computers distributed to different users and departments.
   b. computer cards distributed to different departments.
   c. a mainframe computer doing all the work.
   d. a computer doing nothing but computing.

4. The person who provides passwords for new computer users on the local area network is called:
   a. the chief of security.
   b. the network administrator.
   c. the department manager.
   d. the president of the network user's group.

5. A byte is composed of:
   a. 2 bits.
   b. 4 bits.
   c. 6 bits.
   d. 8 bits.

6. A double-sided double-density disk formatted for the IBM PC will be able to hold approximately:
   a. 360K.
   b. 180K.
   c. 256K.
   d. 512K.

7. To attach a modem to an IBM PC or compatible, its expansion slot must contain a(n):
   a. parallel interface.
   b. synchronous communications adapter.
   c. asynchronous communications adapter.
   d. monochrome video adapter.

8. Memory that retains information even after the computer is turned off is called:
   a. RAM.
   b. ROM.
   c. RIM.
   d. REM.

The Basics of a Local Area Network

ABOUT THIS CHAPTER

This chapter describes the building blocks of a local area network. We will explore how computer workstations are cabled together and how they share resources. We will take a close look at the rules that all local area networks follow to ensure that information is not garbled or lost. Finally, we will look at a number of standards that are helping establish some order to what has been a very chaotic field.

THE CHANGING FOCUS OF LOCAL AREA NETWORKS

As we have seen, a local area network describes a method by which microcomputers can share information and resources within a limited (local) area, generally less than a mile. A LAN requires that the individual workstations (microcomputers) be physically tied together by cabling, usually coaxial or twisted pair, and that some network software reside on a hard disk to permit the sharing of peripherals, data, and application programs.

Until recently, the major use of LANS was to share peripheral equipment such as printers, hard disk drives, and plotters. Since hardware represented the major microcomputer cost in most offices, these early, primitive networks more than justified their cost by ensuring that valuable equipment did not remain idle. Today, some networks (such as Novell's) further increase office savings by allowing the creation of a workstation that does not have a hard disk. A special "autoboot" ROM chip inserted in the IBM PC or compatible enables the computer to become part of the network and use the network's disk drive when it is turned on.

It is difficult to generalize about microcomputer networks because of a lack of compatibility that has plagued the industry despite the efforts by the Institute for Electrical and Electronics Engineers (IEEE) to standardize the ways that information can be transmitted within a network. Even IBM, the industry's acknowledged standard bearer, markets two local area networks that are so different from each other that one meets IEEE standards while the other one does not. In this chapter we will look at the components that all networks require and the various forms the networks can take.

THE INDIVIDUAL WORKSTATION

The individual network workstation can work independently as a personal computer or share network information and resources. Usually it is linked to the network's file server or disk server by a network interface card and cabling.

Most companies decide to install a local area network because they already have a major investment in microcomputers, peripherals, and software. Rather than scrap everything and start over again with a minicomputer, the companies opt to tie their existing equipment together to share hardware and software resources.

Each microcomputer attached to the network retains its ability to continue working as an independent personal computer running its own software. It also becomes a network workstation capable of accessing information located on the network disk server. As *Figure 2-1* illustrates, this ability to function as a network station requires network software in order to communicate with the network server and other network workstations and a special interface (almost always a circuit board) that plugs into one of the microcomputer's expansion slots.

**Figure 2-1.
Workstations
Connected with
Network Interface Cards
and Cabling to Disk
Server**

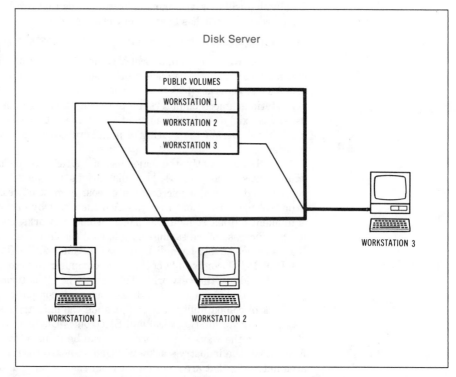

While there are some microcomputers that do not run Microsoft's MS-DOS or PC-DOS, the vast majority of local area networks are designed for IBM PCs or compatibles. In this book, we will assume that an office LAN contains these units and not Apples, Ataris, or other microcomputers that run their own proprietary operating systems.

The workstations in *Figure 2-1* are IBM PCs containing network interface cards. The network program they are using works in conjunction with PC-DOS version 3.1. A cable connects each workstation (through its network interface card) to the network disk server. As we indicated earlier, the workstation's user can choose whether to use the microcomputer as an independent unit or to be part of the network. By simply running the network software program and logging on (identifying oneself with a password as an authorized user) the user becomes an active part of the network.

DISK SERVERS

Some local area networks utilize a *disk server*, a hard disk that contains information that can be shared by the workstations on the network. To the individual workstations, this disk server simply looks like another hard disk drive. If this disk server were designated as drive E, for example, Frank Jones would save his business expense spreadsheet as E:busexp. The E tells Jones's DOS software to send the data to the network hard disk for storage.

This procedure, governed by the workstation's DOS, is identical to the way a PC accesses its own disk drives for storage of files. The procedure is a bit more complex, however, when a workstation wants a particular file residing on the disk server.

IBM PCs and compatibles use a file allocation table (FAT) to keep track of exactly where a particular file is stored. The network disk server keeps its own FAT. Without seeing a copy of this valuable table, an individual workstation has no idea of exactly where one of its files is stored. The disk server sends a copy of this table to the workstation, which stores it in RAM, which is its "work space" when running programs. Using the FAT under DOS, the workstation can access its files on the disk server.

Imagine, though, what would happen if dozens of workstations received copies of the FAT and began saving documents back to the disk server. Each copy of the FAT saved back to the disk server would overwrite (and thus erase) the FAT file that existed prior to the new copy's arrival. It would prove almost impossible to determine which was the original FAT without a safeguard for this important table's integrity.

With a simple disk server, the integrity of its FAT is maintained by dividing up (partitioning) this hard disk drive into several user volumes. Each volume is reserved for a particular workstation's exclusive use, thus preserving the integrity of the FAT for that particular volume. Certain volumes might be established as *public volumes*, but they are usually safeguarded by being classified as "read-only," which means that the individual workstations can view this information but cannot change it. An example of a typical public volume use is the large customer database file for Widget Corporation described in Chapter 1. Several different departments might need to view this information, but the network administrator has declared the file "read-only" so that no one inadvertently changes or destroys the data.

Some networks use a disk server to store files and provide workstations with this information upon request.

A file allocation table helps the disk server keep track of where a particular file is located.

Disk servers partition their hard disk drives into separate volumes for each user. A public volume is available so that different workstations can share information.

FILE SERVERS

A file server uses software to form a shell around the computer's normal DOS. To an individual workstation, the file server simply represents a very large disk drive. It doesn't need to be concerned with a particular file's location.

File servers are far more efficient and sophisticated than disk servers. A file server contains special software that forms a shell around the computer's normal disk operating system. This shell software filters commands out to the file server before DOS can receive them. The file server maintains its own FAT. When a workstation demands a specific file, the file server already knows where the file is because of its FAT. It sends the file directly to the workstation. Note that the individual workstation does not designate the file server as another disk drive as is the case with a disk server. It simply requests a file and the file server responds.

The file server is much more efficient than the disk server because there is no need to send copies of the FAT to each workstation requesting a file. Also, there is no need to partition the network hard disk drive into volumes since the individual workstations no longer need to worry about where a particular file resides. As *Figure 2-2* illustrates, a file server provides great efficiency in a local area network.

Figure 2-2. Workstations Connected to File Server

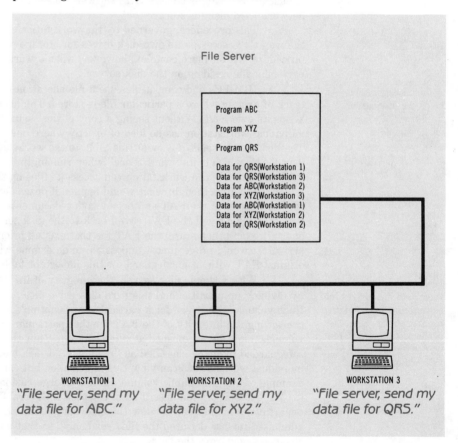

Distributed File Servers

A network may contain one centralized file server or several distributed file servers.

For most office networks, a single file server is more than adequate. This is known as a "centralized server." It functions very much like a minicomputer since all file serving is handled from the one unit with each workstation waiting its turn. If the LAN is designed to handle several departments, such as our Widget Corporation example in Chapter 1, it is usually more efficient to add additional file servers.

These additional units are known as "distributed file servers" because they divide up or distribute the file-serving duties for the entire network. Since all Accounting department workstations use the same accounting programs and access the same data, it would be inefficient to send this information to a file server located several hundred feet away. A distributed file server located right in the Accounting department can speed access time as well as reduce the load on the rest of the network, thus maintaining optimum speed for other users. Accounting personnel no longer have to request files from a centralized file server that also services other network users' requests. Since a file server located in the Accounting department need only concern itself with accounting files, it has fewer files to search through in order to locate requested information, and so can find information much more quickly. Finally, since a file server located in the department sends its files over a shorter distance to the requesting workstations, the information arrives more quickly.

There is one other advantage of distributed file servers. If one file server becomes inoperative, the LAN is not shut down. With sufficient disk space, a single distributed file server can service the entire LAN temporarily.

While distributed file servers provide a number of advantages, they can make security more difficult. The network administrator must now ensure that all file servers are protected from unauthorized entry. We will return to this major issue of network security in a later chapter.

Dedicated and Non-Dedicated File Servers

A dedicated file server is used only for that function while a non-dedicated file server also serves as a workstation. While more efficient, dedicated file servers are more expensive because they cannot serve dual purposes.

In the business world, ironically, dedication is not always prized because it can be very expensive. Some LAN manufacturers extol the price savings they offer because their file servers need not be dedicated. A *dedicated* file server is a microcomputer with a hard disk drive used exclusively as a file server. By dedicating all its memory and processing resources to file serving, that computer usually provides increased network speed and efficiency. When a file server is *non-dedicated*, it is used as a workstation in addition to its file-serving functions. This means that RAM must be partitioned so that some of it is available for running programs. It also means that one network workstation might have to wait for a file to be sent while the user of the file server loads a program from memory.

Because file servers are generally the fastest and most expensive computers in the network, deciding whether to dedicate the unit is difficult. The money that might be saved by not dedicating the unit will more than be lost by the degradation of the entire LAN; the time lost by users of the other workstations soon shows the folly of trying to economize on this critical network element.

PRINT SERVERS

Network print servers enable workstations to share several different printers.

Just as a network file server permits the sharing of a single network hard disk drive, eliminating the need for each of several personal computers to have its own hard disk drive, a network print server can enable dozens of workstations to share various types of printers. A manager might need a letter quality printer for daily correspondence, but once a month need a wide-carriage dot matrix printer in order to print a spreadsheet. An accountant on the same network might use a wide-carriage dot matrix printer daily to produce balance sheets, financial reports, and charts, while only occasionally needing a letter quality printer to write a business letter. With a LAN and its print-serving software, the manager and the accountant may choose any printer on the network.

Printers can be limited to certain users on a network. These local printers usually perform specific tasks.

Having print-serving software doesn't mean that a network station cannot have a dedicated printer. Let's say that a marketing analyst uses a color dot matrix printer almost exclusively to print transparencies of charts. This printer, connected by a parallel interface and cable to the analyst's workstation, can remain a dedicated *local* printer and not a network printer should that serve the best interests of the office. For the occasional report, the analyst can send the word processing file over the network to a letter quality printer.

A second reason for dedicating a printer to a particular workstation is if that particular user needs to print special preprinted, continuous-feed forms. A purchasing agent, for example, might need to print dozens of purchase order forms, while an accounts payable clerk might need to print continuous-feed company checks. It would be time-consuming for each to have to remove the continuous feed forms in order to print an occasional letter.

The network administrator usually will ensure that when a program is installed on the network, it is installed with a default printer driver. This means that the program's files normally will be printed on a particular printer. Word processing programs, for example, routinely might send files to the office letter quality printer or to a laser printer while spreadsheet programs send files to a wide-carriage dot matrix printer.

Print-spooler software enables network users to place files in a buffer for printing at a later time.

Printer-sharing software should contain a *print spooler*, software which creates a buffer where files can be stored until it is their turn to be printed. Think of this as a list of print jobs. As each file is printed, the next file in line takes its place. Sophisticated print spoolers have additional capabilities, including the ability to move a job to the front of the line if it requires immediate printing. On a large office network, time-consuming printing jobs, such as the printing of daily reports, often are placed in the print spooler for printing during the evening so as not to tie up a printer during peak hours.

A problem that occasionally occurs with printer-server software is that some software defaults to a certain type of printer even though there may be times when you require a different printer—a letter quality rather than a dot matrix printer, for example. The network administrator can solve this problem by creating a special *batch file* that automatically loads the program version with the appropriate printer driver. We will discuss this and other DOS network-related issues in a later chapter.

A GUIDE TO LAN CABLING

The local area network must have cabling to link its individual workstations with the file server and other peripherals. If there were only one type of cabling available, the decision would be simple. Unfortunately, there are a number of types of cabling, each with its own vocal supporters. Since there is a considerable range in cost and in capability, this is not a trivial issue. We will examine the advantages and disadvantages of twisted-pair, baseband and broadband coaxial, and fiber-optic cabling.

Twisted-Pair Cable

Twisted-pair cable is by far the least expensive type of network media. As *Figure 2-3* illustrates, this cabling consists of two insulated wires twisted together so that each wire faces the same amount of interference "noise" from the environment. The noise becomes part of the signal being transmitted. Twisting the wires together reduces but does not eliminate the noise.

Twisted-pair cable is inexpensive and easy to install. It is ideal for low-level networks where its lack of speed and limited range are not significant.

**Figure 2-3.
Twisted-Pair Wire
(2 pair)**

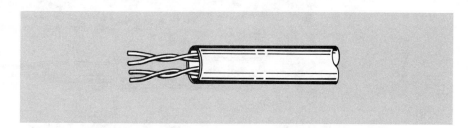

Twisted-pair wire comes in a wide range of gauges and pairs. Wires have an American Wire Gauge (AWG) number, which is based on their diameter. A 26-gauge wire, for example, has a diameter of 0.01594 inch. For network purposes, 22- and 24-gauge cabling are the two most common types of twisted-pair media. The twisted-pair cable is bundled in groups ranging from 4 to 3000 twisted pairs with many networks utilizing 25 pairs. Some local area networks utilize the very same inexpensive unshielded twisted-pair cable used for telephones while others require higher data-grade quality. As one option for its Token Ring Network, IBM supports Type 3 unshielded twisted-pair (telephone) wire, but requires 22 AWG or 24 AWG with a minimum of two twists per linear foot. It *recommends* four twisted pairs when new wire is installed; existing telephone twisted-pair wire must have two spare pairs that can be dedicated to the Token Ring Network.

On the other hand, AT&T's StarLan requires higher data-grade quality. AT&T's network requires two 24-gauge *shielded* twisted pairs, one pair to transmit data and one pair to receive data. The difference in data transmission quality between AT&T's higher grade twisted-pair standard and IBM's Type 3 twisted-pair telephone wire standard is illustrated by the fact that AT&T's workstations may be up to 990 ft (330 m) from a wiring closet while IBM's workstations must be within 330 ft (110 m).

The major limitations of twisted-pair wiring are its lack of speed and its limited range. It can handle data flow of up to approximately one Megabit/second over several hundred feet. For a small local area network with a limited number of users, twisted pair is an ideal choice because it is both inexpensive and easy to install.

Coaxial Cable

Coaxial cable is used in both baseband and broadband networks. While more expensive than twisted pair, it can transmit data significantly faster over a much longer distance.

Coaxial cable is almost as easy to install as twisted pair, and it is the medium of choice of many of the major local area networks. As *Figure 2-4* illustrates, coax is composed of a copper conductor surrounded by insulation. An outer jacket composed of copper or aluminum acts as a conductor and also provides protection. This type of cable is commonly found in the home as an integral part of cable television.

**Figure 2-4.
Coaxial Cable**

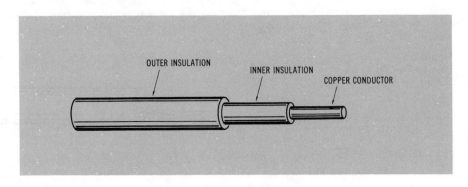

Baseband networks are very fast (10 Mbit/s) but limited to a single channel. It isn't possible to send integrated voice, data, and video signals over baseband networks.

Baseband Networks

Baseband coaxial cable has one channel that carries a single message at a time at very high speed. Its carrier wire is surrounded by a copper mesh and the entire cable's diameter usually is approximately 3/8 inch (in). Digital information is sent across a baseband cable's bandwidth in serial fashion one bit at a time. Depending upon the LAN, it is possible for baseband coaxial cable to handle a data rate of 10 Megabits/second (Mbit/s). Ethernet, the first major local area network with non-proprietary communications interfaces and protocols, uses baseband coaxial cable. Since the Ethernet standard has been supported by both Xerox Corporation and Digital Equipment Corporation, baseband cabling is a popular choice for a LAN medium. Because of baseband's single channel limitation, it isn't possible to send integrated signals composed of voice, data, and even video over baseband cable. One advantage of baseband cabling is that it is easy to tap into this cable and connect or disconnect workstations without disturbing network operations. Although the maximum recommended distance for a baseband LAN is approximately 1.8 miles (3 kilometers), 1500 ft (500 m) might prove to be a more realistic figure if the network is heavily used. While baseband's inability to send integrated signals and its distance limitation must be considered when configuring a network, these disadvantages may not be significant if the primary criteria in media selection are speed of data transmission and cost.

Broadband Networks

Broadband networks can carry integrated voice, data, and even video signals. Because amplifiers are used, broadband has a greater range than baseband.

Unlike baseband, broadband systems have the capacity to carry several different signals broadcast at different frequencies at the same time. This is the approach cable television companies have taken, using 75-ohm broadband coaxial cable. Subscribers can select from several different stations, each broadcasting on its own designated frequency. All broadband systems can utilize a single cable with bi-directional amplifiers as depicted in *Figure 2-5*, or they can use a dual-cable approach. In either case, carrier signals are sent to a central point known as the "head end" from which they are retransmitted to all points on the network.

**Figure 2-5.
Single Broadband
Coaxial Cable with
Bi-Directional Amplifiers**

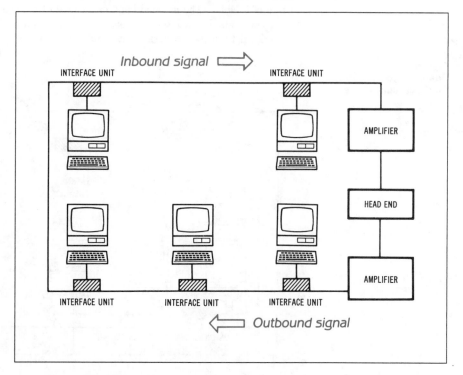

The single cable approach splits a cable by frequency in order to achieve bi-directional transmission of data. Commercial cable companies utilize 6-MHz channels for each communication path. Even with some frequencies designed as "guard bands" between the different channels, it is possible to allocate 346 MHz for forward communications (6 MHz/channel × 56 channels) and 25 MHz for the return data path (6 MHz/channel × 4 channels). The 25 MHz devoted to returning data can be used for several narrow-band channels.

Dual-broadband cable uses one cable for inbound data moving toward the head end and a second cable looped at the head end for the outbound carriers. The full frequency spectrum is available for both inbound and outbound signals. Because of the duplication of cabling, amplifiers, and hardware, dual-broadband cable is much more expensive than the single cable approach, but some networks might require the twice as many usable channels available. Let's take a closer look at this particular broadband approach.

With a dual-cable configuration, coaxial cable forms a two-way highway composed of two bands, each containing several channels. Standard television channels transmit at 6 MHz. Since we have a band with a range of approximately 300 MHz, we can have as many as 50 channels broadcasting at a data rate of 5 Mbit/s. The inbound band carries data from the local area network's *nodes* (individual workstations) to the head end while the outbound band carries data to the network nodes as illustrated in *Figure 2-6.*

**Figure 2-6.
Dual-Broadband Cable
Configuration**

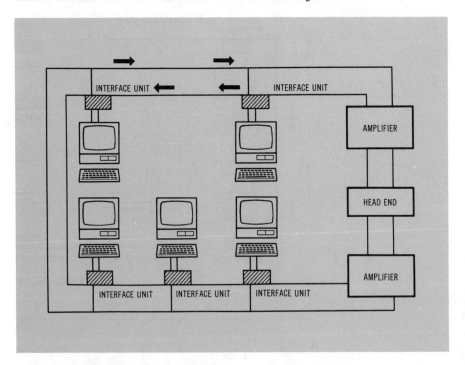

Broadband cable installation requires far more planning than baseband. Since the broadband signals are being broadcast, amplifiers need to be installed to maintain the strength of the signals. In a company with several departments, each department would have a *drop line* with *tap lines* coming off to each node (workstation). The taps contain resistors to ensure that all workstations receive signals at the same strength. If the Widget Company were planning to add an additional building in the future, it would want to include a splitter as shown in *Figure 2-7*. This divides the signal into two paths. Since the splitter was added to ensure future LAN growth, the unused port would be sealed until needed. Because splitters affect transmission quality across the entire network, splitters for anticipated growth should be included in the LAN's initial plan.

**Figure 2-7.
Coaxial Cable
Configuration with
Splitters**

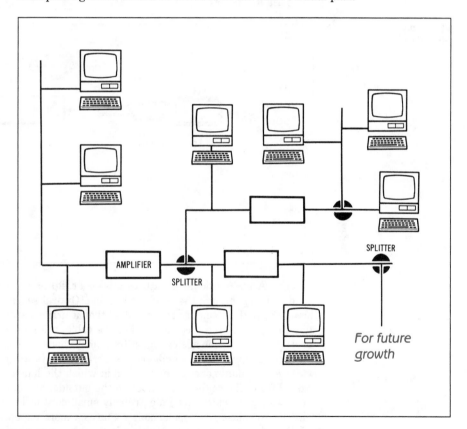

Fiber-Optic Cable

Fiber-optic technology offers immunity from electromagnetic interference and error-free transmission for several miles with the highest level of network security. Unhappily, it is the most expensive medium for use in a local area network.

One of the most exciting media advances in recent years has been the use of fiber optics in local area networks. This new type of data transmission provides a number of advantages over twisted-pair and coaxial cable. In addition to data transmission rates far in excess of either of the other media, fiber-optic cabling is immune to electromagnetic or radio-frequency interference, and it is capable of transmitting signals several miles without loss. This mode of transmission is virtually immune to unauthorized reception. The cable is made of pure glass drawn into very thick fiber to form a core. As *Figure 2-8* illustrates, these fibers are surrounded by *cladding*, a layer of glass with a lower refractive index than the glass in the core.

**Figure 2-8.
Fiber-Optic Cabling**

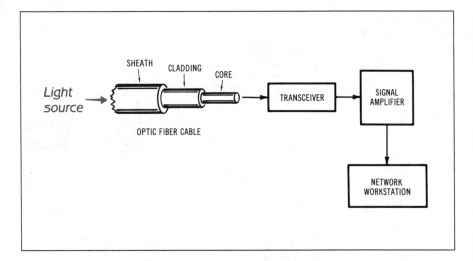

A fiber-optic network uses a laser or light-emitting diode (LED) to send a signal through the core of the cable. Optical repeaters are often used along the path to amplify the signal so that it arrives at its destination at full strength. At the receiving end of the cable, the message is translated back into a digital or analog signal by a photodiode. The cabling consists either of a single fiber (*monomode*), several fibers (*multimode fiber*), or a variation of multimode (*graded index*) in which the index of refraction drops slowly from the center of the fiber to the outside. Monomode fiber has a very wide bandwidth, but its extremely small core makes it extremely difficult to splice. Also, monomode requires a more expensive laser than an LED as a signaling source. Multimode fiber has a smaller bandwidth, but it is much easier to splice. Graded-index multimode fiber is the most expensive medium, but it provides the highest transmission rate over the greatest distance of the three.

Multimode fiber optics for network cabling comes in groups of from two to twenty-four fibers, with groups of two to four fibers the norm. Each fiber is unidirectional since a beam of light is transmitted in only one direction. Two-way communication requires another fiber within the cable so that light can travel in the opposite direction. The American National Standards Institute has established a standard for the physical media-dependent (PMD) layer of the fiber data-distributed interface (FDDI) to work in conjunction with data transmission of 100 Mbit/s. It is possible to achieve rates up to 1 gigabit/second.

It is important that this fiber-optic standard is consistent with the AT&T Premises Distribution Scheme (PDS) as far as the ratio of cladding-to-core (62.5:125 multimode fiber). Therefore companies that have installed AT&T fiber-optic equipment for voice transmission are already cabled for data transmission by local area networks utilizing fiber-optic technology.

At present, fiber-optic cabling is too expensive for most installations and its sophisticated technology makes it difficult to add new workstations after initial installation. But if a company has a serious interference problem, the need for absolute network security, or the need to send signals several miles, fiber optics might be the only solution at present.

NETWORK ARCHITECTURE

Just as there are several different ways to cable a local area network, there are also several different forms a network can take. We call these different shapes the "network architecture" or "topology." Keep in mind that the form of the LAN does not limit the medium of transmission. Twisted-pair wire, coaxial cable, and fiber optics all lend themselves to the various topologies.

The Star

The star topology makes it easy to add new workstations and to provide detailed network analysis.

One of the earliest types of network topologies is the *star*, which uses the same approach to sending and receiving messages as our telephone system. Just as telephone calls from one customer (workstation) to another customer (workstation) are handled by a central switching station, in a LAN star topology, all messages must go through a central computer that controls the flow of data. AT&T's STARLAN is an example of a network utilizing this approach. As *Figure 2-9* illustrates, this architecture makes it easy to add new workstations. Only a cable from the central computer to the microcomputer and its network interface card are needed to tie that workstation to the LAN.

**Figure 2-9.
A Star Network
Topology**

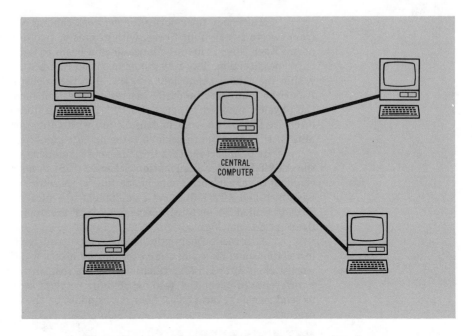

Another advantage of star topology is that the network administrator can give certain nodes higher status than other nodes. The central computer looks for signals from these higher-priority workstations before recognizing other nodes. For networks in which a few key users require immediate response from on-line inquiries, for example, this feature of star topology can be crucial. Finally, a star architecture permits centralized diagnostics of all network functions. Since all messages come through the central computer, it is easy to analyze all workstation messages and produce reports that reveal files utilized by each node. This type of report can prove valuable in ensuring that network security has not been breeched.

The failure of the central computer results in the entire network's failure.

The major weakness of a star architecture is that the entire local area network fails if anything happens to the central computer. This is precisely the same weakness of multiuser minicomputer systems that rely on a central processor.

The Bus

A bus topology is like a data highway. It is easy to add new workstations but difficult to maintain network security. It is often used for low-level LANS that don't require tremendous speed.

A second major network topology is the *bus*. Think of bus, depicted in *Figure 2-10*, as a data highway connecting several LAN workstations. In many such networks, the workstations check whether a message is coming down the highway before sending their messages. Since all workstations share the bus, all messages pass other workstations on the way to their destination. Each workstation checks the address on the message to see if it matches its own address.

**Figure 2-10.
A Bus Network
Topology**

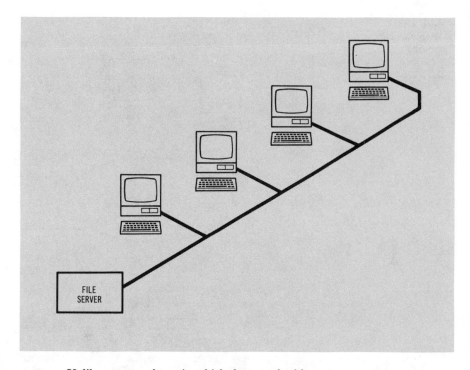

Unlike star topology, in which dozens of cables can congregate near the central computer and cause logistical problems, bus cabling is simple. Many of the low-cost LANs use a bus architecture and twisted-pair wire cabling. Another advantage is that the failure of a workstation doesn't cripple the rest of the network. Gateway Communications' G-Net is an example of a network that uses the bus approach.

A disadvantage of the bus topology is that generally there must be a minimum distance between workstation taps in order to avoid signal interference. Also, there is no easy way for a system administrator to run diagnostics on the entire network. Finally, a bus architecture doesn't have the network security features inherent in a star topology; since all messages are sent along a common data highway, security could be compromised by an unauthorized network user.

The Ring

The ring topology combines advantages of the star and bus. A workstation assumes the role of monitoring all network functions. The failure of one workstation does not result in the failure of the entire network.

Figure 2-11 illustrates a third major type of network architecture: the *ring*. A ring topology consists of several nodes joined together to form a circle. Messages proceed from node to node in one direction only. (Some ring networks can send messages bi-directionally, but only in one direction at a time.) The ring topology permits verification that a message has been received. When a node receives a message addressed to itself, it copies the message and then sends the message back to the sender.

**Figure 2-11.
A Ring Network
Topology**

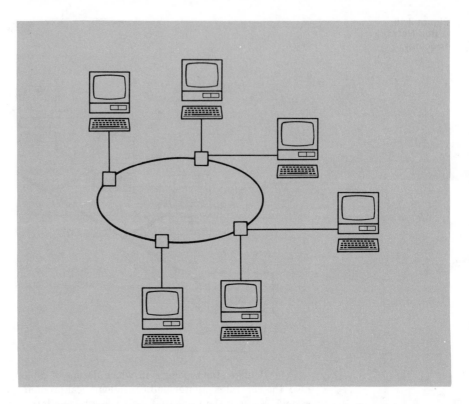

One of the major issues in a ring topology is the need of ensuring that all workstations have equal access to the network. In a *token ring* LAN, a data packet known as a "token" is sent from the transmitting workstation throughout the network. The token contains the address of the sender and the address of the node to receive the message. When the receiving station has copied its message, it returns the token to the originating workstation which then can send the token to the next workstation in the ring.

We will discuss the intricacies of how a token is designed when we examine IBM's token ring network later in this book. It is important to note, however, that for system administration one workstation is designated as the monitoring node in the network. Although this workstation handles all diagnostic functions, if it fails, another workstation may be designated for this task.

There are many advantages to a ring topology. Using bypass software, the network can withstand the failure of various workstations by bypassing them while maintaining the network's integrity. Additional ring networks can be linked together through "bridges" which switch data from one ring to another.

If several workstations are cabled together to form a ring topology, it is extremely difficult to add new workstations. The entire network would have to be shut down while a new node is added and the cabling reattached. There is a simple solution, however. Most token ring networks are now equipped with "wire centers." These connectors, seen in *Figure 2-11*, enable the network administrator to add or remove workstations by connecting or disconnecting them from the appropriate wire centers while the network remains intact and in operation.

NETWORK STANDARDS AND PROTOCOLS

Over the past few years a number of network standards have been developed. Some governing organizations in this field have developed protocols, or rules that ensure compatibility for different vendors' network hardware and software.

We have just looked at the major components of a local area network. If the computers, application software, network software, and cabling were manufactured by the same vendor, there would be little problem in making everything work together smoothly. Today's reality, though, is that network software from one LAN manufacturer usually won't work on a competitor's network and application programs, even cabling must be selected for a specific local area network.

To provide some level of uniformity among network vendors, the International Standards Organization (ISO) has developed *Open Systems Interconnection* (OSI) standards. Different computers networked together need to know in what form they will receive information. When will a particular word begin and when will it end and the next word begin? Is there a way for one computer to check whether its message was garbled in transmission? The OSI model answers these questions and more with a set of standards that in future may result in our confidence that network products from different vendors will work together.

The OSI Model

The OSI standards consist of a seven-layer model that ensures efficient communication within a local area network and between different networks.

As *Figure 2-12* illustrates, the OSI model consists of seven layers of standards. Each of these layers is designed to provide a service for the layer immediately above it. Perhaps an example will illustrate this principle. Whenever someone uses a citizen's band radio to communicate with another person, he or she is using a set of agreed-upon standards very much like the OSI model. Let's look more closely at how Frank's call to Betty follows a series of uniform standards.

By pressing his send button and announcing "Breaker breaker," Frank indicates he wishes to send a message. He then uses a nickname to identify himself before asking for his friend Betty by her nickname: "This is Happy Hacker, can you read me PC Woman?" Having established communication, Frank tells her to "switch over to channel 25 because it's clearer." Betty acknowledges the message, "That's 10-4, Happy Hacker."

Physically, Frank had to press certain buttons to broadcast his message. His use of nicknames established an address for the recipient of his message as well as identifying himself as the sender. Frank then established that his communication was being received clearly (he identified the quality of transmission). After establishing an error-free channel of communication, Frank began talking (with a slight Brooklyn accent) about his new communications program. Betty had to translate Frank's technical

Figure 2-12.
The OSI Model

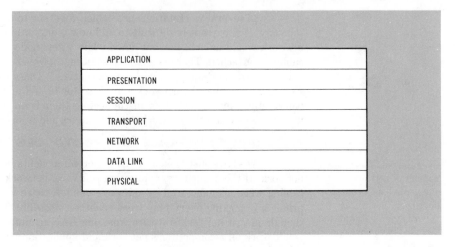

jargon and his Brooklyn slang into standard American English. She could do this because Frank followed certain rules, including using American English grammatical patterns.

Frank followed a series of generally accepted standards while conversing with Betty over their CB radios. The OSI layers of standards only work when all vendors adhere to them and don't bypass any for shortcuts. Note that these standards are not hardware and they are not software; they are simply a set of generally accepted conventions. By dividing the complex procedures necessary for data communications along a network into seven different layers, the OSI model makes it easier to achieve agreement initially on the lower layers and ultimately on the entire seven layers.

The Physical Layer

The physical layer standards cover the hardware standards for network compatibility. These include the voltages used, timing of the data transmission, and handshaking requirements.

The first layer is actually a set of rules regarding the hardware used to transmit data. Among the items covered at this level are the voltages used, the timing of the data transmission, and the rules for establishing the initial "handshaking" communication connection. The physical layer establishes whether bits are going to be sent half or full duplex. Half-duplex transmission is similar to data transmission across a CB. A message is sent and an answer is received. Full-duplex transmission is the simultaneous sending and receiving of data. We will look at this process more closely in Chapter 3 when we examine communications between local area networks and mainframe computers.

Other hardware covered in the physical layer standards includes descriptions of the acceptable connectors and interfaces to media. At this layer, the OSI model is concerned with electrical considerations and with bits (1s and 0s), though the bits have no meaning at this level; that is the responsibility of the next OSI layer—the data link layer.

The Data Link Layer

The data link layer is concerned with packaging data into data frames for transmission.

Earlier we saw that the OSI model has been developed so that each layer provides the layer above it with a key element. The physical layer provides raw bits to the data link, where the bits are given meaning. At this point we no longer deal with bits, but with *data frames*. The data link adds flags to indicate the beginning and ending of messages. At this layer, the standards ensure that data is not mistaken for flags and checks for errors within the data frame. This error checking can take the form of sending information about a data frame to the receiving machine and getting an acknowledgment if everything has been received correctly.

The Network Layer

The network layer is concerned with packet switching. It establishes virtual circuits between computers or terminals for data communication.

This third layer of the OSI model is concerned with packet switching. It establishes virtual circuits (paths between two computers or terminals) for data communications. The network layer takes messages from the fourth layer and repackages them as data packets before sending them to the lower two layers from which they are transmitted. As the destination, this layer reassembles the message. To understand the use of data packets, we need to look at an industry standard found at the lower three OSI model layers, the X.25 standard.

CCITT X.25 Standard

The X.25 standard establishes rules for data packets that are to be sent to public switched networks. The three layers of the X.25 set correspond to the first three protocol layers of the OSI model.

The Consultative Committee for International Telephony and Telegraphy (CCITT) has developed a set of international telecommunications standards. As *Figure 2-13* illustrates, the X.25 standard's three layers (physical, frame, and packet) correspond to the OSI model's first three layers (physical, data link, and network). X.25's physical layer uses the CCITT's X.21 recommendation to define the RS-232 standard for asynchronous data transmission as well as full-duplex point-to-point synchronous transmission between the data termination equipment (DTE) and a public switched network. The frame layer (corresponding to the OSI model's data link layer) is where data is exchanged between a DTE and the network. In the packet layer, corresponding to the OSI's network layer, data is in packet form, which is a requirement for public switched networks. The X.25 standard ensures that information sent from DTE can be understood when received by a public packet network.

These packets contain several discrete forms of information that distinguish one message from another. A packet contains an address field which indicates where it is being transmitted. A control field provides several different kinds of information, including indications that a message is beginning or ending and that the message has been received successfully or an acknowledgment that an error has occurred.

Figure 2-13.
X.25 Standards and the
OSI Model

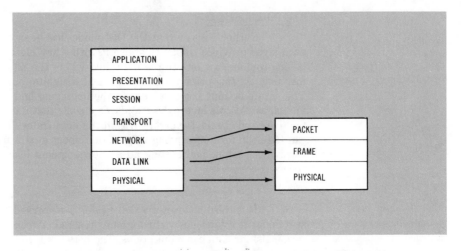

The X.25 standard is designed for packet switching. Using this convention, the network layer of the OSI model functions like a gigantic mailroom. Messages from a host computer are placed in packets, addressed, and sent to the bottom two layers for transmission. Since there may be several different ways (circuits) to route a message to a particular workstation, special routing tables keep track of traffic in order to balance the workload. The major use of the X.25 standard is in conjunction with mainframe communications and public switched networks, a subject we will cover in Chapter 3, when we look at communications between local area networks and mainframe computers.

The network layer contains other conventions in addition to X.25, including procedures for recognizing message priorities and sending messages in proper order. Finally, this layer eases network congestion by preventing a computer from sending information faster than it can be received or stored.

High-Level Data Link Control Procedure (HLDC)

High-level data link control procedure defines the standards for linking a DTE and a DCE.

The X.25 standard found particularly at the data link and network layers of the OSI model defines the standards for linking a DTE and data communications equipment (DCE) utilizing "high-level data link control procedure" (HLDC). Under HLDC, all information is sent in frames. A frame consists of six fields with flags denoting the beginning and ending fields. As *Figure 2-14* illustrates, the flags are identical bit patterns characterized by six consecutive 1-bits. The address field consists of the destination address if the frame is a command and the source address if the frame is a response. The control field contains information indicating whether the frame contains a command or a response. The information field usually contains integral multiples of 8-bit characters, but this is not always the case. We will soon see that this is a significant difference between HLDC and a subset of it used by IBM called "synchronous data link control" (SDLC).

Figure 2-14.
The HLDC Standard

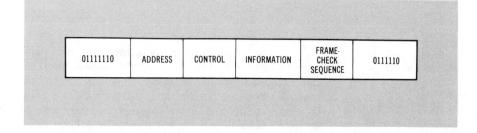

01111110	ADDRESS	CONTROL	INFORMATION	FRAME-CHECK SEQUENCE	0111110

The frame-check sequence field is used to ensure that the receiving station can distinguish information from garbage. It is necessary to have a way to handle situations where information might contain more than five straight 1-bits. How can the receiving station determine whether the data is really information or simply a flag indicating the end of a frame?

Bit stuffing ensures that data in a packet won't be mistaken for control bits.

The solution to this problem is called "bit stuffing." The HLDC protocol ensures that a 0-bit is inserted in any word that contains more than five straight 1-bits. Before the receiving station reads the data, information contained in the frame-check sequence field indicates where to eliminate the 0-bits that have been stuffed into the frame.

The HLDC protocol is designed to handle data exchange between a central computer that controls communications and secondary stations. The central computer is responsible for error checking as well as for polling the secondary stations at designated times. When it receives a signal that a station has a message to send, it sends a poll bit that permits a response from that station. This mode of operation is called "normal response mode" (NRM).

A second mode of operation permits all secondary stations to send messages whenever they desire without waiting for a poll bit from the central computer. This method is called "asynchronous response mode" (ARM).

Synchronous Data Link Control (SDLC)

Synchronous Data Link Control (SDLC) data packets contain some control codes unique to IBM.

IBM computers running under IBM's system network architecture use synchronous data link control (SDLC), a subset of HLDC. While it contains the basic HLDC frame consisting of beginning and ending flags with the same HLDC bit pattern, there are differences between HLDC and SDLC. SDLC's information field contains data that must be integral multiples of 8-bit characters. Also, SDLC contains several commands and responses not found under HLDC. We'll return to SDLC in Chapter 3 when we examine the link between local area networks and the IBM mainframe world of system network architecture.

More about OSI

The Transport Layer

The transport layer is primarily concerned with error recognition and recovery, but it also handles the multiplexing of messages and the regulating of information flow.

The transport layer has many functions including several orders of error recognition and recovery. At the highest order, the transport layer can detect and even correct errors as well as identify packets that have been sent in incorrect order and rearrange them in correct order. This layer also multiplexes several messages together onto one circuit and then writes a header to indicate which message belongs to which circuit. Regulation of information flow by control of the messages' movement also occurs at this layer.

The Session Layer

The session layer is concerned with network management. It handles password recognition, login and logoff procedures, and network monitoring and reporting.

So far, we've seen that the OSI model is concerned with bits and with data messages, not with recognizing particular users on the network. On the session level, the user communicates directly with the layer. It can verify a password typed in by a user and enable a user to switch from half-duplex transmission to full duplex. It can determine who transmits, for how long and how often.

Think of the session layer as the layer concerned with network management. It has the ability to abort a session and so controls the orderly termination of a session. It controls data transfers and it even handles recovery from a system crash. Finally, the session layer can monitor system usage and bill users for their time.

The Presentation Layer

Network security, file transfers, and format functions are dealt with at the presentation layer.

This is the layer of the OSI model concerned with network security, file transfers, and formatting functions. At the bit level, the presentation layer is capable of encoding data in a variety of forms, including ASCII and EBCDIC. The American Standard Code for Information Interchange (ASCII) is a 7-bit plus parity-bit character code for the transmission of data that is the most universally used convention. Since many of the larger IBM computers used Extended Binary Coded Decimal Interchange Code (EBCDIC), the presentation layer must also be able to handle this second standard for data transmission. For true communication, both communicating computers' presentation layers must contain the same protocols. Protocol conversion between computers using different formats is also found at this layer. Most of the word processing functions we associate with the formatting of text are also handled in this layer, including pagination, number of lines per screen, and cursor movement across the screen.

The proliferation of terminals with incompatible codes is treated at this level. A terminal protocol resolves these differences by enabling each data terminal to map the same virtual terminal. In effect, this procedure means that a set of translation tables exists between a local terminal and a remote terminal. The local terminal sends a data structure that defines its current screen in terms of how many characters/line will be displayed. This number can vary considerably; although many terminals routinely display

132 characters/line, other formats are readily available. The data structure goes to the remote terminal's corresponding control object which translates this number into a code that its terminal can understand and implement.

The Application Layer

Network programs found at the application layer include electronic mail, database managers, file-server software, and printer-server software.

For the most part, the functions performed in this layer are user specified. It is difficult to generalize about the protocols found here since different user programs establish different needs. Certain industries such as banking have developed their own standards for this level. Generally, the application layer handles messages and remote logins, and is responsible for network management statistics. At this level, you will find database management programs, electronic mail, file-server and printer-server programs, and operating system command and response language.

IEEE Network Standards

IEEE has developed standards for a bus LAN (802.3), a token bus LAN (802.4), and a token ring LAN (802.5).

Using the International Standards Organization's OSI set of layered standards as a foundation, several IEEE committees have worked to develop a set of standards for local area network topologies and access methods. The committees developed three IEEE 802 standards of particular interest to us: 802.3—the CSMA/CD bus standard; 802.4—the token bus standard; and 802.5—the token ring standard. A fourth standard, 802.6, is concerned with standards for a metropolitan area network, a subject beyond the scope of this book. The complete set of 802 standards may be ordered directly from the IEEE whose address is listed in the bibliography.

Why develop four different and even contradictory standards? The reason is that by 1980, when the 802 committees first met, a wide range of incompatible local area network products already existed. Some vendors had opted for bus topologies while others had chosen token rings or stars. The vendors had also chosen differing methods of avoiding data collisions by network nodes that have information to send: a significant problem for local area networks. So many kinds of local area networks had proliferated because no one topology or data-access method is best for all LAN applications. IBM illustrates this by offering a bus topology network (PC LAN Network) as well as a token ring topology (Token Ring Network); each network is designed to meet a different set of customers' needs. We'll discuss these two networks in Chapter 4.

The major advantage of the IEEE 802 standards to the end user is that they'll eventually result in the standardization of the ISO's physical and data link layers in its OSI model so that hardware from manufacturers that comply with these standards will work together. For network software to work, however, vendors will have to follow the standards established by the higher layers of the OSI model. This may take some time.

IEEE 802.3 and Ethernet

When the IEEE 802 committees began their deliberations, they were faced with a de facto standard, Xerox's Ethernet Local Area Network. By 1980, Intel and Digital Equipment Corporation had joined

Xerox in indicating that all their products would be Ethernet compatible. Rather than require that all local area networks follow the Ethernet standard, an IEEE committee provided 802.3 as an acceptable Ethernet-like standard.

As we indicated, the IEEE 802 committees based its standards on the first three layers of the OSI model. They developed the data link layer into two sublayers: a logical link control sublayer (LLC) and a media access control sublayer (MAC). The LLC standard is very like the HLDC standard we described earlier, while the MAC sublayer is concerned with data-collision detection.

The Ethernet Data Packet

The IEEE 802.3 standard describes a LAN using a bus topology. This network uses 50-ohm coaxial baseband cable capable of sending data at 10 Mbit/s. As *Figure 2-15* illustrates, the committee specified exactly how a frame should be composed. Notice the similarity between this frame and the HLDC protocol discussed earlier in this chapter.

Figure 2-15.
An Ethernet Frame

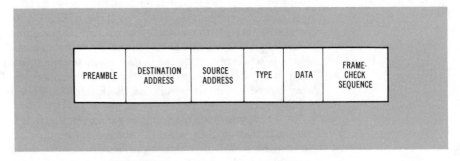

PREAMBLE	DESTINATION ADDRESS	SOURCE ADDRESS	TYPE	DATA	FRAME-CHECK SEQUENCE

The IEEE 802.3 committee defined an Ethernet data packet's format, the cabling to be used, and the maximum distance for the network.

The Ethernet packet begins with a preamble consisting of 8 bytes used for synchronization. The destination address can be a single workstation, a group of workstations, or several groups of workstations. The source address enables the workstation receiving the message to recognize where it came from. The type field is important because there must be a way of designating which type format the data is using. Without this information, it is impossible to decipher the packet when it arrives. The data field is strictly limited; it can hold a minimum of 46 bytes and a maximum of 1500 bytes. Finally, the frame-check sequence field ensures that the data in the other fields arrives safely. In addition to specifying the type of data frames that can be packed in a packet and the type of cable that can be used to send this information, the committee also specified the maximum length of a single cable (1500 ft or 500 m) and the ways that repeaters could be used to boost the signal throughout the network.

CSMA/CD Protocol

Carrier-Sense Multiple
Access with Collision
Detection (CSMA/CD) is a
protocol for defining the
ways that networks will
avoid data collisions.

The IEEE 802.3 committee specified the way that a local area
network using the bus topology should construct its frames of information
and send them over the network to avoid collisions. The protocol is known
as Carrier-Sense Multiple Access with Collision Detection (CSMA/CD). The
CSMA portion of this protocol can be visualized by imagining a network
user who wishes to send a message. In terms of the OSI model that has
been incorporated into the IEEE 802.3 standard, the physical layer of the
user's workstation model generates a signal. It listens to detect carrier
signal from another user who is about to send a message. If no other signal
is detected, the user sends his or her message.

There are problems with this seemingly tidy solution to traffic
control on a network. What happens if two network users are located fairly
far apart? It is possible for them to issue a carrier-sense signal, listen and
hear nothing, and then send their messages only to have the data collide.
To avoid this type of accident, the committee added Collision Detection
(CD) to the CSMA approach. A user listens as he or she transmits a
message. If the user detects a collision, she or he listens for the other
workstation to send transmission and then transmits the message again.

There is still another problem with this approach. Imagine two
drivers who arrive simultaneously at an intersection having four-way stop
signs. Both drivers come to a complete stop, wait a reasonable time, and
then begin to move again only to have to slam on their brakes to avoid a
collision. Embarrassed by the near collision, the two drivers pause before
starting again. Unfortunately, they start again at the same time and once
again narrowly avoid a collision.

While the two drivers' adventure at an intersection sounds like a
silent movie comedy plot, the reality of collision after collision is certainly
not funny to network administrators. To avoid this possibility, network
planners have designed their CSMA/CD approach so that each workstation
waits a different random amount of time after a data collision before
transmitting the message again. After a collision, a special signal called a
jam is sent through the network. This signal ensures that all network
stations, no matter how far apart, are aware that there has been a collision.

After repeated collisions, the network will double its random
delays before permitting stations to transmit again. This approach doesn't
totally eliminate collisions since it is still theoretically possible for two well-
separated workstations to wait different amounts of time and still transmit
messages that collide. These accidents, however, are infrequent and thus
manageable.

Despite the ingenuity of this approach to collision avoidance, there
is one additional consideration. A heavily used bus network utilizing
CSMA/CD can begin to look like a Los Angeles freeway during rush hour.
Even though data is supposed to move at 10 Mbit/s, the doubling and
redoubling of the delay duration after a few collisions can reduce the
network's throughput to as little as 1–3 Mbit/s.

IEEE 802.4 Token Bus

IEEE 802.4 defines a bus topology using a data packet "token" that is passed from workstation to workstation. Only the workstation possessing the token can transmit information, effectively eliminating the possibility of data collisions.

The IEEE 802.4 subcommittee developed a standard for a different type of bus network that doesn't have the contentious approach of the 802.3 model. This type of network is desirable if it is absolutely necessary that there be no data collisions.

Figure 2-16 illustrates the token bus frame format under IEEE 802.4. Primarily, the preamble field synchronizes the signal. The start frame delimiter and end frame deliminator fields define the limits of the frame. The frame control frame carries information from either the LLC or MAC sublayers while the destination and source address fields function identically with those found in the 802.3 Ethernet frame. The destination field can contain a specific workstation's address, a group address for several workstations, or addresses for several different groups (called a "broadcast" address). The information field and the frame-check sequence fields both are identical with those discussed under the 802.3 model.

**Figure 2-16.
A Token Bus Format**

PREAMBLE	START FRAME DELIMITER	FRAME CONTROL	DESTINATION ADDRESS	SOURCE ADDRESS	INFORMATION	FRAME-CHECK SEQUENCE	END FRAME DELIMITER

The token is actually a data packet. A workstation sends the token to the address of the workstation designated to receive it. This station copies the message and then returns the token to the sending station. *Figure 2-17* illustrates how a token is passed in a bus topology. The network maintains a table composed of addresses for each workstation. The address may bear no resemblance to where a station is physically located on the bus network, but it is an indication of the order in which a station will receive the token. A workstation that requires the token frequently because it needs to use the network more than other workstations may be listed several times in the table so that it will receive the token more often. The token is passed from one station to the station with the next lower address. When the station at address 100 sends the token to address 75, it listens to be sure the token was received satisfactorily.

Figure 2-17.
A Token Bus Network

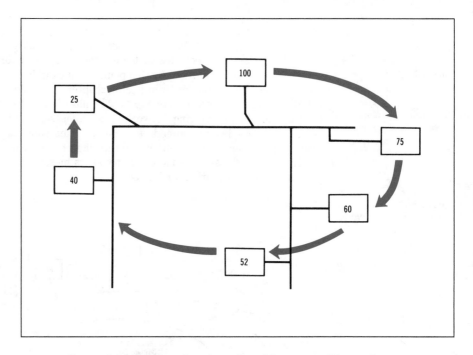

Remember that the token is really a bit pattern. If a station doesn't receive a reply, it sends a second token. If there is still no reply, the sending station sends a special message (called a "who follows" frame) down the network requesting the address of the next station to receive the token. If this fails to elicit a response, it sends a general request through the network asking if any station wishes to receive the token. This is known as a "solicit successor" frame. The sending workstation then changes the address to match this address and sends the token.

Notice that the topology of this 802.4 standard is a bus, yet the token passing is in the form of a logical ring. The lowest address workstation to receive the token will send it back to begin the process all over again. In a smoothly working token bus, each workstation receives the token, inserts the information it wishes to send, and sends it on to its destination, where the workstation copies the information before once again sending the token through the network. Problems can occur with this approach, too.

The most serious problems are caused by malfunctioning hardware that can result in missing tokens or even in multiple tokens. The network controller assumes responsibility for monitoring and error checking to keep such a situation from crippling the network. Other weaknesses inherent in the token bus approach include specific distance limitations; under Ethernet, for example, there are minimum distances required between individual workstations. There are also limitations on how many new workstations can be added to the bus because each new workstation creates a certain amount of signal distortion.

IEEE 802.5 Token Ring Network

IEEE 802.5 defines a token ring network in which workstations pass a token around a physical and logical ring. The token ring uses amplifiers to boost signals so it has a greater range than bus networks.

The IEEE 802.5 standard was developed to cover local area networks with ring topologies that use a token to pass information from one workstation to another. At this point, we'll examine the theoretical basis of this set of standards; in a later chapter we'll take a closer look at IBM's token ring network. As *Figure 2-18* illustrates, the sending workstation in a token ring network places a message on the token and directs it to its destination address. The receiving workstation copies the message and sends the token around the ring until it reaches the originating workstation. This unit removes its message and then passes the token to the next station for its use.

**Figure 2-18.
A Token Ring Network**

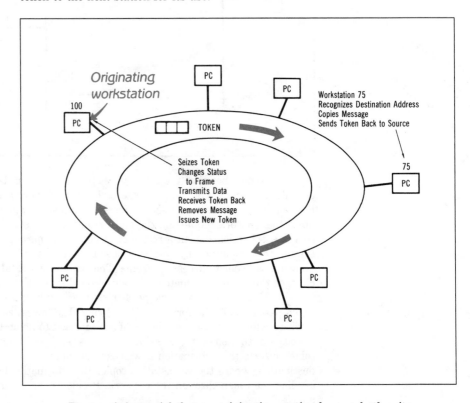

Because it is crucial that an originating station know whether its message has been received, the frame format is slightly different from that of a token bus network. *Figure 2-19* reveals that there is an access control field. This field controls the actual passing of the token. The ending frame delimiter field also contains a new wrinkle. Two bits in this frame are used to indicate whether the station receiving a message recognized the address and whether it actually copied the message successfully.

**Figure 2-19.
A Token Format**

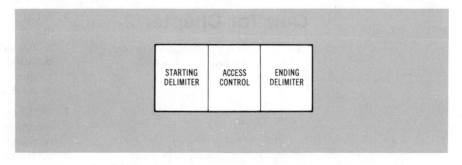

In a smoothly running token ring network, each station receives the token and checks to see if the message is addressed to it. If its address matches, it copies the message and sends the token on by repeating the signal. If the message is for another workstation, it repeats the signal and sends it on. There has to be provision in the network to account for an inactive or defective workstation; otherwise, the entire network would fail. One way to handle this situation is to use hardware that enables the network to bypass a non-transmitting workstation. Earlier we discussed the use of wire centers as a method of keeping the token moving past inactive stations.

A major advantage of a token ring network over a token bus is that it can cover a greater distance without loss of signal since each workstation repeats the signal. Besides the potential problem of a malfunctioning station that is not able to receive or send a message, another negative feature of a token ring network is that large installations require significantly more cable than a corresponding bus topology. In a very large network, however, there may not be another viable alternative. Because of IBM's token ring topology, this type of network is expected to gain at least 70 percent of the local area network market over the next few years.

WHAT HAVE WE LEARNED?

1. File servers offer many advantages over disk servers in a local area network.
2. The major LAN media include twisted-pair wire, coaxial cable, and fiber optics.
3. Broadband coaxial cable can transmit several different messages simultaneously using different frequencies.
4. In a star topology, the entire local area network fails if the central computer fails.
5. CSMA/CD is a method for detecting and avoiding data collisions on a local area network.
6. X.25 is a standard for packet switching with layers of standards corresponding to the first three layers of the OSI model.
7. The OSI model consists of seven layers of standards designed to ensure local area network compatibility of hardware and software.
8. HLDC consists of protocols for placing a message in a packet for transmission.

Quiz for Chapter 2

1. The X.25 set of standards covers how many layers of the OSI model?
   a. One.
   b. Two.
   c. Three.
   d. Four.

2. The OSI model layer that concerns itself with hardware specifications is the:
   a. data link layer.
   b. network layer.
   c. physical layer.
   d. presentation layer.

3. Bit stuffing is used to:
   a. pad insufficient information.
   b. distinguish beginning and ending flags from information.
   c. converting 8-bit words into 16-bit words.
   d. fill a data turkey.

4. When a central computer polls a station to see if it has a message to send, this is an example of:
   a. asynchronous response mode (ARM).
   b. normal response mode (NRM).
   c. infrequent polling procedure (IPP).
   d. polling by authorization (PBA).

5. A protocol is really:
   a. a set of demands.
   b. a set of rules.
   c. a translation book for diplomats.
   d. a call with very high authorization.

6. A CB radio call is very much like:
   a. full-duplex transmission.
   b. half-duplex transmission.
   c. quarter-duplex transmission.
   d. no duplex transmission.

7. In the OSI model, error recognition and recovery is the responsibility of:
   a. the physical layer.
   b. the application layer.
   c. the session layer.
   d. the transport layer.

8. In the OSI model, password verification is the responsibility of:
   a. the session layer.
   b. the physical layer.
   c. the data link layer.
   d. the network layer.

9. Distributed file servers are:
   a. special file servers designed for LANS.
   b. multiple file servers designed to speed up the network.
   c. inexpensive file servers.
   d. file servers also used as work stations.

10. A dedicated file server is:
   a. a hard-working file server.
   b. a file server used as a workstation and as a file server.
   c. a file server used only for serving files to workstations in a local area network.
   d. a file server that never breaks down.

11. A print spooler is:
    a. a buffer used to store files for printing.
    b. the central processing unit.
    c. a printer's spooling mechanism.
    d. a place for assembling and disassembling printer material.

12. To send simultaneous voice and data signals, a LAN should use:
    a. twisted-pair wire.
    b. baseband coaxial cable.
    c. broadband coaxial cable.
    d. two coffee cans with lots of string.

13. A data highway is a good description of which network topology?
    a. A bus.
    b. A star.
    c. A ring.
    d. A token ring.

14. A dead workstation on a token ring network can cripple the network without:
    a. special software.
    b. wire centers or special bypass hardware.
    c. extra tokens.
    d. a dead station token (DST).

15. A broadcast address enables a message to go to:
    a. a single workstation.
    b. a single group of workstations.
    c. several groups of workstations.
    d. a selected peripheral.

16. A jam signal sent through a network means:
    a. the network traffic is too congested.
    b. there has been a data collision.
    c. it's time to go.
    d. the printer's paper feeder is jammed.

17. The IEEE 802.3 standard is closest to:
    a. IBM's Token Ring Network.
    b. Xerox's Ethernet local area network.
    c. a generic star network.
    d. a generic token ring network.

18. For a relatively large network covering a long distance, the best network topology probably would be:
    a. a bus.
    b. a token ring.
    c. a token bus.
    d. a superbus.

19. If interference is a major problem, a network designer should consider:
    a. baseband coaxial cable.
    b. broadband coaxial cable.
    c. twisted-pair wire.
    d. fiber optics.

20. Database management software and electronic mail software would be found in which layer of the OSI model?
    a. the application layer.
    b. the presentation layer.
    c. the data link layer.
    d. the network layer.

Gateways

ABOUT THIS CHAPTER

Microcomputers linked together in a local area network and mainframe computers are of two completely different worlds. In this chapter we'll examine how a microcomputer using a communications gateway can communicate over a LAN with a mainframe computer. We'll take a close look at the mainframe world and how information is handled there and the most common protocols. We'll also examine communications between microcomputers and minicomputers.

Standards for microcomputer communications with mainframes and minicomputers are just starting to emerge. We'll learn about these as well as the different levels of communications possible between microcomputer network user and mainframe or minicomputer. Finally, we will examine how some companies are using their private branch exchange (PBX) phone systems as limited local area networks.

THE WORLD OF SYSTEMS NETWORK ARCHITECTURE (SNA)

IBM's SNA contains several layers of protocols, similar to the OSI model. SNA uses SDLC, a subset of HLDC.

Any discussion of the mainframe world has to begin with IBM's set of specifications for distributed data processing networks. As *Figure 3-1* illustrates, system network architecture (SNA) provides a model composed of network layers very much like the OSI model we studied in Chapter 2. The data flow through SNA is virtually identical with the OSI model except that the frames use the synchronous data link control (SDLC) format rather than the high-level data link control (HLDC) procedure. As we have pointed out, the SDLC frames contain some frames that are transmitted from one node to another throughout an SNA network.

NetView, a new SNA network management program, handles the duties of five former programs much more efficiently.

Recently IBM has replaced five network management programs residing in SNA with a single new program, NetView. NetView provides a centralized management system that performs diagnostics on SNA protocols, communication sessions, and network accounting procedures. It also displays network diagnostic alerts and determines network component failures. NetView can also monitor X.25 traffic in the SNA environment. A new IBM program, X.25 SNA Interconnection, enables SNA networks to carry data under X.25 packet switching protocols.

**Figure 3-1.
Systems Network
Architecture**

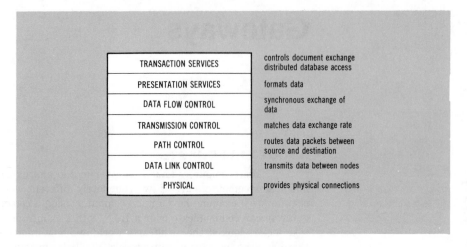

TRANSACTION SERVICES	controls document exchange distributed database access
PRESENTATION SERVICES	formats data
DATA FLOW CONTROL	synchronous exchange of data
TRANSMISSION CONTROL	matches data exchange rate
PATH CONTROL	routes data packets between source and destination
DATA LINK CONTROL	transmits data between nodes
PHYSICAL	provides physical connections

SYNCHRONOUS VERSUS ASYNCHRONOUS DATA TRANSMISSION

While asynchronous transmission sends data 1 byte at a time, synchronous transmission uses frames that permit a stream of data.

Data transmission in the microcomputer world long has taken the form of asynchronous transmission. Serial printers and modems are everyday reminders of how common this form of data communications is. The SNA mainframe world, however, uses the SDLC protocol we discussed briefly in Chapter 2; this is a synchronous method of data transmission. As *Figure 3-2* illustrates, asynchronous transmission is limited to sending characters a byte at a time while the synchronous approach sends continuous information until the transmission is concluded.

**Figure 3-2.
Asynchronous vs.
Synchronous
Transmission**

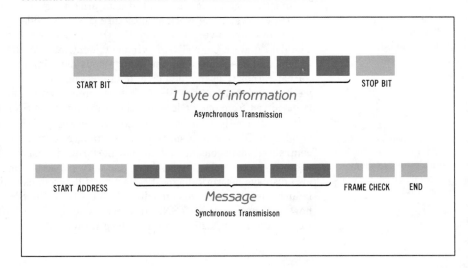

START BIT   *1 byte of information*   STOP BIT

Asynchronous Transmission

START ADDRESS   *Message*   FRAME CHECK   END

Synchronous Transmisison

Some older IBM mainframes use binary synchronous communication (BSC), a protocol that is synchronous but is not the same as SDLC. BSC protocol is character oriented, rather than bit oriented (as is SDLC), and assumes 8-bit characters. We will focus on SDLC protocol machines in this chapter, but it is important to note that several companies, including IBM, market a Binary Synchronous Communication Adapter card and a Binary Synchronous 3270 Emulation program, the keys to tying a microcomputer local area network to an older IBM using BSC protocol.

Logical Units (LUs)

Communication in an SNA network takes place between logical units (LUs). Logical units can represent end users (as does the firmware associated with IBM 3270 terminals, for example) or application programs. Application programs only recognize a terminal's network name, not its physical location. SNA translates the network name into a corresponding address.

Network-Addressable Units (NAUs)

SNA uses network-addressable units (NAUs) to perform a number of network management functions including handling the communications portions of application programs and providing network control. There are three types of network-addressable units: logical units, physical units (PUs), and system services control points (SSCPs). We will examine the latter two types briefly before looking at an actual SNA network in operation.

A physical unit is not actually a physical device. It represents something tangible (a terminal or an intelligent controller, for example) to SNA, which, in effect, deals with the PU rather than with the device itself.

A system services control point (SSCP) serves as the SNA network manager for a single SNA domain. It coordinates communications among network elements, makes sure that the corresponding physical devices are active when two logical units wish to converse, and provides error-checking information.

The Path Control Network

Under SNA, the path control network contains a path control layer and a data link control layer. This network is concerned with traffic flow, transmission priorities, and error recovery. Remember, under SNA, all LUs, PUs, and even SSCPs have different network addresses. The path control network is responsible for identifying the correct addresses of units that wish to converse and then establishing a network path for their conversation.

Logical Units (LUs) can represent end users or application programs.

Network-addressable units (NAUs) consist of logical units (LUs), physical units (PUs), and system services control points (SSCPs).

The path control network identifies addresses of network devices that wish to converse and establishes a path for their conversation.

Sessions

A session consists of a logical and physical path connecting two NAUs for data transmission. NAUs can have multiple sessions.

A session under SNA is a logical and physical path connecting two NAUs for data transmission. SNA thinks of its terminals, controllers, and front-end communication processors as nodes, each having a corresponding PU. If a terminal wishes to communicate with a front-end communication processor, for example, the SSCP would establish a session between the two nodes. Two end users can establish an LU-LU session.

The SSCP controls the activating and deactivating of a session. An application program can maintain several different sessions with different terminals simultaneously under SNA. *Figure 3-3* illustrates the NAU elements found under SNA.

**Figure 3-3.
The NAU Elements
Found Under SNA**

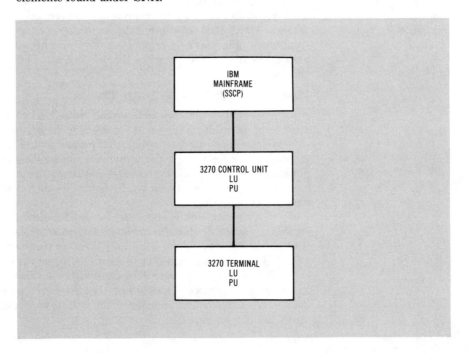

LU 6.2

LU 6.2 contains specifications that ultimately will enable programs written in different languages under different operating systems to communicate with each other.

IBM recently added Advanced Program-to-Program Communications (APPC) to SNA, resulting in development of two new protocols (LU 6.2 and PU 2.1). Earlier we saw that it was possible to have a session between a program and a terminal; now it will be possible to have communication between two programs.

Ultimately, LU 6.2 will enable a microcomputer running a program under one operating system (such as DOS) to communicate with a mainframe computer while retaining its full stand-alone processing capabilities. Underpinning this protocol is the revolutionary concept that different computers running different programs written in different languages under different operating systems will be able to interact with each other.

For years corporations have longed for the ability to download information directly into an IBM personal computer running Lotus 1-2-3. Similarly, there is a real need to be able to take customer files under a DOS program such as dBase III and upload the information directly into a mainframe database.

IBM developed SNA before personal computers were popular. The concept of distributed processing incorporated under SNA was a master-slave relationship. All communication under SNA goes through the main computer. Two users who wish to send information to each other can do so only by going through the mainframe computer. Theoretically under LU 6.2, it will be possible for true peer-to-peer communications. A personal computer as part of an SNA network would be able to address a second personal computer directly without going through the mainframe. Such a path might be particularly valuable if the mainframe should happen to fail.

LU 6.2 overcomes many of the limitations of SNA because it provides a truly generic application program interface (API) between application programs and SNA. Since this interface includes hardware specifications, the network can be thought of as machine independent as long as vendors adhere to these requirements. Rather than the master-slave relationship that has been the norm under SNA, LU 6.2 allows any node in a network session to initiate a session.

IBM has begun to provide tools that will help implement LU 6.2. The Server/Requester Programming Interface (SRPI) is a protocol that allows PC applications to issue requests for services and receive replies from IBM mainframes. This interface permits program-to-program communications under terminal-emulation conditions. SRPI is a subset of the APPC programming interface. IBM has upgraded its mainframe operating systems to work in conjunction with LU 6.2. TSO/E Release 3 is an operating environment upgrade for mainframes running under the MVS/XA TSO/E environment which implements SRPI and allows the mainframe to handle requests for data and services from PCs. IBM has also developed IBM PC Requesters, a product that runs under the new SRPI interface. With this product, an IBM PC will have a DOS menu with which to access databases. The workstation will be able to request data on a record-by-record basis if necessary.

The major problem with LU 6.2 is that existing software packages and hardware do not follow the API guidelines. It will take some time before there are enough programs available to make this new protocol a force in the SNA world.

MICRO-MAINFRAME COMMUNICATIONS

Until the software and hardware that follow LU 6.2 comes along, the main method for micro-mainframe communications will continue to be IBM terminal emulation.

Despite the exciting possibilities of LU 6.2, the dearth of software written for it means that for the foreseeable future microcomputers will continue to communicate with the mainframe world by emulating various IBM terminals. Let's examine several ways, both local and remote, to tie the two worlds together. While our emphasis in this book is on local area networks and on how microcomputers within a network can communicate with each other as well as with mainframes, it is important to understand the options that are available, including those that are limited to a single microcomputer emulating an IBM terminal.

327X Terminal Emulation Via Cluster Controller

An IBM mainframe computer can communicate with various peripherals through a 3274 or 3276 Cluster Controller. The 3274 Controller can connect as many as 32 terminals or printers to the mainframe while only 7 devices can be connected to the 3276. As *Figure 3-4* illustrates, an IBM PC can be connected directly to the mainframe through the cluster controller using coaxial cable and special 3278 terminal emulation software and hardware. The IRMA card in *Figure 3-4* fits into an IBM PC's full-size slot, and it contains RAM, ROM, a 3270 coaxial interface, and a high-speed processor capable of handling 4 million instructions per second. By pressing the PC's two shift keys simultaneously, a user can shift between a DOS application and 3270 terminal emulation.

Figure 3-4.
An IBM PC Connected to a Cluster Controller

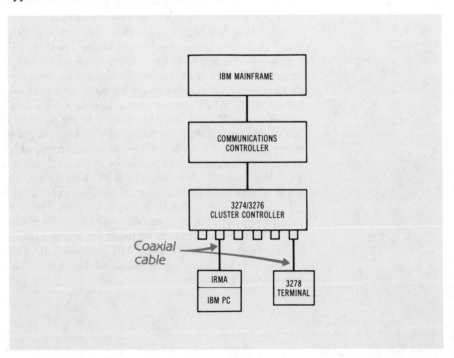

The keyboard and screen on an IBM 3278 terminal are far different than those on an IBM PC. The IRMA software allows the PC user to press keys and have the equivalent 3278 keystrokes sent to the cluster controller. Similarly, the software "paints" the PC's monitor with what appears to be an IBM 3278 display. While the 3278 monochrome terminal is the most common form of terminal emulation, there is also software to emulate the 3279 color terminal. IBM even offers a 3270-PC which really is the IBM PC with a built-in 3270 terminal emulation board and a hybrid keyboard that combines the best features of the two very different keyboards.

The IBM 3270-PC contains a 3270 system adapter that enables it to be connected directly with a 3274 cluster controller by coaxial cable. By using its distributed function terminal mode (DFT), the 3270 can have as many as four host sessions active simultaneously. The user is also able to view the DOS application on the screen. The screen can display all four host sessions simultaneously by creating four separate windows. Since each window in effect represents an entire screen's worth of material, it is possible to use the cursor keys to scroll through the window to see material that is not initially present within the window. Also available on the screen are two *notepads*, in which the user can make notes and store material temporarily.

The 3270 offers both window-to-window copying and file transfer. It is possible to copy the contents of one window to another window. Similarly, files represented within one window host session can be transferred to another window's host session. You cannot copy to a window running a PC-DOS session, however.

Local LAN Gateways

A LAN gateway can be attached via coaxial cable to a 3274 cluster controller to provide a local micro-mainframe connection.

A major limitation of using an IBM PC in 3278 terminal emulation connected to the cluster controller by coaxial cable is that it takes one of the controller's ports. Several PCs connected in this way would severely limit the mainframe's ability to serve all users. But, as is shown in *Figure 3-5*, it is possible to connect a microcomputer local area network to an IBM cluster controller with a gateway using coaxial cable. Any PC in this network has access to 3270 terminal emulation. CXI is one company that offers this coaxial-connect gateway.

Remote Gateways

The more likely micro-mainframe communications situation, however, is illustrated by Widget Company in the first chapter. Many companies have their local area microcomputer network at one location and their mainframe facilities in another location. It is in this situation that LAN gateways prove particularly valuable.

Figure 3-5.
An IBM PC with 3270
Terminal Emulation

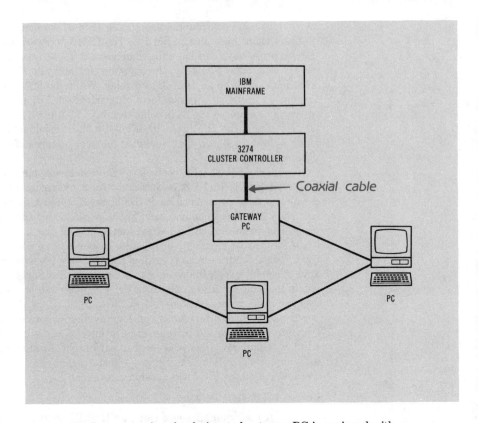

Remote gateways enable local area network users to communicate with a mainframe computer using 3278 terminal emulation over a gateway PC. This gateway emulates a cluster controller and communicates with the mainframe computer via modem.

At the remote site, the designated gateway PC is equipped with a gateway interface board and special gateway software to emulate a cluster controller. As *Figure 3-6* illustrates, each remote PC can emulate a 3278 terminal and use the synchronous modem connected to the gateway PC in order to communicate over a phone line with the mainframe computer. This one gateway server is capable of running as many as sixty-four 3270 emulation sessions. CXI permits sixty-four concurrent host sessions and a data rate as fast as 56,000 bits/second via synchronous modems attached to an IBM 3705 or 3725 controllers. IBM's 3720 communications controller links the mainframe with local area networks. IBM currently offers a special token ring interface to its 3720 controller. It is important to remember from our discussion of the SNA world and the nature of SNA sessions that one user might need three or four editing sessions simultaneously. Often, the network administrator will establish some order of priority for use of these valuable mainframe sessions.

While all the network users theoretically can emulate a 3278 terminal and communicate with the mainframe computer through the gateway PC, several network workstations needing to establish micro-mainframe communications will soon cause a traffic jam. The single gateway PC processing information and transmitting it through a modem communicating over a single telephone line will prove inadequate for this workload.

Figure 3-6.
Remote 3270 Emulation
with a Gateway PC

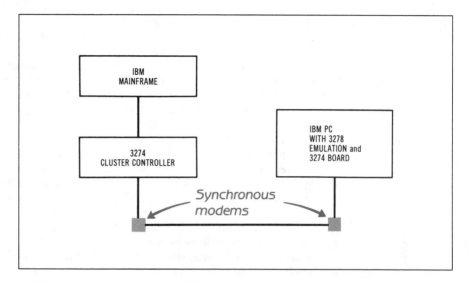

There are a number of ways of alleviating this problem. If the gateway PC is also being used as a workstation, it can be designated as a dedicated gateway and used only for that purpose. If the processing speed of the dedicated gateway PC is still not adequate to handle the workload, a second gateway file server can be installed. Remember, though, that these two servers will be sharing a single modem and telephone line. If this remedy proves inadequate, the only solution left is to install a second network complete with PC workstations, gateway PC, modem, and a second telephone line. The two networks can be connected using a *bridge*, which we'll explore when we look at some specific local area networks.

Micro-Mainframe File Transfers

Many of the micro-mainframe file transfer programs permit only bulk transfer of files. The microcomputer user is not able to select key fields from a mainframe database and retrieve only this very specific information. The more sophisticated file transfer programs permit more selective retrieval of information.

We have seen that it is possible to link workstations in a local area network to a mainframe computer using 3270 terminal emulation and a gateway. The major limitation of this emulation is that an intelligent PC must assume the role of a "dumb" terminal. The terminal-emulation software normally permits on-line inquiry using the mainframe programs and the ability to save each screen of 3270 terminal information.

Unfortunately, this is not the major reason companies want to link their microcomputers with their mainframe computer. Users want to be able to download and upload selected information and not merely dump screensful of information. File transfers in both directions create enormous problems since microcomputer and mainframe are running different programs under different operating systems. A more serious problem, the file structure of micro and mainframe application programs usually differs, with IBM mainframes utilizing an EBCDIC format while microcomputers use an ASCII format. Even more serious are the size limitations of a microcomputer. The microcomputer may not have enough disk space to handle the mainframe's files. Most IBM PCs are still configured with floppy disk drives. Even those units that have hard disk drives are limited; normally 33 megabytes (Mb) is the largest addressable space available under PC DOS. Another major consideration relating to the fundamental micro-mainframe difference in size is that the microcomputer software may not be able to handle the number of records found within a mainframe file.

Many of the leaders in micro-mainframe communications offer file-transfer programs with their 3270 terminal-emulation products. These programs don't permit a user to manipulate the data within a mainframe's application program or to select certain fields; they enable a microcomputer user to download or upload complete files only. With DCA's IRMAlink FT/370, for example, it is possible to transfer files between an IRMA-equipped PC and an IBM mainframe running under IBM's CICS, VM/CMS, or MVS/TSO operating systems. DCA also requires that a magnetic tape be installed on the mainframe side and that it be linked to a terminal controller. It is then possible to transfer files simply by entering the source filename and the destination filename. AST offers the AST-3270/FTS-R, an advanced file-transfer system for the MVS/TSO and VM/CMS environments which provides bi-directional transfer of binary or text files.

Several companies have developed "intelligent links," which tie together their own mainframe programs with major microcomputer software. For example, Information Builders offers FOCUS for the IBM mainframe environment and PC/FOCUS for microcomputers. With these, it is possible to use the mainframe database for distributed processing. PCs tied to a local area network can be used as transaction workstations to enter data. Management Science of America offers Executive Peachpack II, for example, which ties together its mainframe MSA application program's data with Lotus 1-2-3's formats running on a PC. Several vendors offer links to spreadsheets that will accept data interchange format (DIF), the file structure originally used by VisiCalc and still used by many spreadsheet programs.

The lack of uniformity in microcomputer and mainframe software means that until now it has been necessary to purchase separate interfaces (if they were even available) for each vendor's programs. On-Line Software's OMNILINK is a micro-mainframe link that includes software for both the micro and mainframe to address this problem. It includes a file-reformat utility program that automatically converts downloaded data into formats used by Lotus 1-2-3, dBASE III, and several other leading programs. With OMNILINK, it is possible to select criteria and then download only those records within a file that meet these standards.

A few vendors have begun to address the possibilities of LU 6.2 and its potential for facilitating data transfer from microcomputer to mainframe. AdaptSNA LU6.2/APPC from Network Software Associates is just what the name implies—an implementation of LU 6.2 and PU 2.1. It enables a PC-DOS program to communicate directly with a partner program running on a mainframe or minicomputer. This implementation does away with the traditional SNA master-slave relationship and permits peer-to-peer communication. PCs can be configured to participate in IBM's Distributed Office Support System (DIOSS) or another host-based APPC system. CXI's Application Program Interface enables microcomputers to transfer data directly to a mainframe using computer-to-computer communication rather than dumb terminal emulation. Similarly, Rabbit Software has developed Program Interface Module (PIM) which also permits direct transfer of data. Microcomputer users find this process helpful; they don't have to learn mainframe procedures in order to use a microcomputer program.

Remote Job Entry (RJE)

There are many times when remote PCs need to send information in batch form to unattended mainframe computers. While 3270 terminal emulation has become a popular way to communicate with mainframes, remote job entry is often preferable.

Often the primary need for micro-mainframe communications is for the uploading of data after business hours. A company with several retail outlets, for instance, might require its branches to upload sales figures during the evening so that the mainframe computer can digest the information and update its accounting files. IBM originally designed 3270 terminal-emulation protocol for on-line inquiry and remote job entry (RJE) as a method to transfer large amounts of data. RJE contains such features as data compression and compaction to minimize line charges for data transmission.

Network Software Associates' AdaptSNA RJE is a good example of an RJE SNA communications emulator. Emulating an IBM 3770 RJE workstation, this hardware/software package offers a number of desirable features. An applications programming interface permits unattended operation as well as automatic error recovery. In addition to supporting LU-LU and SSCP-LU sessions, the package contains EBCDIC/ASCII conversion tables. It utilizes "on-the-fly" processing and is able to automatically reformat data received from the host computer.

Although great developmental effort has been expended to bypass the inherent limitations of 3270 terminal emulation, particularly its method of dumping one screenful of information at a time, we should note that RJE can still fill a useful niche in micro-mainframe communications.

MICRO-MINI COMMUNICATIONS

Through terminal emulation it is possible for microcomputers individually or as part of a local area network to communicate with minicomputers.

Many microcomputer users prefer to communicate with their departmental minicomputer than with the corporate mainframe. The process is similar to 3270 terminal emulation except that the microcomputers need to be equipped with 5250 emulator boards and file-transfer software in order to communicate with IBM minis and with appropriate software and hardware to communicate with minis from DEC, Hewlett-Packard, and other vendors.

Several major vendors offer this combination of hardware and software. AST, for example, offers the AST-5250/Local Cluster, which enables a PC to function as a local cluster controller. It provides 5250 terminal emulation for as many as four clusters of PCs attached to a "master" controller PC. As *Figure 3-7* illustrates, this controller is connected via standard twinax cable to a host IBM System 34, 36, or 38 minicomputer. The master PC can also be connected via asynchronous modems with remote PCs, which can also use 5250 terminal emulation. It is significant that these modems are capable of supporting speeds up to 9600 bits per second (bps).

Figure 3-7.
Local Microcomputers
Linked to an IBM
Minicomputer

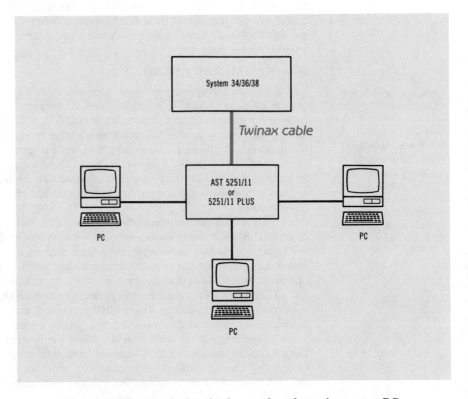

Clustered PCs operate in a background mode to the master PC. This means that one or more of the clustered PCs operates in 5250 emulation mode while the master PC is operating in DOS mode. It is also possible to have concurrent PC DOS and host sessions.

DCA's Smart Alec provides an effective microcomputer link to System 34, 36, and 38 minicomputers. In addition to the 5250/90 terminal-emulation circuit card that fits in a full-size PC slot, the package includes a "splice box," which handles the twinaxial connection, and software for both PC and minicomputer enabling terminal emulation and bi-directional file transfer. One nice feature of the splice box is an external switch that controls switches and jumpers on the circuit card so that the PC need not be opened to reset switches. Smart Alec can emulate a 5251 Model II, or a 5291 or 5292 Model I terminal. The software enables a PC printer to emulate an IBM 5256 system printer. Smart Alec's file-transfer software translates the System 34, 36, or 38 data into some of the more common PC formats including ASCII, DIF, and the Lotus Wks and Wrk formats. As *Figure 3-8* illustrates, Smart Alec supports both local and remote terminal emulation.

Figure 3-8.
Smart Alec Connecting
PCs with IBM
Minicomputers
(Reprinted with
permission of Digital
Communications
Associates, Inc.)

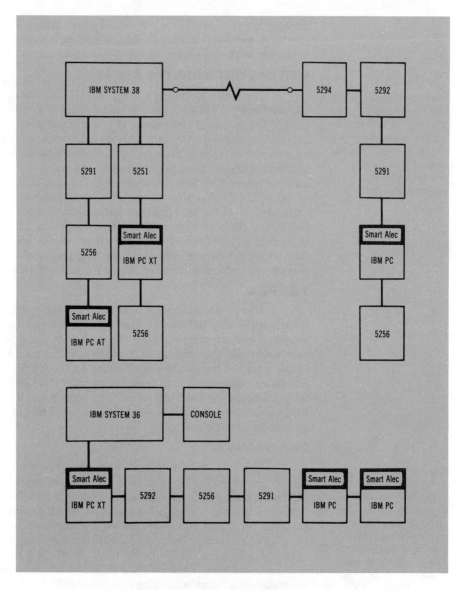

Many of the same file-transfer limitations present in micro-mainframe communications also apply to micro-mini communications. Techland System's Blue Lynx hardware and software addresses many of these problems. Using this board along with DecisionLink's file-transfer software, the micro user is able to perform bi-directional file transfer as well as supporting four concurrent host sessions. On-Line's OMNILINK functions much the same as it does in facilitating micro-mainframe file transfers, permitting the selection of key fields within a minicomputer database for downloading to a microcomputer. Fusion and other companies offer even more sophisticated software that permits the transfer of selected data from as many as eight different files on a System 36.

VIRTUAL NETWORKING SYSTEMS

Banyan Systems has developed VINES software which permits sharing of resources on a virtual network. PCs can actually share a mainframe or minicomputer hard disk.

Banyan Systems has developed VINES software in conjunction with its family of network file servers. As *Figure 3-9* illustrates, VINES permits the accessing and sharing of resources, applications, and information wherever they are located on a virtual network. In a virtual network the differences among microcomputers, minicomputers, and even mainframes are of limited significance to the end user. A microcomputer user can access files from a mainframe as easily as if this information were on her or his PC. The microcomputer can save information onto the "virtual disk" of the mainframe or minicomputer which is also attached to the Banyan file server. Since the software supports LU 6.2, it is quite easy to communicate with other users even if you do not know precisely where they are on the network. The software keeps track of users' addresses and permits electronic mail transfer simply by indicating the receiver's name.

THE PBX

One of the capabilities offered by Banyan's virtual network is that it enables the user to transmit to and receive information from different networks without worrying about the mechanics of the process. To the user, using only the common DOS commands, this complex system seems simple since the complexities are handled by the VINES software. Data processing professionals and telecommunication managers have speculated for years about the feasibility of using an office's telephone system—its PBX—to accomplish not only what Banyan has done but also the integration of voice and data.

PBX History

The PBX has been in use for approximately 80 years. Newer units are completely digital. They are distributed most commonly with twisted-pair wire, but also with coaxial cable and, less frequently, fiber optics.

The PBX has a long history. To understand the concept of a private branch exchange, imagine an office before the PBX. As *Figure 3-10* illustrates, each phone was connected into the trunk cable that carried the signals back to the central office exchange. The PBX simplified this situation. As *Figure 3-11* shows, only a few wires are required to connect the PBX to the trunk. In the late 1800s a first generation PBX phone system was in operation. Bell's 701 family of PBXs launched in 1929 represents the second generation in which operators were no longer needed to handle outgoing calls. A third generation PBX became available around 1980 and featured distributed architecture, non-blocking operation, and integrated voice and data. Sometimes we use the phrase private *automatic* branch exchange (PABX) to differentiate a PBX in which all in-house and outgoing calls are automatically switched. To avoid confusion, though, we'll use PBX to mean the newer PABXs as well.

**Figure 3-9.
Banyan's Virtual
Networking System**
*(Courtesy of Banyan
Systems Incorporated)*

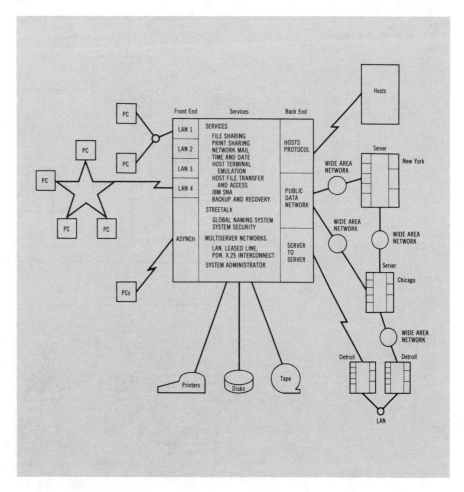

"Distributed architecture" simply means that switching modules are distributed over coaxial cable or fiber optic media. The non-blocking operation is still more promise than reality; the new systems promised that their additional channel capacity made it impossible for them to become overloaded and thus unable to access a call. AT&T allows users the opportunity to select a configuration that can be blocking, non-blocking, or essentially non-blocking. An "essentially non-blocking" configuration means that one in one million attempts to access a call will be blocked.

Integrated voice and data transmission is a topic that we will return to shortly. It is one of the major reasons that companies continue to explore the viability of using the PBX switch to handle all network data and voice needs.

**Figure 3-10.
A Phone System Before
PBX**

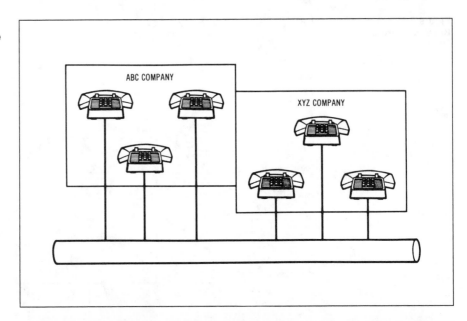

**Figure 3-11.
A PBX Phone System**

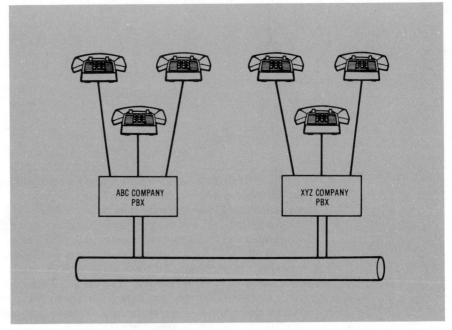

Today there is some debate over whether we now have a fourth generation of PBX. AT&T points with pride to its System 75's high-speed data bus and its ability to handle voice and data simultaneously over the same wire. Other vendors insist that their digital switches are just as sophisticated. For our purposes, it really doesn't matter. What does matter is how the new PBXs work and why they are becoming increasingly popular as alternatives to local area networks.

The coder-decoder is essential to a PBX since it converts a digital signal to analog and an analog signal to digital.

To understand how a PBX digital switch works, it is important to remember that our telephone system sends analog signals over the phone lines. A device called a coder-decoder, or CODEC, converts the voice analog signals into digital form. Many of the newer PBX systems place the CODEC in the telephone handset. As *Figure 3-12* illustrates, this means that all communication to and from the PBX is digital.

**Figure 3-12.
A Digital PBX with the CODEC in the Telephone Handset**

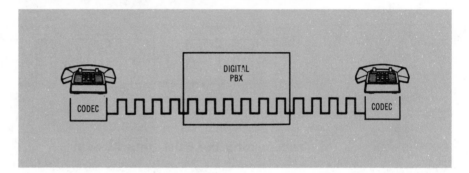

Data Switching Within the PBX

The analog transmission of voice signals is really the transmission of audio frequency sine waves that are equal in frequency and amplitude to the original voice tones. Using *Pulse Amplitude Modulation (PAM)* a telephone system samples the analog voice signal 8000 times/second. This sampling produces pulses of varying amplitude which represent the original signal. As *Figure 3-13* illustrates, the switch amplifies the voice call to regenerate the original signal. There is a problem with this type of signal transmission, however: it is possible to get noise, which can be enhanced as it is regenerated, leading to distortion of the original signal.

**Figure 3-13.
Regeneration of a Sampled Sine Wave as a PAM Stream**

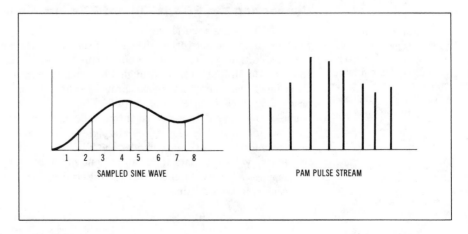

Today digital PBXs have moved a step beyond pulse amplitude modulation. They measure the sampled signals and then digitally encode them. Since these signals are sampled at 8000 times per second and then translated into 8-bit words, PCM produces a bit stream of 64,000 bits/second (bps). As *Figure 3-14* illustrates, this process reproduces the voice signal very clearly.

**Figure 3-14.
PCM Bit Stream**

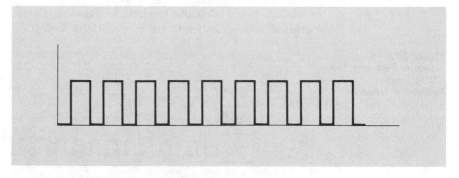

Transmitting the PCM Data Stream

A PBX transmits the PCM data stream along a coaxial cable data bus. This data highway assigns the conversations to time slots using time division multiplexing (TDM).

A PBX uses a high-speed data bus to transmit the PCM data stream. The digital switch's network controller is responsible for monitoring the data highway. Since this coaxial cable highway is capable of transmitting data much faster than the 64,000 bit/second PCM voice signal, several messages are multiplexed over the same path. Each conversation multiplexed onto this bus is given a time slot. This technique is known as "time division multiplexing" (TDM), and the data bus is sometimes called the "TDM bus." AT&T's System 75 PBX has two TDM buses with 512 available time slots. Since two time slots are required for a conversation and some slots are lost in overhead considerations, it is possible to have 236 simultaneous voice conversations. Note that a data conversation takes up three time slots and even more slots on some other PBXs.

Connecting the PBX to Other PBXs and Computer Networks

PBXs can communicate over very high-speed T1 lines at 1.544 Mbit/s. The data is multiplexed using either time division multiplexing or frequency division multiplexing (FDM).

There are several ways to connect digital PBXs to other PBXs or to other computer networks. Most PBXs contain digital multiplex interfaces that enable them to send data to host computers or PBXs over very high-speed (1.544 Mbit/s) T1 links provided by common carriers. Each of the 24 T1 channels can support one asynchronous connection of up to 19.2 Kbit/s or a synchronous connection of up to 56 Kbit/s. As we have learned, TDM is one of the ways data is moved through T1 lines. Rather than assigning data specific time slots along the data highway, a second method, frequency division multiplexing (FDM), divides the T1 channels into subchannels by frequency. Voice and data then can be sent simultaneously over different frequencies. *Figure 3-15* illustrates the difference between these two approaches to transmitting data.

Figure 3-15.
Frequency Division
Multiplexing and Time
Division Multiplexing

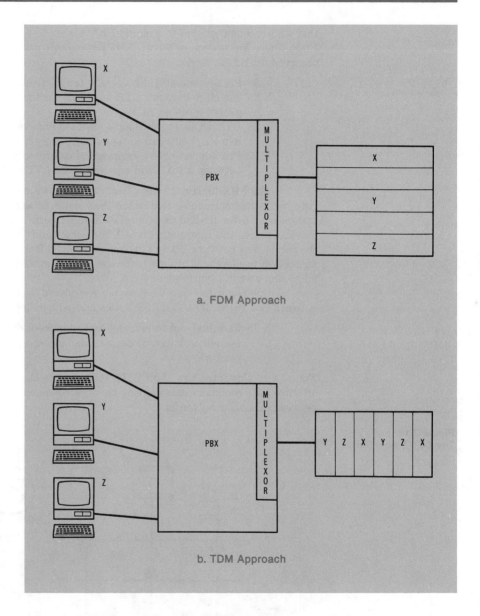

a. FDM Approach

b. TDM Approach

　　In Chapter 2, we discussed the significance of the CCITT's X.25 standard for communication between a computer (a DTE) and a public data network (PDN). We saw that X.25 provided a standard for the packets of information that are transmitted synchronously over a network. In this case, we want to transmit information from a PBX in X.25 packet form to such public data networks as GTE-TYMNET and TELENET. Let's assume that a microcomputer tied to a digital PBX wished to send a message to a PDN. There are several different CCITT standards that would have to be observed for this to work:

X.3   Packet assembly/disassembly facility (PAD) in a PDN

X.25   Interface between DTE and DCE for terminals operating in the packet mode on PDNs

X.28   DTE/DCE interface for a start-stop mode DTE assessing the PAD in a PDN situated in the same country

X.29   Procedures for the exchange of control information and user data between a PAD and a packet mode DTE or another PAD

The PBX functioning as a local area network contains an X.25 gateway. A microcomputer tied to the PBX sends an asynchronous transmission (over RS-232 cable) to a PBX serial port. The PBX X.25 gateway places this information into X.25 packets and transmits them to the public data network. Packet messages received from the PDN are stripped of headers and trailers before being transmitted to the microcomputer in asynchronous form.

One particular case we have not considered is the communication between two PDNs. The CCITT's X.75 standard handles this situation:

X.75   Terminal and transit call control procedures and data transfer system on international circuits between packet-switched data networks

Figure 3-16 illustrates how the CCITT standards work together to ensure effective data communications among network components as well as between dissimilar networks.

**Figure 3-16.
The CCITT Standards**

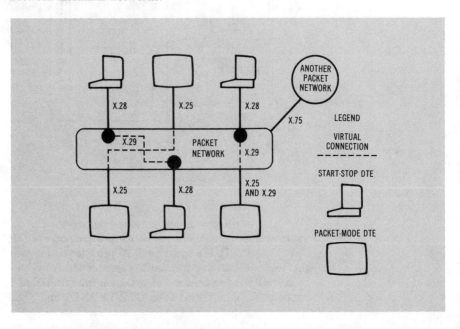

PBX Communication with IBM Mainframe Computers

A PBX offers substantial savings for companies using it for micro-mainframe communications. Its twisted-pair wiring is much more economical than coaxial cable. It also offers protocol conversions from ASCII asynchronous data to EBCDIC synchronous data using SDLC format.

A principal cost normally associated with 3270 terminal-emulation communication with IBM mainframe computers is the coaxial cabling required. A great advantage of using a PBX as a gateway to an IBM mainframe is that the terminals or microcomputers using 3270 terminal emulation can be connected to the PBX by twisted-pair wire. As *Figure 3-17* illustrates, data from a 3270 terminal can be transmitted to the PBX via a special data module that converts this 2.36 Mbit/s stream of data for coaxial cable to the 64 Kbit/s speed that twisted-pair wire can handle.

**Figure 3-17.
Data Can Travel from a
Mainframe to a PBX**

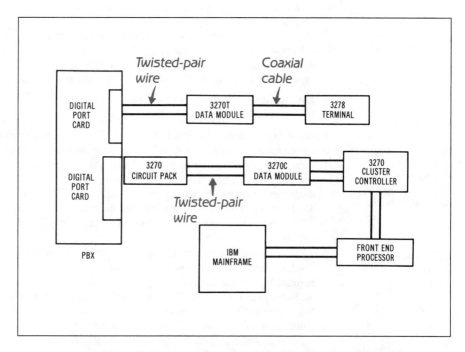

Figure 3-17 also illustrates the way that a PBX can transmit data to an IBM mainframe. Using 3270 circuit packs and a 3270 data module, a System 75 PBX communicates with an IBM cluster controller. Let's assume that the real need for many of the microcomputers linked to a PBX is not so much for on-line inquiry and communication with an IBM mainframe as it is for the uploading and downloading of data. The microcomputers can connect to the PBX through its asynchronous RS-232C ports. The PBX is capable of providing protocol conversions from the micro's ASCII data to IBM EBCDIC-coded 3270 binary synchronous control protocol (BSC) or 3270 synchronous data using the SDLC format.

PBX resource management tools such as modem pooling, station message detail reporting (SMDR) and automatic route selection (ARS) provide useful effective controls for cost-effective management.

If the PBX is situated at a remote site from the mainframe, it offers several advantages as a micro-mainframe communications gateway. One of these is that a PBX features modem pooling. The modems can be accessed through hardware (dialing a specific number for a specific modem) or by software. The software approach automatically selects the fastest modem that the connection between terminal and host can support.

One area in particular where most local area networks have been very weak and where PBXs are very strong is network record keeping. For several years, PBXs have featured station message detail reporting (SMDR) software to enable offices to track each person's phone calls. Law offices, for example, can use this software to automatically charge each call an attorney makes to the client represented. This same SMDR function within a PBX can monitor all microcomputer use of resources and, if so desired, record charges to various workstations or departments for long-distance data line usage.

Another strong PBX resource management tool is automatic route selection (ARS). ARS automatically selects the most economical route for dial-out data calls. Since there are so many different kinds of long-distance lines now available, ARS can save companies substantial amounts of money.

Integrating Voice and Data

A digital PBX can integrate voice and data. Some are able to provide voice messages accompanying the text that flashes across a computer terminal.

Slowly the dream of many telecommunications pioneers is becoming a reality. Digital PBXs are able to integrate voice and data information; some can even send this information simultaneously over the same line. Today a salesperson can call the sales manager using the company's PBX and leave a voice message for the manager to accompany a customer proposal drawn up on a spreadsheet. The sales manager can look at the spreadsheet on a terminal and hear the accompanying message ("This proposal looks strange because of one complication. Let me explain....")

AT&T's 510 BCT Personal Terminal represents the latest technology in integrated voice and data. It also illustrates the effectiveness of using a PBX to perform office network functions.

Several vendors now offer executive workstations that combine the best features of a telephone handset and a computer terminal to provide simultaneous voice and data transmission and reception. *Figure 3-18* shows AT&T's 510 BCT Personal Terminal which combines a telephone with an asynchronous touch-screen terminal capable of providing simultaneous voice and data communication over two pair of twisted-pair wire at selectable speeds from 300 to 19,200 bps.

While a sophisticated PBX such as the System 75 contains hundreds of features, most executives will only use a few of these services. The 510 BCT contains nine feature buttons that can be programmed. The terminal also utilizes cartridges containing 32K of RAM in which to program frequently performed tasks. A busy executive might want to keep a directory of frequently dialed numbers. By simply touching the name of an individual in the directory, the executive will cause the terminal to dial the corresponding number.

Figure 3-18.
AT&T's 510 BCT
Personal Terminal
(Courtesy of AT&T)

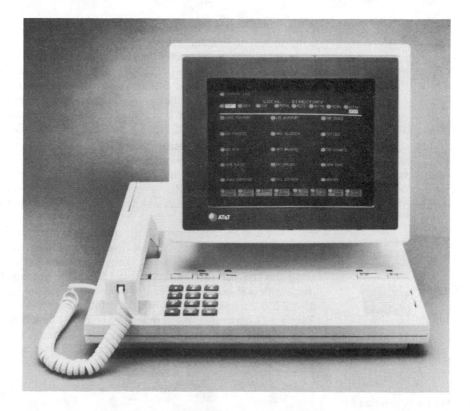

In large companies, a middle manager may receive as many internal calls from other departments as external calls from customers. One integrated voice-data feature that shows the utility of a PBX as a local area network is its ability to match internal caller with a company directory. Imagine how much more efficient communication can be when a caller is greeted by name before introducing her- or himself! The receiver's voice terminal flashes the caller's name as the terminal begins ringing.

ISDN AND THE FUTURE OFFICE

The Integrated Services Digital Network (ISDN) is a CCITT model that provides for the integration of voice and data as well as for a universal interface among networks.

Study Group XVII of the CCITT worked from 1980 to 1984 to develop a set of standards for voice and data integration. The committee took a global view of future telecommunications in developing a plan for an architecture that would provide integrated access to circuit-switched and packet-switched networks and for end-to-end digital transport of data. The Integrated Services Digital Network (ISDN) represents a network of the future that will include truly integrated voice, data, and even video traveling over the same pathways and moving smoothly from one type of network to another.

The ISDN model consists of several channels of multiplexed information transmitted at 64 Kbit/s.

The ISDN concept of a universal interface means that each terminal will understand every other terminal. It will be possible to send information such as interactive videotex and facsimiles at the relatively high speed of 64 Kbit/s. ISDN standards define a digital interface divided into two types of channels. B channels are used for customer information (voice, data, and video) while D channels are used to send signals and control information. These D channels utilize a packet-mode layered protocol based upon the CCITT's X.25 standard.

The two major ISDN interfaces are the basic rate interface (BRI), designed for relatively small capacity devices, and the primary rate interface (PRI), designed for high-capacity devices such as PBXs.

Two major interfaces defined by the CCITT committee utilize the B and D channels. The basic rate interface (BRI) is used to serve devices, such as terminals, with relatively small capacity. A second interface, primary rate interface (PRI), is used for large-capacity devices such as PBXs. Both interfaces utilize one D channel and several B channels transmitting at 64 Kbit/s.

Since the PRI channel structure represents the form most PBXs will take in the future, let's take a closer look at this model. It consists of 24 slots with 23 B channels and 1 D channel. Like the current T1, the maximum transfer rate on the PRI is 1.536 Mb/s. Perhaps this ISDN framework will become clearer if we view it within the context of the AT&T 510 Personal Terminal which combines both voice and data. As *Figure 3-19* illustrates, the terminal is connected by a BRI (AT&T's Digital Communication Protocol) to the digital PBX (System 75). Then, through a PRI (AT&T's Digital Multiplexed Interface), the data is transmitted to a carrier network.

**Figure 3-19.
AT&T's Integration of
Voice and Data**

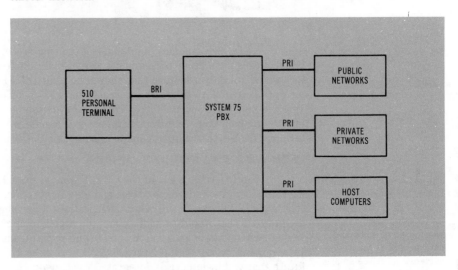

WHAT HAVE WE LEARNED?

1. IBM's mainframe and minicomputers utilize systems network architecture (SNA).
2. Network-addressable units (NAUs) consist of logical units (LUs), physical units (PUs), and system services control points (SSCPs).
3. LU 6.2 provides an application program interface (API) that will permit peer-to-peer communication.
4. An IBM PC or compatible with appropriate hardware and software can emulate an IBM 3270 terminal and communicate with a mainframe via a 3274 or 3276 cluster controller.
5. An IBM PC or compatible can serve as a local area network gateway. The PC is connected via coaxial cable with the cluster controller and provides terminal emulation for an entire local area network.
6. From a remote site, an IBM PC or compatible can emulate a cluster controller and serve as a gateway for a local area network.
7. An IBM PC or compatible can perform remote job entry (RJE) for a local area network.
8. A private branch network (PBX) telephone system can serve as a local area network linking voice and data communications.

Quiz for Chapter 3

1. Under IBM's system network architecture (SNA), the protocol for data packets is:
   a. HLDC.
   b. SDLC.
   c. SPCA.
   d. IMOK.

2. Network-addressable units (NAUs) consist of all of the following, except:
   a. logical units (LUs).
   b. synchronous units (SUs).
   c. physical units (PUs).
   d. system services control point (SSCP).

3. Under SNA, the path control network is concerned with:
   a. traffic flow.
   b. transmission priorities.
   c. error recovery.
   d. all of the above.

4. An IBM PC or compatible can communicate with a mainframe computer via a cluster controller if the PC is equipped with:
   a. a dot matrix printer.
   b. a 30-Mb hard disk.
   c. 3270 terminal emulation hardware and software.
   d. a communications front-end processor.

5. Microcomputers that are part of a local area network can communicate with a mainframe located in the same building by using:
   a. communications software.
   b. an IBM PC or compatible LAN gateway connected via coaxial cable with a cluster controller.
   c. laser technology.
   d. fiber optics.

6. A gateway PC that is used only for this function is known as a:
   a. gateway server.
   b. distributed server.
   c. dedicated gateway.
   d. remote job entry station.

7. A mainframe database file is likely to consist of:
   a. EBCDIC characters.
   b. ASCII characters.
   c. ANSI characters.
   d. eight-bit words.

8. For the uploading of microcomputer information to a mainframe computer, an efficient method is to have the PC emulate a:
   a. 3278 monochrome terminal.
   b. 3279 color terminal.
   c. 3770 remote job entry workstation.
   d. 3705 front-end processor.

9. To communicate with an IBM System 34, 36, or 38, the PC should emulate a:
   a. 3770 remote job entry workstation.
   b. 3278 monochrome terminal.
   c. 3279 color terminal.
   d. 5250 terminal.

10. A PBX stands for a:
    a. public broadcasting exchange.
    b. public branch exchange.
    c. private branch exchange.
    d. preferential broadband exchange.

11. Converting analog signals to digital transmission and digital signals back to analog is performed by a(n):
    a. operator.
    b. transformer.
    c. coder-decoder.
    d. switchboard.

12. A digital PBX measures and samples signals 8000 times per second and translates these signals into 8-bit words using a process called:
    a. pulse amplitude modulation (PAM).
    b. pulse code modulation (PCM).
    c. public data network (PDN).
    d. pulse amplitude authorization (PAA).

13. A technique for transmitting a data stream through a coaxial cable bus by assigning time slots is known as:
    a. pulse code amplification (PCA).
    b. time division multiplexing (TDM).
    c. frequency division multiplexing (FDM).
    d. pulse code modulation (PCM).

14. A T1 high-speed link is capable of transmitting data at a maximum speed of:
    a. 64 Kbit/s.
    b. 19.2 Kbit/s.
    c. 1.544 Mb/s.
    d. 15 Mb/s.

15. The standard used for transmitting packets of information to a public data network is:
    a. 802.3.
    b. X.25.
    c. X.3.
    d. 802.6.

16. A network manager can monitor the data usage of each network user when a PBX serves as a local area network by using the following PBX feature:
    a. ARS.
    b. SMDR.
    c. CCITT.
    d. X.25.

17. The integrated services digital network (ISDN) will provide:
    a. integrated voice and data information.
    b. an interface between different networks.
    c. several channels of multiplexed information at 64 Kbit/s.
    d. all of the above.

18. Under the ISDN model, small-capacity devices such as terminals will use the:
    a. basic rate interface (BRI).
    b. primary rate interface (PRI).
    c. universal rate interface (URI).
    d. terminal rate interface (TRI).

19. The maximum transfer rate under PRI is:
    a. 1.536 Mb/s.
    b. 64 Kbit/s.
    c. 19.2 Kbit/s.
    d. 56 Kbit/s.

20. Under the ISDN model, a high-capacity device such as a PBX would use a:
    a. primary rate interface (PRI).
    b. basic rate interface (BRI).
    c. T1 line.
    d. all B channels.

The IBM PC Network and Token Ring Network

ABOUT THIS CHAPTER

Having discussed how local area networks work in theory, it is time we looked at how they actually work. Since IBM is the acknowledged leader in this field, we will look at its two major LANs: PC Network and the IBM Token Ring Network. We'll examine the hardware, the network architecture, the software, and the overall network operations.

PC NETWORK: HARDWARE

PC Network is a broadband local area network that uses the same coaxial cable used for cable television. It is designed primarily for a departmental environment in which workstations are located relatively close together. Using IBM's own cabling kits it is possible to link seventy-two workstations within a 1000-ft (330-m) radius. Companies that need to connect more workstations over a greater distance need a different frequency translator and cabling system. Sytek, the broadband network developer who worked closely with IBM in developing PC Network, is able to supply these components. We'll see later in this chapter, however, that companies with these requirements are probably better served by selecting the IBM Token Ring Network developed specifically to address such needs.

The PC Network hardware consists of a network translator unit (NTU) for frequency translation, an eight-way splitter to connect up to eight nodes, base expanders for more than eight nodes, and adapter cards for each node. The network uses the same coaxial cable used by cable television companies.

The PC Network consists of a network translator unit (NTU) which provides broadband frequency translation from the return channel to the forward channel for the network. This unit connects by way of a directional coupler to an eight-way splitter to which workstations are attached via cabling that connects to the network adapter cards placed in the workstations' expansion slots. *Figure 4-1* illustrates a basic PC Network configuration.

Using the eight-way splitter, the NTU can be connected with up to 8 workstations. Each workstation can be a maximum of 200 ft (60 m) from the splitter. using *base expanders* and IBM's short (1 ft or .3 m), medium (400 ft or 120 m), or long-distance cabling kits (800 ft or 240 m) an additional sixty-four workstations can be connected. *Figure 4-2* illustrates the use of a base expander.

**Figure 4-1.
Basic PC Network
Configuration**

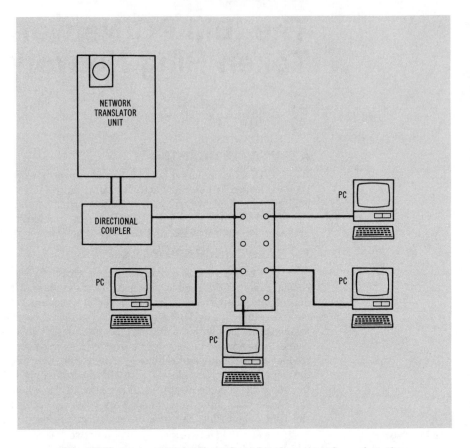

The NTU has both a
receive channel (50.75
MHz) and a send channel
(219 MHz). It boosts
signals before forwarding
them to the appropriate
workstation along the PC
Network bus.

The NTU receives signals broadcast by the network workstations
through the modems found on their network adapter cards. The NTU
receives these signals at a 6-MHz channel centered at 50.75 MHz and
retransmits these signals across the network at a different 6-MHz channel
centered at 219 MHz. The workstations receive all these signals and
determine whether the particular message is directed to them or not. The
NTU can also boost signals before retransmitting them in order to maintain
a balanced network.

While the NTU receives and then transmits every network
message, it is not a network file server or central processor. The IBM PC
Network utilizes a bus topology without a master computer. While this bus
architecture is very simple, it does require significant planning before
installation. It is a good idea, for example, to utilize only half the ports in
the network's eight-way splitters to ensure room for future growth.

**Figure 4-2.
PC Net Configuration
with a Base Expander**

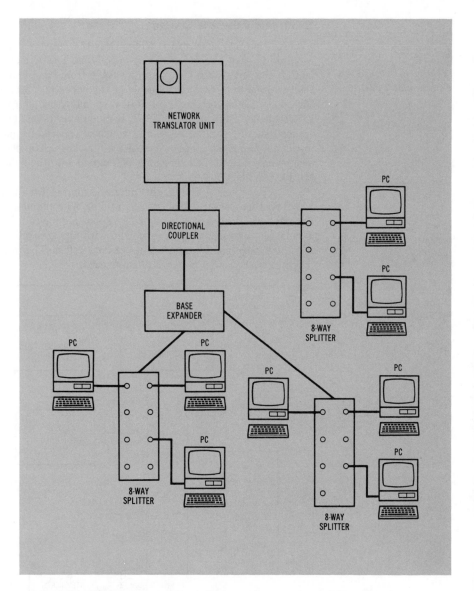

All workstations on the PC Network are potential file servers if they have at least 320K of RAM. Given proper access, any network user can retrieve files located on any other user's hard disk. File servers need not be dedicated although dedicated file servers are significantly faster.

Network Adapter Cards

The Network Adapter Cards (NAC) are the "brains" of the PC LAN. They contain a modem and use frequency shift keying (FSK) to achieve 2 Mbit/s transmission speed.

The real heart of PC Network is the network adapter card (NAC) required in each workstation's expansion bus. This circuit card includes a modem that translates the digital message from the PC into RF signals that are sent over the coaxial cable at the speed of 2 Mbit/s to the NTU. The modem achieves this transmission speed by use of a technique known as "frequency shift keying" (FSK). It modulates 1s and 0s during transmission by shifting between two closely spaced frequencies. Since the modem is *frequency agile*, it cannot handle other channels. The NAC must also be able to translate incoming RF signals into their digital form so that the PC can display them.

Designed by Sytek, this network adapter card utilizes an Intel 80188 microprocessor as well as an Intel 82586 communications controller. Sytek's serial interface controller is responsible for collision detection and avoidance. By comparing bits received with bits transmitted, the controller identifies discrepancies as evidence of data collisions. *Figure 4-3* is a block diagram of the actual network adapter card.

Figure 4-3.
Block Diagram of PC Network Adapter Card
(Courtesy of Sytek)

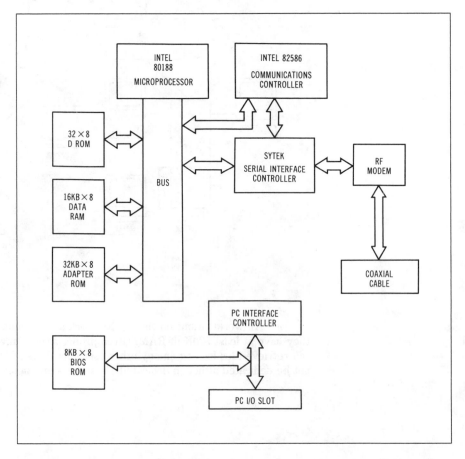

The network adapter card's communications controller is responsible for conversion between RF signals and digital data. It is also responsible for arranging data into packets for transmission. The packets are framed with flag control characters, much like the HLDC protocol. Both the start and the end of a frame contain the same flag pattern: 01111110. The protocol uses a variation of bit stuffing known as *"zero insertion."* This technique inserts a 0 after five straight 1s. Upon receipt of the data packet, the 0 is stripped away.

The ROM on each NAC contains a unique 48-bit address. When a data frame is transmitted, the first 48 bits of the frame after the start flag consist of the destination address. Each node's NAC checks a data packet to see if its ROM address matches the destination address. If it does, the accompanying message has reached its destination. If nodes share a group address a data packet sent with a group address may find several users as part of the group. Their addresses will share a least significant bit 1.

As the "brains" of the PC Network, the NAC also provides end-to-end error detection and recovery by use of a 32-bit cyclic redundancy check (CRC) sequence. The CRC frame is generated when a message is transmitted and then is checked upon receipt.

The NAC contains the NETBIOS (Network Basic Input/Output System) in ROM. Included in the NETBIOS functions are an interface to DOS, network management, and error checking.

A major feature of the network adapter card is the presence of the NETBIOS (Network Basic Input/Output System) interface between IBM PC DOS-compatible applications and the network adapter controller. It is this ROM software that is responsible for managing all network traffic for that particular workstation, enabling the NAC hardware to perform the functions we have discussed so far, including collision and error detection, transmission of data packets, and reassembly of data upon receipt of a packet. The NETBIOS also determines when a message has ended or when a station has failed to respond within a given period of time (timeout).

When we discuss the Token Ring Network later in this chapter, we will distinguish between the NETBIOS for that network and that for PC Network. The implementation of NETBIOS for the Token Ring Network is a superset of the PC Network, so an application program that runs correctly on a PC Network should run correctly on the Token Ring Network. The converse, however, is not necessarily true although both networks use the same IBM PC Local Area Network Program.

THE IBM PC NETWORK PROGRAM (PC LAN PROGRAM)

Since the IBM PC Local Area Network Program functions on both PC Network and the Token Ring Network (with the proper NETBIOS), we'll take a close look at the many features offered by this powerful yet easy-to-use software package. The program was originally called the PC Network Program, but IBM has changed its name to the PC Local Area Network Program, perhaps to distinguish the program from the network hardware. The program permits the sharing of disk drives and printers as well as the sending and receiving of messages and files. For beginning network users, there are a series of menus within menus. More experienced users may wish to use network commands to send and receive information.

PC Local Area Network Program Configurations

The PC Local Area
Network Program
requires users to indicate
when entering the
network how they wish to
configure their
workstations. The four
configuration options are
redirector, receiver,
messenger, and server.

The PC Local Area Network Program has four different configurations: redirector (RDR), receiver (RCV), messenger (MSG), and server (SRV). The *redirector* configuration restricts the user to certain activities. It accepts requests for applications directed to servers and passes the requests along to the servers. It accepts and passes along data and sends messages. The *receiver* configuration includes the redirector. It also receives and logs in messages. This represents a minimum user configuration. A full user would usually opt for the messenger configuration, which provides full-screen message editing and forwarding capabilities as well as all the functions of the redirector and receiver. The server configuration includes all the functions of the messenger, redirector, and messenger configurations as well as the ability to control disk drives, directories, and printers.

Beginners will automatically go to the main menu, depicted in *Figure 4-4*, and not concern themselves with configuring their systems; they will depend upon the normal defaults built into the network. For more experienced users, however, the Net Start command permits them to customize their own workstations.

Figure 4-4.
The PC Local Area
Network Program Main
Menu *(Courtesy of*
International Business
Machines Corporation)

IBM PC Network

Main Menu - Task Selection

1. Message tasks

2. Printer tasks

3. Disk or directory tasks

4. Print queue tasks

5. Network status tasks

6. Pause or cancel the network setup

1 Choice
Enter- Continue   F1- Help
Esc- Exit

Experienced users will change their network configuration based upon the amount of memory needed to run specific application programs, the need to share additional resources, and the need for additional memory to hold long messages in a buffer.

Why would you want to reconfigure the workstation? There are many reasons for changing the normal default values. The network default value for use of network devices, for example, is five. If you will need to use more than five network devices to perform certain operations, you would need to reconfigure your workstation. Similarly, if you need to share more than five of your workstation devices with the network, you would also reconfigure. Finally, network default values for the size of the buffer used for printing (512 characters), the size of the buffer used to hold messages (1600 characters), and the number of network computers (10) that will be using your devices are also likely to need to be changed from time to time.

The RAM installed on a network workstation can limit its ability to serve other network functions. To serve as a file server, for example, a network workstation needs to have at least 320K of RAM for DOS and the PC Local Area Network Program. A network user who wanted to run a program that requires 320K as well as use the workstation as a file server would need to install 640K of RAM to serve both purposes. As a file server, then, this workstation would be able to share its disk drives, directories, and printers, while as a workstation it would be able to share in those resources found on other workstations.

The messenger configuration requires a minimum of 256K of RAM for the PC Local Area Network Program and DOS. In addition to being able to send and receive messages, a workstation with this configuration is also able to transfer messages to other computers and to save messages directly to a file by logging them in. We will soon see how easy it is to send a message on this network.

If you decide to configure your workstation as a receiver, you will need 192K of RAM for the PC Local Area Network Program and DOS in order to send and receive messages, save these messages by placing them into a log file (rather than have to view them the moment they are received), and share network disk drives, directories, and printers.

The redirector configuration, on the other hand, only requires 128K of RAM. It allows a workstation to send messages and to share network disk drives, directories, and printers. This is the only configuration that cannot both send and receive messages.

The IBM PC LAN Network *User's Guide* provides a handy description of the configurations and their major functions. It is summarized in *Table 4-1*.

**Table 4-1.
Configurations and
Functions**

Configuration	You can use the PC Network Program to:
Server (320K RAM required)	Send messages Use network disks, directories, and printers Receive messages Save (log) messages Use network request keys Receive messages for other names Transfer messages to other computers Share your disks, directories, and printers
Messenger (256K RAM required)	Send messages Use network disks, directories, and printers Receive messages Save (log) messages Use network request keys Receive messages for other names Transfer messages to other computers
Receiver (192K RAM required)	Send messages Use network disks, directories, and printers Receive messages Save (log) messages
Redirector (128K Ram required)	Send messages Use network disks, directories, and printers

In order to see why a network user would choose one configuration over another, it is useful to examine how these options are presented in the PC Local Area Network Program menu format. As we indicated earlier, *Figure 4-4* illustrates the main menu. Notice that help is available by pressing the <F1> key. We'll go through the options and examine how the network works.

It is important to realize that the PC LAN Network keeps track of machines and not of people. Each network workstation must have a name so that other network users can address it. This name can be up to fifteen letters. Sometimes one name is not enough. The PC Network Program permits a maximum of sixteen names for a particular workstation. If several people in Accounting share a workstation, for example, the workstation could have the name "ACCOUNT" as well as individual names of departmental users.

Message Tasks Available Under the PC Local Area Network Program

Figure 4-5 illustrates the way that messages are edited prior to being sent on the PC Network. Notice that the use of the asterisk (*) results in the message being sent to all network workstations. A message can be up to 1600 characters in length (80 characters/line × 20 lines). The one exception is a *broadcast message*. Broadcast messages are sent to all computers on the network and are limited to 128 characters. This message screen editor is capable of "word wrap" so that words are not hyphenated at the ends of lines. Because of this feature, some messages might look unprofessional with a series of short lines interspersed with long lines. The <F3> key will adjust a paragraph and make it look more even. Notice that in the lower right corner of the screen the number of free characters is tracked.

**Figure 4-5.
Screen for Editing
Messages** *(Courtesy of
International Business
Machines Corporation)*

```
                              Send Messages

         Send the message to: (* for all computers) Bill

         Type the message below:

         This is a test to see it work.

         Ctrl-Enter Send message          Esc- Previous menu or Exit
         Tab- cursor to next field        Ctrl-PgDn - Erase message
         Ctrl-Home - Return to Main Menu  F3 ADJUST PARAGRAPH F4 VIEW MESSAGES
         F1 - HELP   F2 - COMMAND LINE

         Message sent . . . and successfully received    Characters free 1571
```

The message function of the PC Local Area Network Program is a good example of how the program uses the IBM PC's special keys and function keys. The <F1> key is always the key to use when requesting additional information. The <Tab> key is always used to move the cursor from field to field. The <Esc> key is always used as a way to exit a menu or move backwards and view a previous menu screen. The <Ctrl> and <Home> keys can be pressed simultaneously to bring a user back to the program's main menu.

When a user completes editing a message, he or she sends it by pressing the <Ctrl> and <ENTER> keys simultaneously. The PC Local Area Network Program does have a number of safety features built in to help network users avoid making serious mistakes. A user who inadvertently presses the <Esc> key before sending the message doesn't lose the message because the program asks that the key be pressed again for confirmation.

Notice that the PC Local Area Network Program asks for a specific name for the addressee (the message's destination). Many network administrators publish a directory of network users and their network names to prevent confusion when it comes to sending messages. It is likely, for example, that a large company would have more than one Bob. Users in other departments might know Bob but not know his last name. So it is practical for the individual workstation NAC to be able to handle sixteen different names. Since Bob handles payroll for the company, his workstation might have PAYROLL as one of its names.

The PC Local Area Network Program has a number of ways of handling incoming messages depending upon how users have configured their network workstations. When configuring the workstation a user may have chosen to use the network request keys. *Figure 4-6* illustrates the message the user will receive when one arrives. If the user presses the <Ctrl> and <Break> keys, the message will be put into a waiting area. The user can go through the message tasks menus to view this message at a later time. Because buffer room is limited, however, users should view their messages frequently and then erase them. If the user had chosen to view the message when it arrived, he or she would have pressed the <Ctrl> <Alt> <Break> keys. After viewing this message, the user presses the <Esc> key to return to his or her work. Note that these three network request keys normally perform a far different function. Except in the instance when a user receives a message-waiting signal, these three keys pressed simultaneously will interrupt whatever the user is doing and go directly to the network menus. After making the desired network menu selections, the user is returned to whatever he or she was doing prior to pressing these keys.

**Figure 4-6.
PC LAN Program
Signals Incoming
Message** *(Courtesy of
International Business
Machines Corporation)*

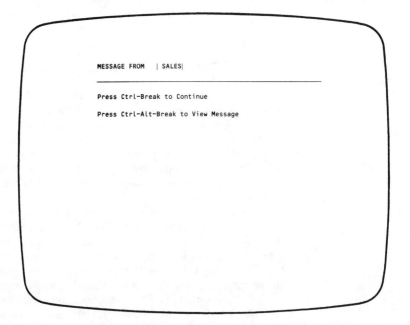

The third alternative when receiving messages is to configure your workstation so that incoming messages are automatically saved to a "log" file. Then, at your convenience, you use the DOS command TYPE to view your messages. With this option your workstation will "beep" when a message arrives but not disrupt your current activities. If you are using a receiver configuration, messages are automatically logged to your workstation console and displayed unless you specify that they be sent to a log file. Without the use of this log file, your current work is disrupted and you may need to continually refresh your screen to eliminate the "garbage" from messages. You may also have messages sent to a logged printer rather than file, but the printer must be dedicated to this function and cannot be shared with other network users.

Figure 4-7 illustrates how messages are viewed on the PC LAN Program. Notice, once again, that the same function keys used on the Send Messages screen are used on this View Messages screen. Two additional options (Save Message and Print Message) can also be performed by using function keys. Notice that PC Local Area Network distinguishes between waiting messages (messages stored in memory) and saved messages (messages already saved and logged to a file).

**Figure 4-7.
Receiving Messages on
the PC LAN Program**
*(Courtesy of International
Business Machines
Corporation)*

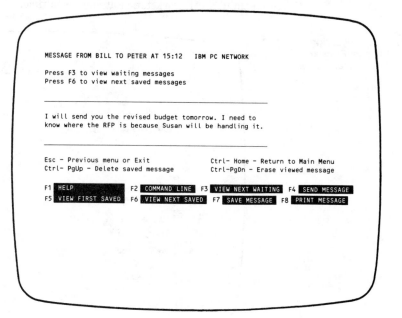

```
MESSAGE FROM BILL TO PETER AT 15:12    IBM PC NETWORK

Press F3 to view waiting messages
Press F6 to view next saved messages


I will send you the revised budget tomorrow. I need to
know where the RFP is because Susan will be handling it.


Esc - Previous menu or Exit              Ctrl- Home - Return to Main Menu
Ctrl- PgUp - Delete saved message        Ctrl-PgDn - Erase viewed message

F1 HELP                    F2 COMMAND LINE  F3 VIEW NEXT WAITING  F4 SEND MESSAGE
F5 VIEW FIRST SAVED        F6 VIEW NEXT SAVED  F7 SAVE MESSAGE     F8 PRINT MESSAGE
```

It is possible to have the network save all incoming messages so that you won't be disturbed. It is also possible to receive messages for another user. A third option permits users to forward their messages to another node if they need to work there.

The additional message commands indicate the power of this PC LAN feature. If you are faced with a deadline and don't wish to be interrupted, you can tell the network to start saving messages. The network will continue to do this until told otherwise.

Another common need in an office is for someone to "cover" for another employee. Let's say that Bill and Susan are working on an important project. Susan must go to a meeting but asks Bill to cover for her so that they can act on the message as soon as it arrives. Bill can give the network the command to let him Start receiving messages for another name and indicate that Susan's messages should be sent to him. When Susan returns, Bill selects the Message Task entitled Stop receiving messages for another name.

Many large firms have the call-forwarding option on their PBX telephone systems. PC Network has a similar feature in its message program. If Bill needs to spend the day working in the Accounting department, he can use the Forward messages to another computer option and have all messages sent to that particular computer (ACCOUNT). *Figure 4-8* illustrates the PC LAN Network menu that would be used for this purpose. When he returns the following day, he selects Stop forwarding messages to another computer. Up to twelve names may be in use on a network workstation at any given time.

Figure 4-8.
Message Forwarding
with PC LAN Program
(Courtesy of International Business Machines Corporation)

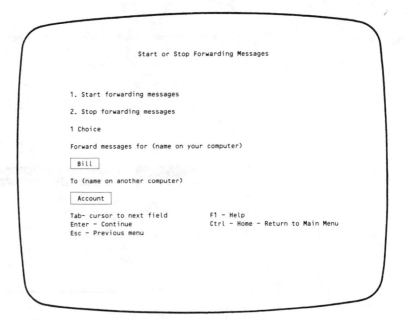

```
                      Start or Stop Forwarding Messages



       1. Start forwarding messages

       2. Stop forwarding messages

       1 Choice

       Forward messages for (name on your computer)

         Bill

       To (name on another computer)

         Account

       Tab- cursor to next field        F1 - Help
       Enter - Continue                 Ctrl - Home - Return to Main Menu
       Esc - Previous menu
```

Printer Tasks under the PC Local Area Network Program

It is possible to share up to three printers with the network. Printers may be designated as shared or as local. There are queues for each printer.

As we see in *Figure 4-4*, the second option available from the PC LAN Program Main menu refers to Printer tasks while the fourth option refers to Print queue tasks. We'll examine both options to see the degree of control over network printers available under the PC Local Area Network Program.

Every printer attached to a workstation using the PC LAN Program has to be designated as a local printer (limited to that workstation) or as a network printer. Even more significant, the PC Network Program's print management functions control all printing so network print commands must be used. A workstation user can't use a PRINT command, for instance, even with the local printer, but must use the network NET PRINT command.

As *Figure 4-9* illustrates, six printer options are covered under the Printer Tasks menu. A user may share up to three printers with the network. It is possible, though, to declare a printer a shared printer but not provide the name of the printer to other users, resulting in a printer that performs as a local printer but utilizes the network print management program.

Figure 4-9.
Printer Tasks Menu
(Courtesy of International Business Machines Corporation)

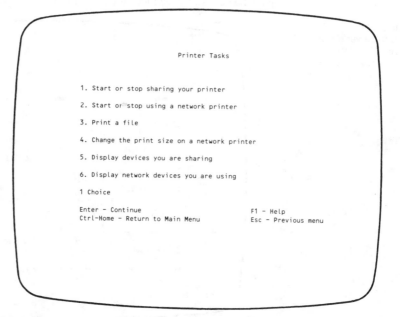

```
                              Printer Tasks


        1. Start or stop sharing your printer

        2. Start or stop using a network printer

        3. Print a file

        4. Change the print size on a network printer

        5. Display devices you are sharing

        6. Display network devices you are using

        1 Choice

        Enter - Continue                      F1 - Help
        Ctrl-Home - Return to Main Menu        Esc - Previous menu
```

Why would anyone decide not to share a printer with the network? If you have a major printing job that must be completed as quickly as possible, you won't want to wait your turn. There is also a limit of twenty-nine devices that can be shared with the network at a given time. You might wish to share a device such as a plotter or a modem and thus need to remove one of your printers from the network.

Printer Server

Each server requires 256K of RAM and supports three printers. Users may place up to 100 files in the printer queue table from which they will be printed in order in *background mode* while the computer's processor continues to perform other functions.

Network application programs are designed to send print jobs automatically to the printer queue. This queuing process isn't obvious; with low levels of network printing activity, the printing of a file might seem to be almost instantaneous.

The PC Local Area Network Program permits separate queues for each of the network printers. A user can request the status of any printer queue. As *Figure 4-10* illustrates, it is possible to check or change the print queue from a menu. Option 6 will cause the particular entry you have highlighted to "Print Now" rather than wait for its turn in the queue. The program allows users to set up a *separator page* that will print out between files indicating who printed the file, the name of the file itself, and the date and time. Files that are still "spooling" are still being sent to the printer queue. Their status cannot be changed until they finish spooling.

Figure 4-10.
Printer Server's Print
Queue *(Courtesy of*
International Business
Machines Corporation)

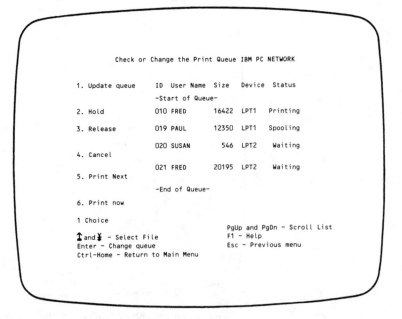

```
              Check or Change the Print Queue IBM PC NETWORK

    1. Update queue      ID  User Name  Size   Device  Status
                             -Start of Queue-
    2. Hold              010 FRED       16422  LPT1    Printing

    3. Release           019 PAUL       12350  LPT1    Spooling

                         020 SUSAN        546  LPT2    Waiting
    4. Cancel
                         021 FRED       20195  LPT2    Waiting
    5. Print Next
                             -End of Queue-

    6. Print now

    1 Choice
                                        PgUp and PgDn - Scroll List
    ↑ and ↓ - Select File               F1 - Help
    Enter - Change queue                Esc - Previous menu
    Ctrl-Home - Return to Main Menu
```

The IBM PC Local Area Network Program has a number of printer control commands. The NET PAUSE PRINT [=printdevice] causes the network sharing of a specific printer to pause. NET CONTINUE PRINT [=printdevice] resumes network printing. Certain server commands would also achieve these results, but we'll look at those when we examine the server functions found on the PC LAN Program.

Sharing Disks and Directories with the Network

The third option under the PC Local Area Network Program's main menu is "Disk or directory tasks." The tasks consist of the following choices:

1. Start or stop sharing your disk or directory.
2. Start or stop using a network disk or directory.
3. Display devices you are sharing.
4. Display devices you are using.

The PC Local Area Network Program permits the sharing of directories but not files. You must place a file in its own directory if you wish to share the file. Your decision to share a directory is not automatically sent as a message to other network users. The PC Local Area Network Program assumes that you will make the availability of this directory known to the people who need to know about its existence and who may need to use it.

To share application programs with other users, IBM suggests placing the programs in one subdirectory. The PC Local Area Network Program has an Installation Aid utility program that will create this subdirectory, install the application programs, and mark each program file "Read Only." Because some application programs have files that require read/write/create access, the usual practice with the PC Local Area Network Program is to create several user subdirectories, each of which contains copies of these files. The Installation Aid utility will create private subdirectories for each user who wants to run these application programs.

You can establish a password for a particular directory or subdirectory that you are sharing. Let's assume you wished to share a sensitive directory (TOPSEC) with a remote computer user named JEAN. You've decided to use the password ABCXYZ. You would enter the following:

```
NET SHARE JEAN=C: \ TOPSEC ABCXYZ
```

This information could be placed in an Autoexec.bat file with an asterisk (*) replacing the secret password. When the batch file actually runs, the network will prompt you for the password.

There are additional steps that can be taken to increase security. A file server's physical location offers additional control. A controller, keeping sensitive payroll records on an IBM PC AT that is also used as a file server, can take the precaution of locking the machine. Some companies save valuable data to disks that are stored under lock and key.

Virtually all network activities under the IBM PC Local Area Network program can be accessed by direct commands as well as through the system of nested menus. This means that an experienced user who wished to share a directory with the network could use a command (NET SHARE) to do so. The network command structure uses the DOS hierarchical file structure naming conventions. This means that if Bill wished to make his budget reports found in his drive C directory named \ BUD \ BUDRPT available to the entire network, he would use the following command:

```
NET SHARE \ BUD \ BUDRPT
```

A problem with this arrangement is that network users who want to access this file have to provide its exact path. A user who wanted to treat Bill's directory as his own drive D, for example, would have to type the following:

NET USE D: \ \ BILL \ BUD \ BUDRPT

Bill could make everyone else's work easier by using a network name for his directory. Let's assume that the network users already refer to Bill's famous budget reports as the "87 Budget Report." He could provide the network name BUDGET:

NET USE BUDGET=C: \ BUD \ BUDRPT

Now other network users who want to access this directory as their D directories, for example, could type the following:

NET USE D: \ \ BILL \ BUDGET

Users who wish to share their entire disk rather than certain directories can do so by sharing their root directory (C:\ ). Everything in this C drive directory, including all subdirectories, will then be available to other network users. *Figure 4-11* illustrates how Bill could go about sharing a customer list found in one of his subdirectories with the rest of the network.

Figure 4-11.
**Sharing a Directory with
the Network** *(Courtesy of
International Business
Machines Corporation)*

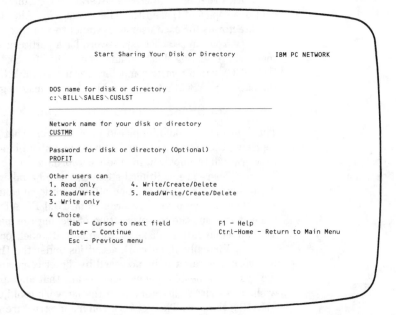

```
          Start Sharing Your Disk or Directory        IBM PC NETWORK


    DOS name for disk or directory
    c:\BILL\SALES\CUSLST
    _____

    Network name for your disk or directory
    CUSTMR

    Password for disk or directory (Optional)
    PROFIT

    Other users can
    1. Read only          4. Write/Create/Delete
    2. Read/Write         5. Read/Write/Create/Delete
    3. Write only

    4 Choice
         Tab - Cursor to next field        F1 - Help
         Enter - Continue                  Ctrl-Home - Return to Main Menu
         Esc - Previous menu
```

As *Figure 4-11* shows, the IBM PC Local Area Network Program permits five combinations of user access to the directories being shared with the network:

1. Read only
2. Read-Write

3. Write only
4. Write-Create-Delete
5. Read-Write-Create-Delete

The program's default value is Read/Write/Create/Delete. A user who wished to share a directory and pressed the <ENTER> key at this point would provide this level of access for all network users. Users who only need to view information can be limited to "Read only" status while other members of your particular project or department might require the full "Read-Write-Create-Delete" privileges. The PC Local Area Network Program doesn't provide the level of security that a more sophisticated program such as Novell's NetWare provides. Any user who knows the password (PROFIT) for Bill's device (in this case, his disk drive containing this subdirectory) will be able to access the material. Of course, Bill could decide not to share this directory; in which case, network users wouldn't be able to access the files in the directory even though they might have access to the disk drive.

There is one additional way around the PC Local Area Network Program's limitation in providing the same level of security for all network users. It is possible to offer this same subdirectory to the network several times with several different network names and device passwords. A company controller, for example, might want to set up the payroll subdirectory so that certain individuals would access it under one network name with read-only privileges while a payroll clerk who needs to alter hours-worked and hourly rate fields would use a different network name and have greater privileges.

Saving Time when Starting the PC Local Area Network Program

The PC Local Area Network Program enables you to save your configuration values established when you first entered the network in an Autoexec.bat file. If you indicate you wish to save your network setup, the program saves the optional parameters you have established, including which resources you wish to share with the network and which resources you currently are using. If you are receiving messages for additional names, this will continue when you enter the network the next time.

There are questions that you need to ask yourself before saving your network setup under the PC Local Area Network Program. Since memory is a very valuable resource that affects the network's speed and ability to respond to network users' requests, you need to decide precisely what you plan to be doing the next time you enter the network. If you are expecting an important lengthy report, for example, you might have to change the buffer size for your messages from 512K bytes to 60,000 bytes. This decision, in turn, may affect your ability to run a large application program and still serve as a network server.

The IBM PC Local Area Network Program enables the user who is sharing resources to adjust the time and memory allocation of network functions versus local functions. The tasks the user performs on his or her own machine are known as "foreground tasks" while those tasks performed by other network users are called "background tasks." A network timer provides intervals composed of timer ticks of 18.175 milliseconds. The network's normal default value of 5/4 allocates almost equal time to foreground (5 intervals) and background (4 intervals) tasks. Five intervals are equivalent to 90.875 milliseconds (5*18.175 milliseconds). The "Time-Slice Intervals" (TSI) parameter defines the way the server will divide its time. The file server performs a foreground task until it reaches the time to perform a background task. It then checks to see if there is a background task to perform. If there is, it temporarily halts what it is doing and begins performing the background task.

While the file server is incapable of multitasking and really only performs one task at a time, it switches back and forth so many times within a second that the results may seem to be multitasking. Despite this speed, there are some file-server tasks that can cripple the entire network's speed. One example is disk formatting. During this relatively lengthy procedure the file server will not release DOS to enable the time-slicing procedure to work. Obviously, file servers should not be used to format disks. If foreground and background tasks are allocated larger numbers, the network response will seem erratic. It may seem to take forever for certain tasks to be performed.

Other Ways to Boost Network Performance

Additional parameters can be adjusted in order to maximize PC Local Area Network performance. These include the amount of memory used for disk sharing, print spooling, and background print performance. The receive request buffer (/RQB), for example, can be adjusted to specify the maximum buffer available for file transfer between file server and network workstations. The larger the number specified for /RQB, the more data the file server can send at a time to the workstation. The result of this larger value for /RQB is that the file server doesn't need to perform as many send operations and thus can perform other network procedures more quickly.

The request buffers parameter (/REQ) determines how many user requests can be handled at any given time. This value can vary from 1 to 3 with 2 serving as the default figure. The larger this parameter, the more requests that can be processed and the faster the network performance. While a 2 requires 16K bytes of memory, a 3 requires 48K bytes.

Network print buffer parameters can also enhance performance under the PC Local Area Network Program. The print buffer parameter (/PRB) specifies how much of a print file the printer server can keep in memory at a time before it has to retrieve more of the file. The default value of 512K bytes is sufficient unless there is very heavy printer activity on the network. Similarly, the print priority parameter (/PRP) is used to specify how much of the foreground task interval is to be used for printing files while the server computer is performing other tasks. The default value for this parameter is 3, but a network user who wants greater responsiveness from the server computer should specify a 1 or 2.

THE IBM TOKEN RING NETWORK: OVERVIEW

While PC Net might be adequate for a small office environment, IBM does offer a more powerful, faster, local area network that is capable of much greater expansion. The IBM Token Ring Network uses a star-wired ring topology and follows the baseband-signaling and token-passing protocols of the IEEE 802.5 standard. The network utilizes unshielded twisted-pair telephone wire designated by IBM as type 3 cabling. It is also possible to use IBM's type 1 or type 2 cable as well as fiber optics. The Token Ring Network operates at 4 Mbit/s and supports up to 260 devices using shielded twisted-pair or 72 devices using telephone twisted-pair wire.

While both the Token Ring Network and PC Net run the PC Local Area Network Program, the two are quite different with respect to the NETBIOS and hardware. While PC Net uses a NETBIOS found on ROM portions of the adapter cards that are required on each network workstation, Token Ring Network uses a NETBIOS software program that is loaded into each machine. Whereas PC Net uses a simple bus architecture, where there is always some danger of data collision, Token Ring Network's topology allows only one network workstation at a time to have the token required to send messages.

HARDWARE REQUIRED FOR THE TOKEN RING NETWORK

The PC Adapter

The Token Ring Network requires an adapter card in an expansion slot in each workstation. *Figure 4-12* illustrates the configuration of the circuit card. There is an exchange of data buffers and control blocks between the network workstation's RAM and the adapter card. The card's RAM is actually mapped into the workstation's memory in a section IBM refers to as "shared RAM." This technique reduces the overhead required for I/O between adapter card and workstation.

**Figure 4-12.
Token Ring Adapter
Card Structure** (*Courtesy
of International Business
Machines Corporation*)

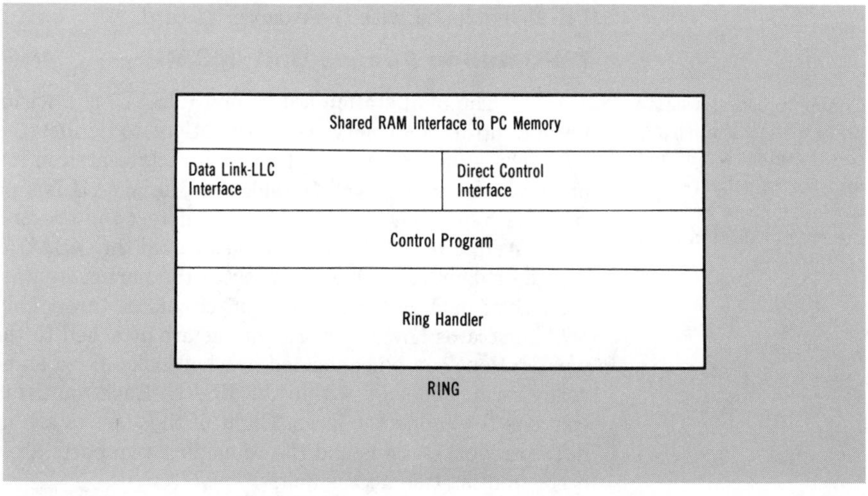

Shared RAM Interface to PC Memory	
Data Link-LLC Interface	Direct Control Interface
Control Program	
Ring Handler	

RING

The Token Ring Adapter Card contains microcode to provide error checking, token generation, address recognition, and data transmission.

Figure 4-12 also shows the two interfaces found on the adapter card. The data link-LLC interface contains some microcode (ROM) that supports these logical link control functions as defined by the IEEE 802.2 standards. The direct interface provides a way for a user program to read information maintained by the adapter card.

The adapter card located in each workstation handles token recognition, data transmission, frame recognition, token generation, address recognition, error checking and logging, time-out controls, and link-fault detection. One workstation's adapter is designated as the *active token monitor* in contrast to the other adapters, which function as passive monitors. This station is responsible for error-recovery procedures should the normal token activity become disrupted. Note that any of the remaining workstation's adapter cards can assume the active role should something happen to the active token monitor.

The adapter card comes with two diagnostic programs. The adapter diagnostics program is used *before* the adapter card is attached to the ring. It checks the adapter and the attaching cable and ensures that the card is able to perform self-diagnostics successfully. A second program checks the adapter card after it has been connected to the ring and ensures that it is able to perform the functions required to connect it to the ring media. The adapter itself is able to detect such permanent errors as loss of receive signal and then generate a notification signal to initiate automatic network recovery. Recoverable errors, such as bit errors in the transmitted message, are detected by the adapter for subsequent reporting to a ring diagnostic program.

There are actually two different Token Ring Adapter cards available from IBM. The Token-Ring Network PC Adapter is the choice for workstations in a self-contained token ring network. There is a second option, the Token-Ring Network PC Adapter II, which enables the attachment of IBM PCs, IBM Industrial Computers (7531, 7532, 5531), and System/36 computers. PCs are attached directly to the token ring through this adapter while the System/36 is attached to the ring through an IBM PC AT equipped with the Adapter II card.

Multistation Access Unit (MSAU)

The multistation access unit (MSAU) is a wiring concentrator that permits up to eight network workstations to be inserted or deleted from the network.

The multistation access unit (MSAU) is a wiring concentrator that permits up to eight network workstations to be inserted or bypassed on the ring. The unit is mounted either on a rack located in a nearby wiring closet or in a housing on a wall or tabletop. The MSAU is a passive device that contains bypass circuitry designed to detect the presence or absence of a signal from a network workstation. Should the MSAU detect a defective device or damaged cable, it bypasses the particular workstation to avoid the loss of data and the token that circulates throughout the ring. *Figure 4-13* illustrates how the workstations are attached to the MSAU. Although workstations can be connected in what looks like a star architecture, it is really a ring topology within the MSAU. Each multistation access unit contains ten connector jacks. Eight of these ports are used to connect network workstations and the remaining two ports are used to connect other multistation access units.

Figure 4-13.
Multistation Access
Unit with Three
Workstations

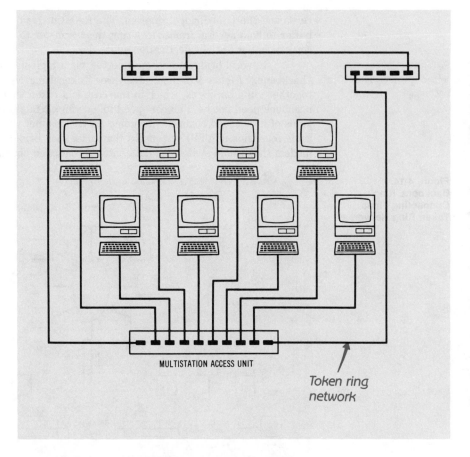

MULTISTATION ACCESS UNIT

Token ring
network

TOKEN RING NETWORK CONNECTIVITY

A principal strength of the IBM Token Ring Network is that IBM provides the hardware and software required to connect this network with other networks, PBX systems, remote PCs, and mainframe computers. We'll see how easy it is to connect the network to the rest of the world.

Network Bridges

A network node (usually an IBM PC AT) serves as a bridge to connect two more token ring networks together. The bridge computer contains network adapter cards for each network and the appropriate bridge software.

Two IBM Token Ring Networks can be joined, using a *bridge*. In fact, bridges can connect several token ring networks, each of which can contain up to 260 workstations. Bridges appear to be a normal node on a ring, but they route frames of information between rings by examining the destination addresses contained on the frames. As we'll see when we examine how the token is passed from node to node within a ring or through a bridge to other rings, the destination addresses identify a specific ring as well as a workstation within that ring. To perform this high-speed data transfer, the bridge is normally an IBM PC AT or a selected model of IBM industrial computer containing two Token-Ring Network Adapter II cards and the IBM Bridge program. The RAM in this bridge serves as a buffer to hold several frames awaiting their transfer to the network nodes corresponding to their destination addresses.

Several bridges can be joined together by a backbone.

Several bridges can be connected via a high-speed link known as a "backbone." *Figure 4-14* illustrates three Token Ring Networks joined together via a backbone, which in this case is a token ring itself. The backbone need not be a higher-speed token ring; it might consist of other kinds of high-speed channels, including an RF channel within a broadband cable television (CATV) system. In that case, each bridge would consist of a modem that would switch the data onto a broadband channel.

Figure 4-14.
Backbone Ring
Connecting Three
Token Ring Networks

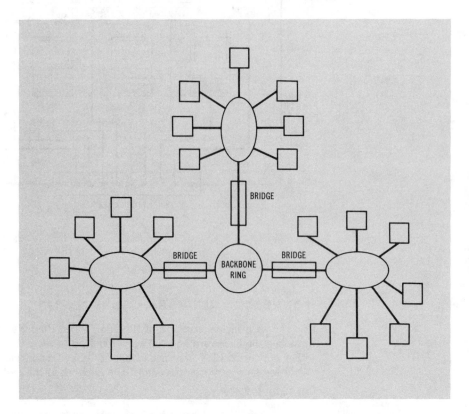

Connecting PC Network and the Token Ring Network

The Token-Ring Network/PC Network Interconnect Program running on a dedicated PC workstation with adapter cards for both networks can serve as a bridge.

A company might need to connect a PC Network, which could be performing a departmental function, with a larger Token Ring Network that encompasses all the company's activities. IBM offers the Token Ring Network/PC Network Interconnect Program to serve this purpose. It is necessary to dedicate an IBM PC running the interconnect program and the NETBIOS program for this. Adapter cards from each network are installed in two of the PC's expansion slots, and workstations in one network can share resources of the other network through this "bridge" PC.

The Interconnect Program can handle up to sixteen application names for each network. This means that the maximum number of attaching devices on one network that can be identified to the other network is sixteen. Some applications, however, require the use of multiple names. For example, the file-server function on the PC Local Area Network Program requires the use of three names, so a maximum of only five file-servers on one network can be identified to the other network. Because of this limitation, it might be necessary to run multiple Interconnect programs in order to identify all of the devices that workstations need to address. The Interconnect program permits a maximum of 32 active sessions. When a name on one network connects with a name on the other network, two sessions are created, one for each network. During the program's configuration phase, it identifies the devices on each network and stores them in a configuration file. The operational phase of the program is concerned with receiving information from one network and forwarding it to the other network.

While the Interconnect program is running, it monitors a number of on-line data. It is possible, for example, to check the status of any adapter on either network. Since PC Network and the Token Ring Network require different kinds of status reports, there are different screens for each network's adapters. It is also possible to examine interconnect status. This means that the program will display a list of network names that are currently connected. The network administrator can select a connected network pair and examine traffic statistics involving that particular session.

Connecting a Token Ring Network with System/370

It is possible to connect Token Ring Network workstations with IBM's System/370 world of systems network architecture. A 3725 communication controller with token ring adapters can connect as many as eight Token Ring Networks to an IBM mainframe computer. Workstations on these networks could then communicate with the mainframe computer using 3270 emulation mode. A gateway workstation on these networks could be connected to an IBM System/370 via the network connection with the 3725 or directly with an SDLC adapter card, the PC 3270 Emulation program, and cabling. The gateway station can also function as a normal workstation depending on the amount of gateway activity. The gateway unit can also function as a network print server or file server.

Connecting a Token Ring Network with System/36

Since the System/36 serves as IBM's major offering at the departmental level, it is logical that the company would provide a connection between System/36 and the Token Ring Network so that a mid-size company would be able to integrate all its data communications. A System/36 can be directly attached to a Token Ring Network through an IBM PC AT functioning as a communications controller. With an optional PC Support/36 Workstation feature, network workstations can emulate

IBM 5250 terminals and access System/36 files, libraries, and folders. Assuming the System/36 is connected with a System/370, a network workstation can access the System/370 through the System/36. In this scenario it would be possible for a PC network workstation to operate independently and run DOS programs, emulate a 5250 terminal, and establish multiple System/36 sessions, or it could emulate a 3278 and communicate with the System/370.

Connecting a Token Ring Network with Series/1 Computers

By the time you read this book, IBM will also offer an IBM Series/1 PC Connect program. This gateway program, and the necessary hardware, provides a link between the Token Ring Network and the Series/1 computers enabling workstations to use Series/1 resources. Consisting of an S/1 controller card, a PC channel extender card, cabling, and software, this file-server/print-server package permits workstations to access Series/1 high-density disks and high-speed printers. It also establishes a logical connection through the Series/1 with System/370 host application programs.

The SNA Advanced Program-to-Program Communication (APPC)

The Advanced Program-to-Program Communications (APPC) program provides a program-to-program protocol (LU 6.2) that permits peer-to-peer conversations between applications running on an IBM PC, a System 36/38, System 370, Series 1, and another IBM PC. While this program does not provide direct connectivity between sessions on the Token Ring Network and sessions on the SDLC link, it does provide an application programming interface so that a program can be written to communicate between these logical units.

Asynchronous Communications for the Token Ring Network and PC Network

IBM offers an Asynchronous Communications Server program that enables workstations on the Token Ring Network or PC Network to access ASCII applications via switched communication lines. By using this program network, administrators can link workstations in their IBM network with a Rolm CBX II, a PBX, or to public-switched networks. Each Asynchronous Communications Server gateway station provides up to two dial lines, and it is possible to have more than one of these non-dedicated gateway stations on a network.

The Asynchronous Communications Server program runs in background mode. It is able to establish outbound calls to such services as the IBM Information Network, The Source, and Dow Jones News/Retrieval Services. Because modems are shared resources on the network, the program provides cost-effective service to workstations that need this type of information. If all phone lines are being used, the program provides queuing of these requests. The program also accepts inbound calls directed toward particular workstations running communication programs; it provides transparent ASCII data transfer between the caller and the network workstation. While this program operates on both the PC Network and Token Ring Network, it will work on PC Network only if the PC is configured for re-director functions.

It is also necessary for an external ASCII device that wishes to communicate to a network workstation to be able to perform a two-step procedure in order to establish communications. Because remote asynchronous devices cannot have direct access to resident functions such as file servers, print servers, or message servers, after establishing contact with the asynchronous communications server, the caller must be able to provide the name of the network workstation. Some electronic mail programs that have their own private protocols won't work with this software. Other programs that cannot use the asynchronous communications server for this reason include host security applications that require the ability to disconnect and then immediately call back.

Connecting a Token Ring Network with a PBX

Just as AT&T has integrated its local area networks with its PBX telephone systems, IBM has accomplished much the same thing between its Token Ring Network and Rolm's CBX II telephone equipment through the Asynchronous Communications Server and a number of digital interfaces such as Rolm's DataCom Module (DCM), Integrated Personal Computer Interface (IPCI), Integrated Personal Computer Interface AT (IPCI/AT), or Data Terminal Interface (DTI).

Attachment to a Rolm PBX such as the CBX II permits network workstations to share the CBX II's resources, including its modem pooling report capability. An even more significant reason for considering this connection is the ability of the CBX II to switch among several different computer systems, including those with different protocols. With this PBX and protocol converters such as IBM's 3708, 3710, or 7171, an office having several different types of equipment, including PCs and other ASCII terminals, can bridge the communication gap between IBM and the rest of the world that uses ASCII.

IBM sees this Token Ring Network connection with Rolm's CBX II as a way for PC workstations to access IBM office systems including DisplayWrite/370, PROFS, and Personal services/370. Because of the CBX II's architecture, it is able to operate attached ASCII terminals at much higher speeds than in the past. An IBM 3161/3163 and Rolm workstations such as the Cedar, Cypress, or Juniper can operate at up to 19.2 Kbit/s through an IBM protocol converter. *Figure 4-15* illustrates the many different devices that can be connected to the Token Ring Network.

Figure 4-15.
IBM Token Ring's
Connectivity *(Courtesy of*
International Business
Machines Corporation)

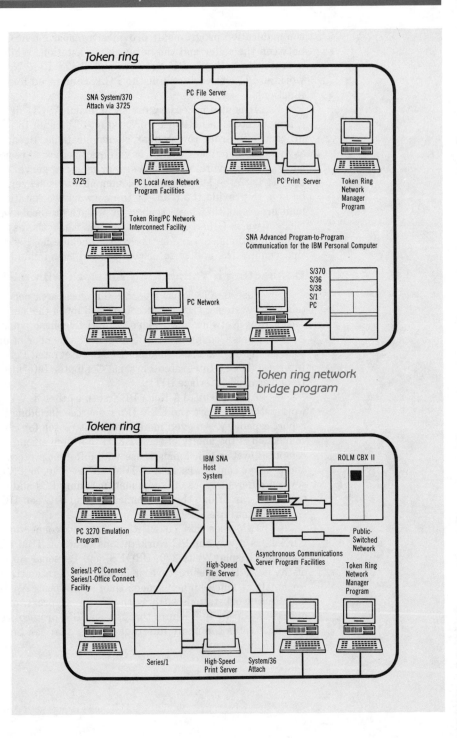

Printing in the Token Ring Network

As we pointed out earlier, the PC LAN program offers printer-server functions including a printer queue. IBM offers an additional program, the IBM Local Area Network Print Manager, to connect the Token Ring Network with its very fast and powerful 3820 laser printer.

DATA TRANSMISSION ON THE TOKEN RING NETWORK

Unlike the PC Network which is a bus topology utilizing Carrier Sense Multiple Access with Collision Detection (CSMA/CD) to avoid collisions, the Token Ring Network is a non-contention network. Only one network node can send information at any given time because of the nature of the token ring architecture. We'll look now at how information is transmitted and received on the network and at how network problems are diagnosed.

Information to be sent across the network is formatted into frames. *Figure 4-16* illustrates the fields found within these frames. Notice that the frame contains both the destination node address and the address of the source workstation. In very large networks with multiple rings tied together with bridges, an optional routing information subfield (RI) follows the address fields and indicates the sequence of bridges that must be transversed to reach the correct ring.

**Figure 4-16.
Token Ring Information
Frame**

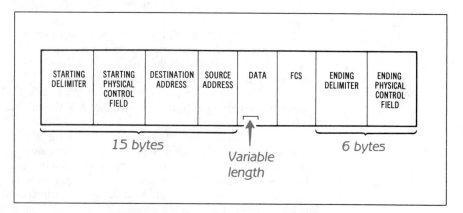

When a mailbox's flag is up, the mail carrier knows that there is a letter to be picked up. In much the same fashion, the token that circulates around the ring has a bit sequence that tells the various nodes whether it is carrying a message or is free to be used. The first byte of the physical control field and the starting delimiter field and ending delimiter field compose a special token identifier. One of these bits is known as the "token bit," because when it is set to 0 the token is ready to be used. When a node has information to send, it captures the token and adds the source and destination addresses as well as the other fields seen in *Figure 4-16*. It then changes the 0 to a 1 indicating that the frame is now an information frame.

The information frame moves through the ring until it reaches the destination node. The workstation recognizes its own address in the destination address field. It copies the information that has been sent and returns the token to the sender. The sender removes the header (the first 15 bytes) and issues a new token. The frame is now ready to circulate to the next node that needs to send a message. Each network node gets a chance to use the token because no one node is allowed to transmit continuously.

Errors can occur on a token ring network and IBM has developed some safeguards that prevent network downtime. As we learned in our discussion of adapter cards, the circuit cards which are required in each node perform such tasks as frame recognition and token generation. A node designated as the active token monitor runs the IBM Token Ring Manager program, which monitors the network for transient errors and permanent errors. A "transient" error is a "soft" error, often intermittent, that can usually be corrected by retransmission. Transient errors are detected by a node by monitoring all frames and verifying the validity of the frame-check sequence that accompanies the message. Each node keeps track of these errors and reports them if they exceed a threshold amount. An operator can use a function called "Soft Error Conditions" to display the conditions of all stations reporting transient errors. The node detecting these errors sets the error-detected flag in the physical trailer portion (6 bytes) of the frame.

In contrast to soft errors are permanent errors, which represent a serious threat to the network's continued operation. When a node sends a message and receives the token back, it examines it to see if the address-recognized flag has been set by the destination node. If the flag has not been set, the location of the defective node is identified. The wire concentrators are able to bypass such faults in the network and keep the network operating.

A complete disruption of the network signal can be caused either by the complete failure of a receiver and/or transmitter of an active node or by a break in the wiring. The next network node downstream from the defective node sends out a special network signal called a "beacon". This frame contains the address of the node sending the special message as well as the address of the node immediately upstream from it (presumably the defective node). The normal response to this signal is for the wiring concentrator involved to bypass the defective node. Breaks in the actual wiring of the network may not be as easy to resolve. The entire ring may have to be reconfigured to bypass a particular break. Since each node has the ability to perform self-diagnostic tests that can identify errors in its own wiring, it is a good idea to run these tests if there is no obvious break apparent in the network wiring.

WHAT HAVE WE LEARNED?

1. The PC Network is a broadband LAN utilizing coaxial cable.
2. The network adapter cards for PC Network contain modems as well as the NETBIOS, the "brains" of the network.

3. PC Network workstations can be configured as redirector, receiver, messenger, or server.
4. The IBM Token Ring Network requires a NETBIOS software program.
5. It is possible to connect Token Ring Network and PC Network with the Token-Ring Network/PC Network Interconnect Program using a dedicated workstation with adapter cards from both networks.
6. It is possible to connect Token Ring Network with a PBX through an asynchronous communications server and a digital interface.
7. Token Ring Network can be connected directly to an IBM mainframe and minicomputers.
8. The Token Ring Manager program monitors the network for both transient and permanent errors.

Quiz for Chapter 4

1. PC Network is a broadband network that uses which medium?
   a. Fiber optics.
   b. Coaxial cable.
   c. Twisted pair.
   d. RS-232 serial cable.

2. The actual broadband frequency translation on the PC Network is handled by the:
   a. adapter cards.
   b. network translation unit.
   c. eight-way splitters.
   d. base expanders.

3. Since this is a broadband network, PC Network utilizes modems located:
   a. in the network translator units.
   b. in the network adapter cards.
   c. in the base expanders.
   d. in the eight-way splitters.

4. The modems are able to achieve 2 Mbit/s speed on the network by use of:
   a. frequency shift keying.
   b. modulating and demodulating signals.
   c. bit stuffing.
   d. accelerating bit packing.

5. On PC Network, the interface between PC DOS applications and the network adapter controller is known as:
   a. SNA.
   b. BIOS.
   c. UNIX.
   d. HLDC.

6. The PC Network configuration limited to accepting requests for applications directed to servers and the passing of these requests along to the servers is:
   a. the messenger.
   b. the redirector.
   c. the receiver.
   d. the server.

7. Network request keys on PC Network consist of:
   a. <Ctrl>-<Alt>-<Break>.
   b. <Ctrl>-<Alt>-<Del>.
   c. <Ctrl>-<Esc>.
   d. <Ctrl>-<PrtSc>.

8. The PC LAN command to share resources is:
   a. LINK.
   b. SHARE.
   c. NET SHARE.
   d. JOIN.

9. Programs in PC LAN are normally set up with the following default:
   a. Read-Write-Create-Delete.
   b. Read Only.
   c. Read-Write.
   d. Write-Create-Delete.

10. Tasks a user performs on his or her own machine are known as:
   a. background tasks.
   b. foreground tasks.
   c. remote tasks.
   d. server-initiated tasks.

11. The Token Ring Network's topology follows which standard?
   a. IEEE 802.3.
   b. IEEE 802.4.
   c. IEEE 802.5.
   d. IEEE 802.2.

12. Token Ring Network's wiring concentrators are found on its:
    a. adapter cards.
    b. network translation cards.
    c. multistation access units.
    d. active network monitors.

13. Two token ring networks can be joined together with a:
    a. backbone.
    b. bridge.
    c. spinal tap.
    d. T1 high-speed connection.

14. Several bridges can be joined together with a:
    a. backbone.
    b. bridge.
    c. spinal tap.
    d. T1 high-speed connection.

15. To establish peer-to-peer conversations between applications running on an IBM PC and a System 370, IBM provides:
    a. modems.
    b. an asynchronous communications server.
    c. the Advanced Program-to-Program Communication program.
    d. synchronous connections.

16. To establish cost-effective calls between network workstations and services such as The Source and Dow Jones News/Information Network, IBM provides:
    a. SDLC Protocol.
    b. an Asynchronous Communications Server.
    c. HLDC Protocol.
    d. Dow Jones software.

17. When a network workstation wishes to use a token, it must check to see:
    a. if the token bit is set to 0.
    b. if the token bit is set to 1.
    c. if the token bit has been removed.
    d. if the token beacon signal is on.

18. Transient network errors are:
    a. vagrant bits looking for a free transmission.
    b. errors caused by user mistake.
    c. errors normally corrected by retransmission.
    d. errors that extend across a bridge to a second network.

Novell's Local Area Network Systems

ABOUT THIS CHAPTER

In this chapter we'll survey the many different local area network solutions offered by Novell. We'll examine Novell's hardware (primarily its file servers and network interface circuit cards) as well as the intricacies of the network software (NetWare) it offers. Because Novell is one of the few local area networks to offer true file servers and sophisticated network security, we will take a close look at these two issues and what they mean to both the network user and the system administrator. We will examine the many utility programs available under NetWare including the electronic mail system. Finally, we'll look at Novell's system fault tolerant versions of NetWare, software designed to prevent network failure.

NOVELL'S PHILOSOPHY

Novell's approach to serving the local area network user is unique. While the company does offer its own LAN hardware including file servers, tape backup units, add-on disk drives, and communications servers, its LAN software (NetWare) is what has made Novell an industry standout. NetWare runs on virtually any IBM or compatible and works with all the major LAN vendor hardware including AT&T, Corvus, and 3Com. NetWare is clearly the most sophisticated software offered for microcomputer LANS. Novell's philosophy is to complement the other local area networks rather than to compete with the other vendors. Does a major corporation insist on purchasing IBM's Token Ring Network? Novell is happy to supply compatible NetWare to enhance the token ring performance of the system.

TOPOLOGY

Novell supports a variety of network architectures including a star, a string of stars, a token ring, and a bus.

Novell offers several different starter kits that can be configured, depending upon the hardware you select, as a star, a string of stars, a token ring, and even a bus. The compatibility of the different versions of NetWare software ensures that companies forced to change their hardware or their network topologies because of unplanned growth or other considerations will not have to start all over again with new application programs and incompatible data.

The Star (S-NET Server Systems)

Novell's S-NET system is a star network using a proprietary 68000 microprocessor-based file server. It provides very fast response for a limited number of users.

As *Figure 5-1* illustrates, Novell's S-Net system is a star configuration with the individual workstations connected to the file server by dual twisted-pair wire coming from the network interface cards (NICs) residing in the expansion unit of each PC or compatible. Note that Novell makes it economical for companies that don't need independently functioning IBM PCs. It is possible to use a unit without a disk drive as long as the Novell Remote System Reset PROM is installed. This chip allows a workstation to boot directly from the network and use the network's hard disk drive for data storage. The PROM is available for virtually all Novell networks. The S-Net file server has slots in which RAM expansion boards can be placed, expanding to a maximum of 8 Mb of RAM and supporting a maximum of twenty-four workstations. There are ports for twenty-four physical connections, but the file server can handle up to a hundred logical devices. The RAM boards are available in 1-Mb or 4-Mb configurations. Each S-Net file server can support five printers and a maximum configuration of 2 gigabytes (2000 megabytes) external storage. One important consideration here is that volumes cannot exceed 128 megabytes; a company with thousands of inventory transactions that need to be kept together might find this limitation unacceptable.

Figure 5-1.
Novell's S-Net System Server Configuration
(Copyright, 1986, Novell, Inc., all rights reserved)

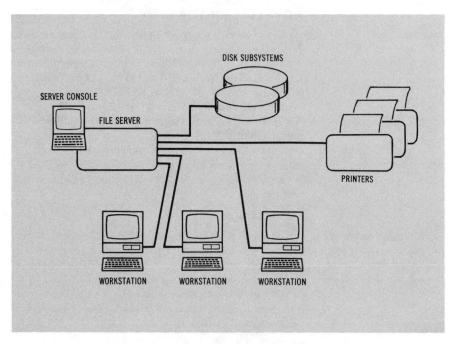

All S-Net file servers are dedicated; they cannot be used as workstations. The file-server chassis contains two serial ports for attaching the system console and a serial printer. The system console is actually a user-selected terminal. S-Net and NetWare support most of the major terminals, including TeleVideo, Lear Siegler, Wyse, and ADDS Viewpoints. Basically, Novell requires a terminal capable of displaying a page of 1920 characters (80 columns by 24 lines) with a standard 96 ASCII character set and cursor control functions for clearing the screen and providing direct cursor addressing. There are also ports available for attaching the maximum of twenty-four workstations via dual twisted-pair cable; each workstation requires an NIC in its bus.

It is possible to link several file servers under S-NET using Novell's Advanced NetWare 68 operating system. Connecting two file servers requires two twisted-pair wire connections between them and uses two ports on each file server.

Twenty-four workstations may not be enough for some companies. Using the Advanced NetWare 68 operating system, it is possible for S-Net to utilize up to 2 gigabytes (Gb) of disk storage and connect several file servers. *Figure 5-2* illustrates how several file servers can be joined. Each LAN card in the file server can handle up to eight workstations. Novell recommends that file servers be connected with cables to two ports of each file server. This means that each of the file servers could serve a maximum of twenty-two workstations, or a total of forty-four workstations. A significant limitation of S-Net is that the maximum cable length between workstation and file server is 1500 ft (450 m). The S-Net server may be up to 50 ft (15 m) away from the console.

The S-Net system has all the advantages and disadvantages of a star topology. It is easy to add a new workstation because it only entails connecting dual twisted-pair cabling from the workstation's NIC to an empty port in the file server. Another advantage of this topology is that the failure of a single workstation will not affect the entire network. Since there is a central file server with a dedicated cable connecting it to a specific workstation, it is relatively easy to perform system diagnostics and pinpoint whether a particular workstation's interface card or its cable is defective. The major disadvantage of this architecture, however, is that the failure of the file server can result in the entire network's failure. This is one reason that a chain of distributed stars appeals to many network administrators.

ARCNET's String of Stars

ARCNET's distributed star architecture provides the many advantages of the star topology with the added protection that a failure of a single file server will not bring down the entire network.

One way to enjoy the advantages of a star topology's power and speed and expand to several dozen users without worrying about a total network failure is to use Novell's software with ARCNET's distributed star architecture. Using Standard Microsystem's ARCNET Network Interface Cards and Novell's T286A or T286B file servers, it is possible to support up to 128 active workstations per server. Workstations may be up to 4000 ft (1200 m) from the file server because they are connected with RG-62 coaxial cable, the same cabling used by IBM's 3270 mainframe system. Facilities that already use an IBM mainframe can realize a tremendous savings in network installation costs since the bulk of their cabling is already in place.

Figure 5-2.
Novell's Multiple Server
S-Net Configuration
(Copyright, 1986, Novell,
Inc., all rights reserved)

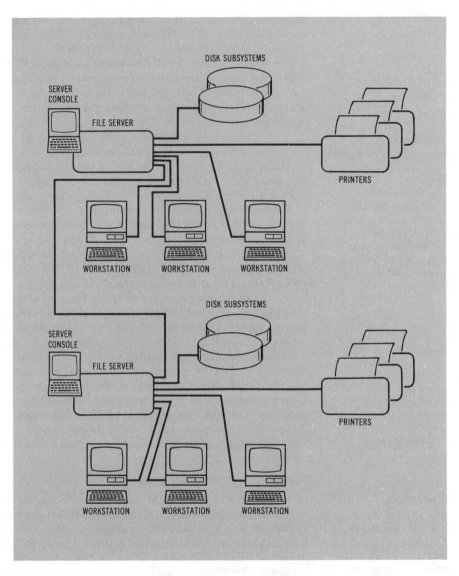

As *Figure 5-3* illustrates, the ARCNET/Novell system provides a series of active and passive hubs that use a modified form of token passing to produce a string of interconnected stars. In effect, the network is a logical ring but a series of physical stars that utilize token-passing technology. Because the active hubs contain repeaters to boost a signal, there may be up to 2000 ft (600 m) between devices. The passive hubs, on the other hand, permit only a maximum of 100 ft (30 m) between devices because they simply split a signal. It is not possible to connect passive hubs together. The maximum trunk length for the entire network is 20,000 ft, or approximately 4 miles (mi) or 6 kilometers (km). Theoretically, this network could support a maximum of 255 IBM PCs or compatibles. The network is capable of transmitting data at 2.5 Mbit/s.

Figure 5-3.
Example of ARCNET
Topology *(Copyright, 1986, Novell, Inc., all rights reserved)*

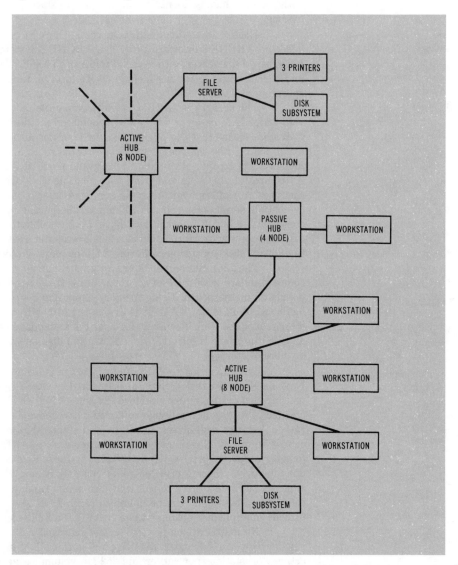

The token-passing procedure is designed to give all workstations access to data transmission. The token is constantly circulating. The workstation with the token sends its message and waits for a signal acknowledging receipt of the packet. If there is no acknowledgment, it sends the same message again. If there is still no acknowledgment within a designated number of micro-seconds, a *reconfiguration burst* is sent through the network. The station with the highest identification number always times out first. It receives the token and sends it to the workstation with the next highest identification number to start a new round of token passing.

Novell offers both the 286A and 286B file servers. These 80286-based servers offer zero wait-states and ports for adding disk subsystems.

Each workstation and file server in the ARCNET-based network needs an ARCNET interface card. The ARCNET system includes its own 80286-based file server, either the (T)286A or (T)286B. The "T" designation means that both file servers include 60-Mb internal tape cartridge drives operating at 4 Mb/s.

The (T)286A is an IBM PC AT-compatible unit with 1 Mb of zero wait-state RAM resident on the fully populated motherboard. The zero wait-state means that the microprocessor operates at its top speed. With expansion boards, this memory can be boosted to an impressive 9 Mb. The file server is capable of running in protected mode at 8 MHz. It includes six AT-compatible I/O slots and two PC-compatible slots. One major advantage that the 286A offers over other file servers is that it supports two PC-compatible serial ports and one PC-compatible parallel port. The 286A comes with a 30-Mb internal disk drive. It is possible to add an optional disk coprocessor board to provide a small computer system interface (SCSI) to external disk subsystems offering 2 Gb or more of storage.

The 286B file server offers additional memory and I/O slots. It comes standard with 2 Mb of zero wait-state RAM resident on the fully populated motherboard. Using memory expansion boards, this can be increased to 12 Mb of RAM. It is available in 109-Mb and 183-Mb mass storage models. A disk coprocessor board is a standard item in the 286B, so an SCSI interface is included to add external disk subsystems offering 2 Gb or more of storage.

Novell offers two different disk drive subsystems. The NDS2 houses two drives while the NDS4 houses four drives.

The expansion to 2 Gb of disk storage is achieved by using Novell's NetWare Disk Drive Subsystems. The NDS2 is a storage unit housing two drives, either standard (23 and 47 Mb) or high-capacity (109 and 183 Mb). It is also possible to house a disk drive and a tape drive rather than two disk drives, but high- and standard-capacity disk drives cannot be mixed. Novell also offers a larger unit, the NDS4, which houses four high-capacity drives (109 or 183 Mb) or three high-capacity drives and one tape drive. Since a disk controller can only handle two disk drives, adding a third disk drive to this unit also means adding a second disk controller. These units can be linked to reach 2 Gb of storage. The units provide multiple-disk channel access with 30–35 millisecond access speed.

No matter which file server you select, the ARCNET hardware running Novell's Advanced NetWare 286 is capable of handling a hundred active workstations per server and 252-Mb volume servers. Since several stars can be distributed by connecting the different file servers, it is possible to enjoy the power and speed of the star topology without the danger of the entire system failing if a file server fails. This kind of arrangement of file servers is known as a "multiserver network." With

Novell's software it is possible to link together two or more multiserver networks to make an "internetwork." The use of multiple file servers provides the measure of safety that most system administrators desire.

Proteon's ProNET's String of Stars

One of the fastest Novell local area networks is Proteon's ProNet system of distributed stars. This network can achieve 10 Mbit/s transmission speed and is able to use twisted-pair wire, twinax, or fiber optics. It is also easy to add and remove workstations because the network uses wire centers.

Novell has designed its Advanced NetWare Operating System to work in conjunction with Proteon's p1300 network communications card. The Proteon ProNET system of distributed stars is capable of being implemented by twisted-pair wire, twinax, and fiber optic cabling.

As *Figure 5-4* illustrates, the ProNET system is a star-shaped token-passing ring configuration that is capable of achieving data transmission at 10 Mbit/s. Proteon uses a series of connection boxes known as "wire centers," each of which can connect four, eight, or twelve workstations. A major advantage of this wire center approach is that it is easy to add or remove workstations from these connection boxes without disturbing network operation. Wire centers can be connected to other wire centers to create the "string of stars" effect that many system administrators want. This is accomplished by equipping the wire centers with repeaters for long wire center-to-wire center path lengths. With fiber-optic cabling a maximum cable length of 1.5 mi (2.5 km) is possible. Fiber-optic Proteon networks use intelligent level-converter boxes that bypass or partition the ring into the optimum number of separate subrings given the particular path failure. As *Figure 5-5* illustrates, there is a dual redundant fiber-optic link available that uses two pairs of fibers and switches to the backup pair in case of failure. Note that the file servers for this system are either 8086- or 8088-based microprocessors. Many companies have found the 8086-based COMPAQ Deskpro and AT&T 6300 Plus to be ideal file servers. The principal advantage of the Proteon hardware running Novell's NetWare is that it represents one of the fastest LANs available. Its major disadvantage is that it is a difficult system to install, requiring a good deal of preliminary system analysis and planning.

The G-Net Bus

Many simple network needs can be satisfied with Gateway Communications' G-Net system. This low-cost linear bus topology uses coaxial cabling. Network response time can be enhanced by using distributed file servers.

Many businesses don't require an elaborate local area network. A word processing department, for example, might have five or six typists located in the same room who need to share certain documents and forms. Because most word processing takes place within a workstation's own processor and requires a minimum amount of file-server response, a simple bus LAN topology is often more than adequate for this environment.

Figure 5-4.
Sample ProNET
Topology *(Copyright,*
1986, Novell, Inc., all
rights reserved)

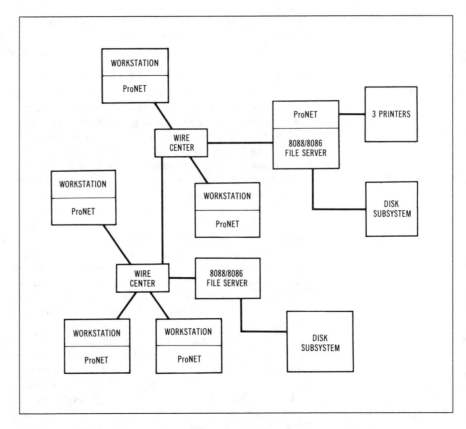

Novell's G-NET uses the Gateway Communication NICs for the IBM PC and compatibles. This circuit card occupies an expansion slot in each workstation. The G-NET system uses standard coaxial cable which enables the network bus to be up to 4000 ft (1200 m) long with 75-ohm terminators at either end. The bus approach utilizes a CSMA/CD approach for avoiding data collisions on its baseband cable. A workstation that wishes to send a message to the file server listens to see if anyone else is using the data highway. If no other workstation is using the bus, it transmits its message. The maximum speed possible for data transmission on this system is 1.43 Mbit/s. As in the case of most Novell LANs, users have two options in designing their network configuration. They can use an 8088- or 8086-based microcomputer as a file server with Novell's NetWare/86 network software. The second option is to select Novell's NetWare 286 software and an 80286-based microcomputer as a file server (an IBM PC AT or compatible). The Compaq Deskpro 286 has been certified by Novell as an excellent substitute for the PC AT. As *Figure 5-6* illustrates, the major advantage of a bus topology is its simplicity and its cost effectiveness.

Figure 5-5.
Dual Redundant Ring
(Copyright, 1986, Novell,
Inc., all rights reserved)

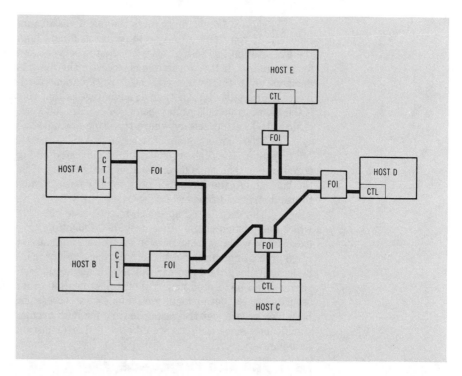

Figure 5-6.
G-NET's Linear Bus
Topology

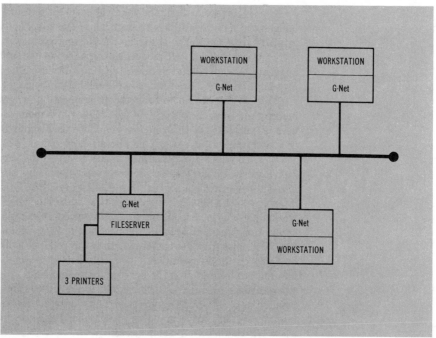

Figure 5-6 also illustrates the major disadvantage of a G-NET bus topology. If you think of bus architecture as a data highway, it is clear that the workstation furthest away from the file server has to wait the longest for a response. If the workstations closer to the file server make heavy demands on it, the response time for workstations further away will increase dramatically. Another disadvantage is that the entire network fails if the trunk cable fails at any point. On a large network, it can be very difficult to locate precisely where the cable has failed.

There are a couple of ways to maximize the effectiveness of a G-NET system. The file server should be dedicated and as fast as possible (an 80286 rather than an 8086 or 8088 microcomputer). If selected users along the bus require the same files on a regular basis, it might prove worthwhile to use distributed file servers.

The distributed approach might prove effective in an office in which one portion of the office uses the accounting programs almost exclusively while another portion uses office automation software, including word processing, spreadsheet, and database programs. One file server could be located along the bus near the accounting section while a second file server could be located near the office automation group. Assuming proper security access, both groups would be able to access the information on both file servers, yet the response time for both groups would improve significantly since the data would have a shorter distance to flow along the data highway.

NETWARE AND THE CONCEPT OF A FILE SERVER

NetWare is designed for true network file-server support. To understand how this differs from much of the LAN software currently available, it is helpful to study how a file server functions under Novell's software. Under the OSI model, Novell's file-server software resides in the application layer while the disk-operating software (DOS) resides in the presentation layer. In effect, the file-server software forms a shell around the DOS so that it is able to intercept application program commands before they can reach DOS. As we will see in a moment, the workstation user is not aware of this phenomenon. The user simply asks for a data file or a program without worrying about where either is located.

To understand this interaction between file server and the individual workstations, let's look at what happens when a workstation issues a request for a particular file. As *Figure 5-7* illustrates, the network interface to the network file server (the "interface shell") resides in each workstation. It is responsible for intercepting DOS commands from an application program. When an application program requests a specific file, the shell must first determine whether the request is for a local file (residing on the workstation's own disk drives) or a network request for information located on a file server. If the information is located on the workstation's own drives, the request is passed back to DOS where it is handled as a normal I/O operation. The workstation user notices the red light on the disk drive go on as a particular file is located and loaded into the workstation's CPU for processing.

Figure 5-7.
Network Interface Shell
(Copyright, 1986, Novell, Inc., all rights reserved)

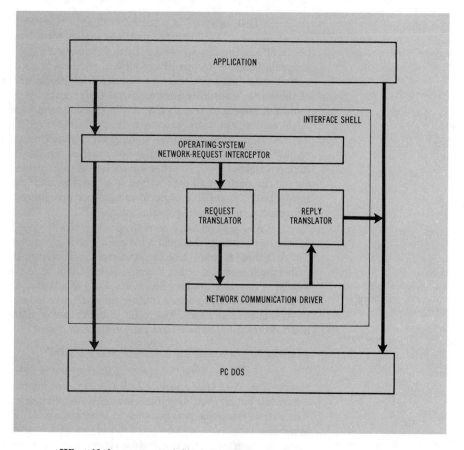

What if the requested file is located on a file server? In this case, the request translator issues a "read" request to the file server which locates the file and transmits it to the workstation in the form of a reply packet. The packet is received by the reply translator, which converts this information into a form that DOS on the local workstation can handle. DOS then provides the application program with this data. Notice that the workstation user is completely unaware of the internal mechanics of this operation. The network file server is so fast that the local and the network response will appear to be equally fast.

Techniques for Speeding Up the File Server

Directory hashing is a method of mapping and indexing directories and their files to minimize the number of entries a file server must examine in order to locate a specific file.

Novell's NetWare uses a number of techniques to speed up the response time of its file servers. One technique is "directory hashing," which can be likened to an efficient indexing system. The software maps all the directory files and keeps all of this information in RAM. When a workstation requests a particular file, the file server need only examine a few directory entries to locate the particular file. Since this information is in RAM and not on disk, it is a very fast procedure.

Disk caching is a
technique for keeping
often requested files in
RAM for rapid response
to workstation requests.

"Disk caching" is a second technique Novell uses for rapid file-server response. It illustrates just how intelligent a Novell file server can be. In effect, the file server anticipates future workstation file requests and keeps an image of frequently requested portions of its drive in RAM. When a workstation makes a second request for additional material from this area of the server's hard disk drive, it is already located in RAM and does not require a second hard disk access. Since disk access is in milliseconds while RAM access is in microseconds, a "smart" file server's use of disk caching can represent significant time savings for network users. Second and third requests for information that has been cached can be processed one hundred times faster. Another advantage of disk caching is that the file server can perform all disk writes as a "background" operation, which means that it is capable of performing other procedures while sending this information to requesting workstations.

Elevator seeking is a
technique enabling the file
server to determine the
order in which to execute
file requests based upon
the current location of the
disk heads.

Another technique used to speed up Novell's file-server response time is "elevator seeking." Imagine a file clerk who is given a series of files to locate. The first three files are Johnson, Anderson, and Jackson. If the clerk actually pulled the files in this order, it would be inefficient since two of the files are located in the same drawer. Elevator seeking is a technique in which the file server executes requests in a manner most effective in relation to the current position of the disk heads. The result is an increase of throughput of up to 50% and a decrease in the wear and tear on the disk drives.

FILE MANAGEMENT UNDER NETWARE

NetWare allows the system administrator to define who has access to specific files. We'll take a look at how a department might establish its users in a moment, but an even more fundamental issue to address is the nature of the files themselves. Some programs might be single-user MS-DOS or PC-DOS applications that certain users want to use in a multiuser environment. The system administrator can designate a program or file as shareable (capable of being shared) or non-shareable (restricted to one user at a time). NetWare also contains a default file-locking function which means that these single-user programs could be accessed by different users, one at a time.

If a file is non-shareable, different users can view the file in read-only mode, but they cannot write to it while it is being used in read/write mode by a specific user. Programs or files designated as shareable with record-locking capability operate in a true multiuser fashion; several users can read and write to them simultaneously as long as only one user is writing to a specific record at a time. One feature of NetWare is that an application program can specify all the records it needs before telling the file server to lock these records. This technique ensures that two application programs needing overlapping records cannot create a deadlock in which both wait for records that simply are not available.

Setting Up Directories under NetWare

NetWare uses a hierarchical file structure. A diagram of this structure would resemble a mature tree with main branches having smaller branches, which, in turn, have even smaller branches of their own. As an example, imagine that the Widget Company has just installed a Novell network with several distributed file servers. Now it is time to set up some directories on the first file server.

Let's assume that Sales and Personnel will be using this file server. Beth and Barbara are the two sales administrators and Phil, Paul, and Peter handle personnel functions. As *Figure 5-8* illustrates, Widget has named its first file-server FS1. Under the Sales directory are two subdirectories: Beth and Barbara. Each sales administrator has created subdirectories under her directories. Beth has created the subdirectories EASTERN.RGN, CUSTOMER.LST, and WESTERN.RGN. Notice that under WESTERN.RGN Beth has created two additional subdirectories: SALES.RPTS and PROSPECTS. Barbara has not yet created as many subdirectories, but she certainly has that option in the future.

**Figure 5-8.
NetWare's File
Structure**

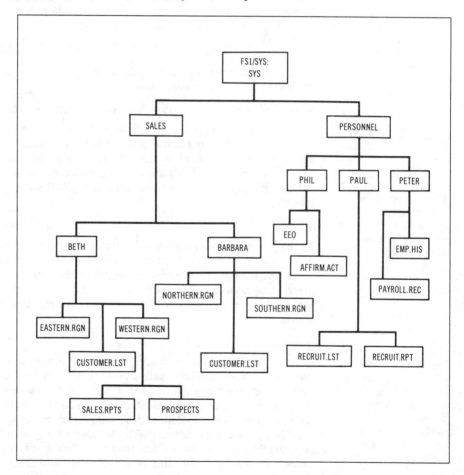

The Personnel department has created directories for each of its administrators. Since Phil, Paul, and Peter all have distinct functions, each has created two subdirectories to handle his specialized reports. Within the directories and subdirectories of both departments the system administrator will load appropriate files. Under Beth's CUSTOMER.LST directory, for example, will be found the following files: CURRCUST.E, CURRCUST.W, OLDCUST.E, and OLDCUST.W. To send a letter to former Widget customers living in the western region in order to announce a new program designed to entice them to again buy widgets, Beth writes a form letter and performs a mail merge with the file OLDCUST.W.

When designating subdirectories, Novell follows the convention that a slash ("/") or a backslash ("\") must be used to separate a directory from its subdirectory. The names of all succeeding subdirectories must also be separated in the same manner. To indicate the pathway for OLDCUST.W, for example, Beth would type:

FS1/SYS:SALES/BETH/WESTERN.RGN/CUSTOMER.LST/OLDCUST.W.

Since we have written a pathway for OLDCUST.W, the last directory named is the directory we wished to specify.

Mapping Network Drives: A Novell Shortcut

Network drives are logical and not physical drives. By assigning directories to specific network drives, a user is able to move quickly from directory to directory without having to remember the exact pathways.

NetWare requires that directories be assigned to a specific network drive. Network drives point to network directories and not to physical disk drives. Each workstation may assign twenty-six logical drive letters (A through Z). Let's assume that we want to assign the WESTERN.RGN directory to network drive F. We would type the following:

MAP F:=FS1/SYS:SALES/BETH/WESTERN.RGN.

Typing the colon following the drive letter assigns this directory to the drive. Now we can type F: from a DOS prompt to go directly to this directory. By assigning frequently used directories to different network drives it becomes a simple matter to jump back and forth among files without having to remember pathways and correctly type in the long names.

Search Drives Save Time

Search drives permit users to locate files even though they might know in which directory the files reside. It is even possible to locate files on other file servers using this technique.

One of the most common network error messages indicates that a file cannot be found. This usually means that the file doesn't exist in the directory in which you are working. Often you cannot remember exactly where it resides. To avoid this situation, use NetWare's search drives. The software permits you to define up to sixteen search drives (Search1:, Search2:, etc.). Search drives enable the operating system to locate program files in directories other than your default directory. By placing universally used programs in a public directory and then mapping a search drive, the file server locates these programs when they are requested even if they are not in the current directory from which the request is made. A major advantage of this approach is that rather than copy the same program into several people's individual directories, a single copy can be accessed by people from their current directories since the copy is mapped to a search directory.

Search drives can also be mapped to directories on different file servers. The result is that a system administrator can make file-access painless for novice users since all they need to do is to specify a particular file or program that has been mapped to a search drive. Even if the file is located on a distant file server, it will appear on the user's screen as if it resided on his or her local disk drive.

SYSTEM SECURITY

While vendors who only market network security systems may offer more elaborate systems, Novell's NetWare offers by far the most extensive security system available as part of a network package. NetWare provides file-server security in four different ways: the login procedure, trustee rights, directory rights, and file attributes.

The Login Procedure

NetWare requires a valid username, file-server name, and password at the login procedure.

NetWare provides security at the login stage by requiring a valid username (user identify) and a valid password. As a matter of convenience, the network administrator normally allows the user to use his or her first name as the username. Fred's username then is simply FRED. The user must also know which file server he is using. Fred's login to file-server FS1, for example, might look like this: LOGIN FS1/FRED. (NetWare doesn't care if users use uppercase, lowercase, or a combination.) NetWare now waits for a password to be typed. The software doesn't announce the correctness or incorrectness of the login at this stage, but all three variables must be correct to clear this security level. For security reasons in the event of an unacceptable login, NetWare will not indicate whether the username, file server, or password is incorrectly typed. Let's observe Fred's login procedure. We'll begin with Fred typing the command:

```
LOGIN <ENTER>
Enter your login name:
FS1/FRED <ENTER>
Enter your password:
```

For security reasons, Fred's password will not appear on the screen when he types it. One important point to make here is that the password is associated with the user and not with the machine. With his username and password, a user can work on any available workstation.

Trustee Rights

Each user has up to eight usage rights assigned by the network supervisor.

The network administrator, referred to by Novell as the "network supervisor," is responsible for the network's security as well as its operation. The supervisor makes each user a "trustee" and provides each with specific rights in certain directories. These rights normally extend through all subsequent subdirectories unless the supervisor specifically limits a user's access. These rights may be extended to the user either as an individual or as part of a user group. The range of eight possible trustee rights is listed here:

Read from open files
Write to open files
Open existing files
Create (and simultaneously open) new files
Delete existing files
Parental (create, rename, and erase subdirectories of the directory)
Set trustee and directory rights in the directory
Set trustee and directory rights in its subdirectories
Search the directory
Modify file attributes

Users can be given any combination of these rights. A user with Read, Open, and Write rights, for example, can open a file, read its contents, and write to the file. Without Search rights, however, the user would have to know the name of the file in order to access it; he or she would be unable to search for it. Notice, also, that without the Delete right, a user would be powerless to delete any existing files.

NetWare trustee security has many different levels and potential combinations. A user needs Parental rights as well as Delete rights, for instance, to delete an entire subdirectory. The network supervisor also establishes directory security. Normally, when a directory is established, all trustees enjoy all directory rights, but the supervisor can, if needed, limit these trustee rights within the directory. For example, within a specific directory, all or certain users might be limited to simply reading and not changing information. A "maximum rights mask" for a directory means that users enjoy all eight trustee rights within that directory. Since this is a mask, only those user rights that are also directory rights will match and represent a particular user's rights within the directory.

Through network equivalencies a supervisor can set the trustee rights of a particular user as equivalent to the rights of a particular user group or groups or a number of different individuals.

The network supervisor assigns each user to a user group and then may assign trustee rights directly to the entire group. These rights may also be assigned to user groups indirectly through *equivalencies*. A user or user group may have up to thirty-two security equivalencies. The supervisor may establish that one user group may have all the rights already found within another user group; the two groups become equivalents. The supervisor may set up a group called "Everyone" and make all user groups' rights equivalent with this group. Obviously, this is more efficient than setting rights for each user. All members of the word processing pool, for example, are part of the same user group and share the same trustee rights. A supervisor temporarily setting an assistant's rights as equivalent to his or her own would enable the assistant to function as the supervisor.

A user's total rights comprise those as an individual user, plus those as part of a user group, plus all the trustee rights of any other users or user groups for which this user has a security equivalence.

File Attributes Security

A user who establishes a file can set the attributes for that file using the FLAG command. File attributes prevail over individual trustee rights.

NetWare security permits a user to determine whether an individual file may be modified. Let's assume that Frieda has been having trouble with other network users changing the contents of a particular file (CUSTCONFIG). Her rights include Modify privileges for this file's directory. Using the FLAG command, she restricts the file's use to Read-only. Frieda is in her default directory where the file resides, so to effect the change she types:

FLAG CUSTCONFIG SHAREABLE READ-ONLY <ENTER>

Now the CUSTCONFIG file can be shared by other users who can read but not change the contents. Frieda could have changed all the files in her default directory to the same shareable read-only status by typing:

FLAG *.* SHAREABLE READ-ONLY <ENTER>

There are four different combinations of attributes that a user can select for a file or group of files with the FLAG command:

Shareable, Read-only
Shareable, Read-write
Non-Shareable, Read-only
Non-Shareable, Read-write

By typing FLAG and pressing <ENTER> within a directory you can see a list of the flags on files within the directory.

File attributes take precedence over trustee rights because NetWare uses a logical AND function to determine final rights. Let's assume that Stan has Read and Write rights as a user. The CUST file has been flagged as Shareable, Read-only. NetWare examines Stan's user rights and the file's attributes using an AND function that accepts only those terms that appear in both lists. Since the Read function appears in both lists, Stan can only read the CUST file.

NETWORK UTILITIES

The four levels of network security we have been discussing are all handled by NetWare's powerful series of utility programs. At this point we'll examine the two utility programs that are used in conjunction with network security: SYSCON and FILER.

The SYSCON Utility

SYSCON enables users to view information about the file servers they are logged into, their login procedure, the user groups that include them, and their trustee rights and network security equivalencies. This utility permits changing these variables with proper network security.

The SYSCON utility is used for system configuration. It handles many of the security functions we have been discussing, such as establishing passwords, user groups, access to file servers, trustee rights, and equivalencies. Because some of its functions can be performed by non-supervisors, SYSCON is loaded into the SYS: PUBLIC directory. SYSCON is a menu driven program. From DOS, typing SYSCON and <ENTER> gives the Available Topics menu shown in *Figure 5-9*. Notice that even though you might not be a network supervisor you can still view information regarding your own status on the network. Frieda, for example, can select the File Server Information option and see a server's name, its NetWare version, the number of connections supported, the number of workstations in use, the number of volumes supported, and her workstation's network and node address.

**Figure 5-9.
SYSCON's Available
Topics Menu**

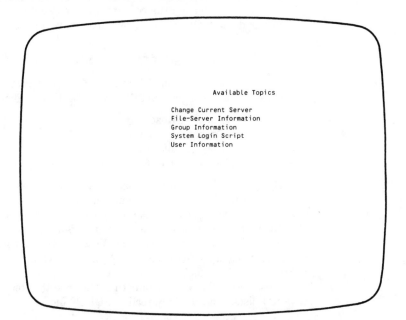

```
                         Available Topics

                    Change Current Server
                    File-Server Information
                    Group Information
                    System Login Script
                    User Information
```

By selecting Group Information, Frieda can verify the groups she currently belongs to. A Personnel department, for example, might want to make all staff members part of the PERSONNEL group, which entitles them to Read-only privileges. So any person in the department could look up a personnel file for basic information, but only certain members of the department would have individual trustee assignments enabling them to change a file.

Novell's NetWare allows users to examine their own security equivalences and trustee assignments. In *Figure 5-10* Frieda has chosen to examine her security equivalences and discovered that she has security equivalences with Chris, Everyone, and Personnel. As we saw earlier, this system makes it easy to add new users and duplicate trustee rights without having to list each of several dozen files that a user should be able to retrieve. A new Personnel department clerk who will cover Frieda's assignments during her summer vacation can be given security equivalence to Frieda, automatically giving the clerk all the group as well as the individual rights Frieda now enjoys. When Frieda returns from vacation, the clerk can be given a security equivalence to another department clerk.

**Figure 5-10.
NetWare's Security
Equivalencies**

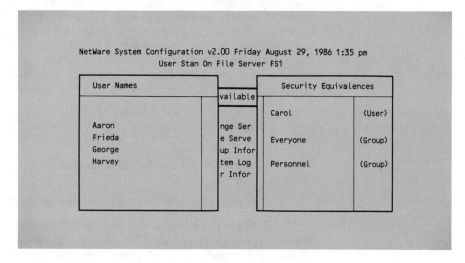

NetWare System Configuration v2.00 Friday August 29, 1986 1:35 pm
User Stan On File Server FS1

User Names		Security Equivalences	
	vailable		
Aaron	nge Ser	Carol	(User)
Frieda	e Serve		
George	up Infor	Everyone	(Group)
Harvey	tem Log		
	r Infor	Personnel	(Group)

NetWare's Login Scripts

Login scripts permit network users to have their network search drives automatically mapped, key information displayed upon logging in, and the proper disk-operating system software loaded into their network workstation.

At any given time, a user can use the NetWare utilities menu to examine his or her login script and make any necessary changes. The login script is a shortcut, a way to tell NetWare how to go through a preassigned set of steps to customize the network's environment for you and to display certain information when you login to the network. We'll see in a moment that it is possible to have a different login script for each file server that you use and for different days of the week as well. While it is possible for each user to design an individual login script, one of the major advantages of this procedure is that the network supervisor can set up a login script for a new user that will shield the novice from the intricacies of a network environment. The SETLOGIN command defines a login script.

While NetWare permits the mapping of different search network drives, this information is erased each time the user logs off the system. One of the major uses of a login script is to provide NetWare with this information automatically when the login script is executed. A login script for Peter might include the following:

```
map *1=sys:Paul
map *2=sys:super
map *3=sys:public
map *4=sys:system
map *5=sys:fs1/sys:Sales/Cust.Lst
```

With this login script, Peter is able to access files in different directories without even knowing where these files exist. By typing Cust.Lst, for example, Peter will retrieve this information without knowing the full pathname. As a new user, Peter need not even know what a pathname is as long as his network supervisor has set up this login script for him.

NetWare provides that a number of different variables can be placed in a login script, including the time, day of the week, month, and year. The login script can also identify the specific file server the user is addressing. Scripts use a command language that is clearly explained in Novell's documentation. The commands include an IF...THEN combination that permits you to individualize scripts for each day of the week. Frieda, for example, might want to remind herself of a staff meeting that is always held Mondays at 10:00 A.M. She could have the following login script:

```
IF DAY OF WEEK="Monday" THEN
WRITE "Another week. Don't forget the staff meeting at 10
AM."
```

When Frieda logs in on a Monday morning, her computer screen will display the following:

```
Another week. Don't forget the staff meeting at 10 AM.
```

You can individualize each day's script not only with the date and time and standing appointments, but also with the actual set of procedures normally performed that day. A payroll clerk may only go through the actual check-printing routine on the 1st and 15th of a month. The script could specify that if the date were the 1st or the 15th the network should log the clerk into a different file server where the check-printing program resides, load the program, and make sure that the appropriate printer is on-line. The clerk would only need to use the correct login name and password to begin the check-writing procedure.

The INCLUDE command enables you to link a number of text files and place them in a login script.

Another useful login script command is INCLUDE. This command enables you to establish a series of text files that can serve as subscripts for your login. It is possible to have as many as ten levels of INCLUDE commands accessing different subscripts. There are a number of very practical uses for these subscripts. Let's say that several people are working on a project with a tight deadline. Although some of these individuals are scattered throughout a large four-story building and others are at remote locations, it is essential that they all know the progress of the project on a daily basis. A project manager could establish an announcements file under the PROJECT directory. Each night before leaving work (or even late at night from home with the proper remote equipment), the project manager could use the word processing program to write a text file that addressed all members of the team. Each member's login script then would have an INCLUDE command to access this file. As a team member, Frieda's login script might include the following:

```
IF DAY OF WEEK="Monday" THEN BEGIN
WRITE "Another week. Don't forget the staff meeting at 10
```

AM."
INCLUDE SYS:PROJECT/ANNOUNCEMENTS
END

NetWare's interpretive shell permits workstations with different operating systems to share information.

NetWare, and its login script procedure, addresses a critical problem for many major companies, the proliferation of types of computers and of operating systems. On a NetWare file server, differing operating systems can share files because of the interpretive shell. CP/M 86 files can coexist with PC-DOS 2.1 and MS-DOS 3.1 files. A company can establish an identifier macro command within users' login scripts to ensure that a user whose software is PC-DOS 2.1, for example, loads the proper 2.1 versions of his programs and not 3.1 programs. Novell suggests the following LOGIN script to map search directories for differing machines and operating systems:

MAP S2:=SYS:PUBLIC \ %MACHINE \ %OS \ %OS VERSION

The FILER Utility

FILER permits users to display and change key information about directories and files that they control. For security, a user may specify which directories and files will *not* appear when the contents are listed.

The FILER menu utility program controls volume, directory, file, and subdirectory information. Earlier we discussed a situation in which Frieda wanted to ensure that other users did not change a file within a directory she had established. To do so, Frieda can change the directory's maximum rights mask or change the file's attributes. Let's assume that Frieda wished to make the change at the directory level. She could examine the maximum rights mask for that current directory using the FILER utility. The maximum rights consist of the following:

Create New Files
Delete Files
Modify File Names/Flags
Open Existing Files
Parental Rights
Read From Files
Search For Files
Write To Files

Frieda places the selection bar (displayed on the screen) on the right she wishes to delete and then presses the <Delete> key. NetWare will ask if she wishes to revoke this particular right (Yes or No). When she presses her <Select>, the right is revoked and removed from the maximum rights mask.

The FILER utility also permits adding or deleting trustee rights for a particular directory and viewing and deleting file attributes. A security feature available under FILER is the capacity to specify a directory exclude pattern. A network supervisor, for example, could establish a network directory exclusion pattern for all directories whose names begin with PROJ. This would mean that the even more secretive information for the Jove, Jupiter, and Saturn projects (PROJJOV, PROJJUP, and PROJSAT) would not be displayed with a directory listing. It is also possible to specify a file exclusion pattern within directories. Let's say that within the directories of each of the secret projects is a budget file

(PROJ.BUD) only the project manager needs to see or use. A file exclusion pattern for the .BUD pattern ensures that even those users with sufficient security to enter the project directories won't be able to see the budget files when they request a listing of all the files in that particular directory.

PRINTER UTILITIES

QUEUE permits network users to specify the order in which files are to be printed as well as which printers are to be accessed.

NetWare contains a rich assortment of printer commands that are probably the most sophisticated among those for local area networks. NetWare contains a QUEUE menu utility as well as specific commands such as SPOOL and KILL PRINTER, and several form feed instructions. Let's begin by examining the QUEUE menu utility.

This one utility program controls all the print queues for all the file servers on a NetWare LAN. It is possible to spool as many as a hundred files to a queue and easily reorder jobs waiting in the queue. If Fred has been working on several spreadsheets and wants to see the print queue to see in which order they are to be printed, he selects DISPLAY PRINT QUEUES. As *Figure 5-11* illustrates, he would see the sequence, the file name, and the username for each item to be printed. It is not possible to delete another user's files from this queue unless you have supervisor rights. The QUEUE utility also permits you to choose a file server, volume, and directory to display the files available to print. You may then select which files you wish to print.

**Figure 5-11.
NetWare Printer Queue**

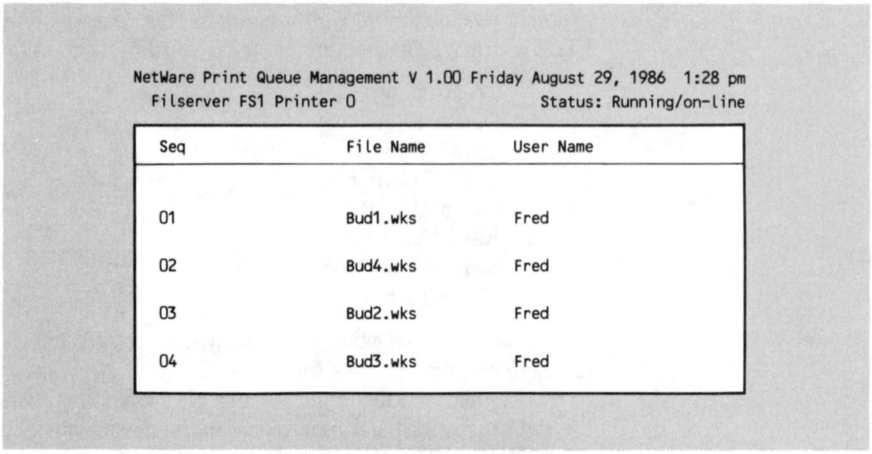

```
NetWare Print Queue Management V 1.00 Friday August 29, 1986  1:28 pm
   Filserver FS1 Printer 0                      Status: Running/on-line
```

Seq	File Name	User Name
01	Bud1.wks	Fred
02	Bud4.wks	Fred
03	Bud2.wks	Fred
04	Bud3.wks	Fred

The QUEUE utility permits you to select as many *spool flags* as you wish in order to specify how the files should be printed. You may indicate, for example, whether you wish to have a specific banner (located in a file) printed prior to the printing of a file. You may also specify whether you wish to delete the file after printing it, how many copies of the file you wish to print, what type of form you wish to print, the number of the printer you wish to print from, and whether or not you wish to expand the tabs to spaces. Using the QUEUE utility, it is possible to display printer information as well as queue information.

The SPOOL command must be used under NetWare if a file cannot be sent directly to a network printer. You must also use SPOOL to use the <Shift>/<PS> keys to "dump" a workstation screen to a network printer station. If Frieda wanted to print five copies of a budget worksheet on file server 1 to printer 1 (a dot matrix) using form 75 (a spreadsheet format) without any banners, she would specify the following:

SPOOL S=FS1 C=5 F=75 P=1 N.B.

Note that Frieda can keep several different printing formats (memo, sales report, etc.) on file and simply specify which format she requires for a particular spooled document.

NetWare offers several other printer commands that simplify network printing. FORM CHECK aligns continuous-feed, preprinted forms in any printer. This command causes a row of asterisks to be printed on the form showing the vertical print position. After using this command to align the paper, a FORM SET command ensures that the printer will automatically set the second form to the correct printing position. KILL PRINTER enables a network supervisor to erase all print jobs from a specific printer's queue. Since this command affects everyone on the network, it should only be used by the supervisor. Files can be rerouted from a defective printer without using this command by using the STOP PRINTER and REROUTE PRINTER commands.

NetWare's QUEUE program is menu driven for those users who require a menu. But it is possible to use the various print commands with their very English-like syntax without taking the time required to go through several menus. An experienced user who wishes to change the priority of a print job, stop a printer to change a ribbon, reroute a print job to another printer and then start the same printer again would type the following commands:

CHANGE QUEUE 2 JOB 4 TO PRIORITY 1
STOP PRINTER 2
REROUTE PRINTER 2 TO PRINTER 0
START PRINTER 2

ELECTRONIC MAIL

NetWare's electronic mail system (EMS) enables users to send and receive a variety of information, including files, memos, documents, and letters.

Every time a user starts on a file server, a mailbox is created for him or her. By typing MAIL, users are able to send and receive mail and view the mail residing in their mailbox. While NetWare's electronic mail has its limitations, it is a simple system to operate. Let's follow the normal procedures a user would use in creating a message and sending it to another user.

Fred has decided that he needs to send a note about PC servicing to his colleague Bob. He creates a note by typing the following:

EDIT PCNOTE <ENTER>

The cursor moves to the top of the editing screen and waits for Fred to type the note. Fred writes his note and then saves it by pressing the F2 key. He then sends the document to Bob. Notice that EMS permits an English-like grammar.

SEND DOCUMENT PCNOTE TO BOB <ENTER>

Novell's electronic mail includes files, documents, letters, and memos. Fred could have written a memo and commanded (SEND MEMO TO BOB) or even an express memo (SEND EXPRESS MEMO). An express memo message will flash across Bob's screen informing him that he has received a message.

Novell's electronic mail system permits users to send an identical message to all users on the network by typing:

SEND DOCUMENT PCNOTE TO ALL USERS <ENTER>

If the network supervisor has established a number of groups on the network, it is possible to use this feature with electronic mail. Fred can send his note to those users who have local printers and have been placed in a group that receives notes about servicing and support:

SEND DOCUMENT PCNOTE TO LOCALPRINTERS <ENTER>

If Fred isn't sure if certain employees are part of the local area network, he may type either of the following commands to learn who's in the network.

LIST USERS <ENTER>
LIST GROUPS <ENTER>

When Fred logs in on the network, his login script indicates whether he has mail. Assuming that he does, Fred would normally type the following:

OPEN ALL MAIL <ENTER>
LIST <ENTER>

Notice that the EMS requires that you open all mail before you can list it or read it. Fred decides to read a document from Phyllis spelling out her recommendations for the company's Arizona operations (BUDGET RECOMMENDATION):

READ BUDGET RECOMMENDATION <ENTER>

After reading the report, Fred decides that he needs to file it for later access. He closes the document and uses the PUT command to place the document into a DOS file:

CLOSE BUDGET RECOMMENDATION <ENTER>
PUT BUDGET RECOMMENDATION TO BUDGET.AZ <ENTER>

Fred can use his word processing program to retrieve this file, format it, and incorporate it as part of a much larger budget report for the entire western region.

With EMS, it is easy to remove electronic mail that is no longer needed. To remove a memo reminding him that a staff meeting has been rescheduled, Fred types:

REMOVE STAFFMEMO <ENTER>

The EMS makes it equally easy to remove all messages of a certain type. Fred can clean out his electronic mailbox by removing all his staff memos by typing:

REMOVE MY STAFFMEMOS <ENTER>

Because EMS understands many English synonyms, Fred could have used TRASH or ERASE for the same results.

What makes the EMS very powerful is that date/time qualifiers can be used. If it were 5:00 P.M. on September 1st and Fred wanted to remove from his electronic mailbox all but that day's mail or all of the mail he had already read that day, he could have typed:

REMOVE ALL MAIL MAILED BEFORE SEPTEMBER <ENTER>
REMOVE EVERYTHING MAILED BEFORE 4:00 PM <ENTER>

With EMS it is easy to distribute messages to members of different groups in different departments. If a sudden deadline means that secretaries in the Marketing department will have to work extended hours, an electronic message can be addressed as follows:

ALL MARKETING SECRETARIES

If everyone in Marketing needs to be notified that their hours will be extended, the memo could be sent this way:

ANYONE IN MARKETING

Notice that people can be members of several groups simultaneously. A female Marketing department secretary is a member of at least these three different groups (females, Marketing department, secretaries). She might receive a message sent to all females informing her that the insurance company has changed its rates for pregnancy insurance, for example.

Novell's EMS is limited in certain ways. When you reply to an item that you receive, your reply includes the full text of the message you received, taking up needless disk space. Also, it is difficult to print messages that you receive. Present options are either to do a screen dump of the information one screen at a time or to save the information in a file and print that file. Both are time-consuming procedures. Also, in a large facility with multiple file servers the EMS becomes cumbersome. It is necessary to run the MAIL program on the particular file server to which you want to send a message. Despite these limitations, the EMS is a valuable feature of NetWare because it is so easy to use and it is included without charge.

NETWARE BRIDGES AND GATEWAYS TO OTHER NETWORKS

Bridge Software

Novell's Bridge software permits the linking of two networks. A bridge PC must contain the network interface cards for both networks as well as the Bridge software.

NetWare makes it possible for networks to communicate with other networks as well as with IBM mainframes. A bridge connects networks using different hardware. One network, for example, might use IBM's broadband PC LAN Network while another network uses ARCNET's circuit cards. NetWare provides Bridge software, which permits these two networks to share information. The software resides on a bridge unit, usually a dedicated IBM PC. The computer must have at least one floppy disk drive and two available expansion slots to hold the PC LAN Network and ARCNET adapter cards. The cards are cabled to their respective networks. The bridge is designed to remain invisible to both sets of network users.

SNA/Gateway for Micro-Mainframe Communications

Novell's SNA/Gateway hardware and software provides micro–mainframe communications through a gateway PC. This non-dedicated unit provides IBM 3270 emulation for the entire network. The gateway software also has the ability to perform file transfers and disk and printer spooling. It supports up to thirty-two concurrent sessions.

Novell provides a gateway board that resides in a PC providing IBM 3270 or 3770 emulation for all the computers that are part of the local area network. Novell does not require that the gateway unit be dedicated. This may not be an issue for LANs that plan heavy micro–mainframe communications, however, since it is possible to have multiple gateway PCs on the same local area network. Each gateway has a unique name, and users select the gateway they wish to use. The SNA Gateway board supports eight, sixteen, or thirty-two concurrent SNA LU sessions using just one communication line. This is possible because of the sophisticated 32016 32-bit National semiconductor chip the board utilizes. The board comes with 512K of self-contained memory and the ability to switch sessions and even suspend them ("session hold") and return to DOS whenever needed. *Figure 5-12* illustrates how the gateway PC connects the network with the IBM mainframe by use of modems.

With the Novell NetWare SNA/Gateway, which supports SNA/SDLC protocol, it is possible to use modems, modem eliminators, or leased lines and to achieve speeds up to 19.2 Kbit/s. The software supports file transfer as well as printer sharing, host-initiated printing, and disk spooling. The PC gateway unit emulates a 3274 cluster controller.

Asynchronous Communications Server

Novell also offers an asynchronous communications server (ASC) which can handle up to four wide area network interface modules. An IBM PC, PC AT, or a compatible serves as the host unit. *Figure 5-13* illustrates how this communications server works. The individual workstations tied to the communications gateway unit are able to establish a virtual circuit to a host or modem. The workstation emulates a TeleVideo 925 or DEC VT 100 terminal and has the ability to transmit ASCII files.

Figure 5-12.
Sample NetWare SNA
Configuration *(Copyright, 1986, Novell, Inc., all rights reserved)*

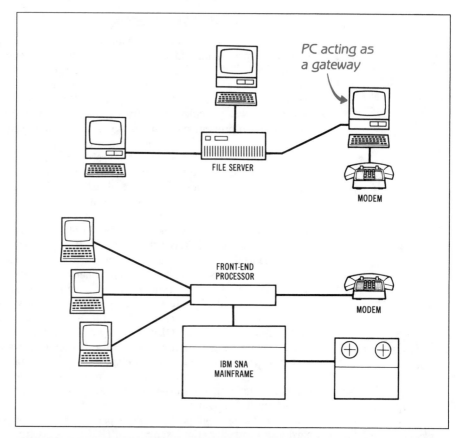

Figure 5-13.
ASC Configuration
(Copyright, 1986, Novell, Inc., all rights reserved)

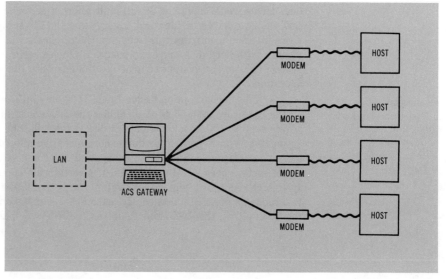

SYSTEM FAULT TOLERANT NETWARE

Novell offers three levels of System Fault Tolerant NetWare. Features include the duplication of file allocation tables, disk drives, and even the file server.

Any company that relies completely upon computers for information processing is fearful of a system failure. Novell has developed System Fault Tolerant NetWare to overcome this potential disaster. This special version of NetWare comes in three different levels, each with progressively more protection. What makes Novell's approach so unusual is that while it has provided the software tools to provide hardware duplication (to prevent downtime), the user may purchase off-the-shelf hardware in order to realize a significant cost savings.

The Level I NetWare offers protection against partial destruction of the file server by providing redundant directory structures. The file server maintains extra copies of file allocation tables and directory entries on different disk cylinders for each shared network volume. If a directory sector fails, the file server immediately shifts to the redundant directory; it then uses a feature known as a "hot fix" to place the bad sector in a bad block sector table and stores the data in another location. Not inconvenienced, the user is not even aware of this automatic procedure. When a Level I system is powered up, it performs a complete self-consistency check on each redundant directory and file allocation table. It performs a read-after-write verification after every network disk write to ensure that data that is written to the file server is re-readable. Level I software also includes a VOLFIX utility program that scans the surface of a disk looking for potential surface faults. It then ensures that the file server will bypass potential trouble spots and place data on safe areas.

Level II software includes the protection offered by Level I plus a number of additional features. At this level, Novell offers two options to protect the LAN against the total failure of the file server. The first option is *mirrored drives:* supporting two duplicate hard disk drives with a single hard disk controller. For example, an IBM PC AT with two 30-Mb hard disk drives would have one 30-Mb fault tolerant server. NetWare requires that the two drives be identical. Every time the file server performs a disk write function it mirrors this image on the duplicate file server. It also verifies both hard disk drives to ensure complete accuracy. If there is a system failure, the system switches to the mirrored file server and resumes operations.

With duplexed drives the disk controller, disk drive, and even the cables and interfaces are duplicated. Because both drives perform disk reads, file-server performance is virtually doubled.

The second option under Level II is for *duplexed drives:* virtually all the hardware is duplicated including the disk controller, interface, and power supply. If a disk controller or disk drive fails, the system automatically switches to the duplexed alternative and records this fact in a log. The performance of a duplexed system is far superior to that of a single system because of *split seeks.* If a certain file is requested, the system checks to see which disk system can respond more quickly, and if two requests occur simultaneously, each drive handles one of the disk reads. In effect, this technique doubles the file-server performance.

The Transaction Tracking System ensures that the data integrity of a database is maintained if the network is disrupted in the middle of a database transaction.

Level II also includes a Novell feature known as the transaction tracking system (TTS), which is designed to ensure the data integrity of multiuser databases. The system views each change in a database as a transaction that either is complete or is not. If a user is in the middle of a database transaction when the system fails, the TTS rolls the database back to the point just before the transaction began. This action is known as "automatic rollback." A second procedure performed by the TTS is "rollforward recovery," which means that the system keeps a complete log of all transactions to ensure that everything can be recovered in the event of a complete system failure.

Level III software incorporates all features from Level II and adds a duplicate file server connected by a high-speed bus. If a file server fails, the second file server immediately assumes control over network operations.

WHAT HAVE WE LEARNED?

1. System Fault Tolerant NetWare is designed to provide redundancy of key hardware and software elements to prevent a network from failing.
2. S-Net is Novell's star topology network built around its own 68000 Novell file server.
3. G-Net is a bus topology network that utilizes a CSMA/CD approach to data-collision avoidance.
4. Three techniques NetWare uses to speed up its file-server response time are directory hashing, disk caching, and elevator seeking.
5. By mapping network drives and utilizing the principle of search drives, a user can retrieve a file without knowing where it is located.
6. NetWare's many levels of network security include the login procedure, trustee rights, directory rights, and file attributes.
7. New network users can immediately enjoy all the rights of another network user if they have the same network equivalencies.
8. NetWare users can learn information about their login scripts by using the SYSCON utility.
9. Using the FILER utility, network users can establish directory- and file-exclusion patterns.
10. Novell's electronic mail system (EMS) enables users to send a variety of mail to specified groups or individuals.
11. Novell's NetWare Bridge software and hardware permit two networks to be linked.
12. Novell's SNA/Gateway software and hardware permit up to thirty-two concurrent SNA sessions with an IBM mainframe computer.
13. NetWare can search for potential bad disk sectors and then avoid them using the VOLFIX utility program feature of system fault tolerant software.
14. The integrity of a database is maintained even in the event of network failure by the Transaction Tracking System (TTS).

Quiz For Chapter 5

1. ARCNET uses a series of active and passive hubs tied together with:
   a. fiber optics.
   b. twisted-pair wire.
   c. coaxial cable.
   d. lasers.

2. NetWare file servers keep often-requested files in RAM for rapid response to requests. This is known as:
   a. directory hashing.
   b. disk caching.
   c. elevator seeking.
   d. rapid response retrieval.

3. NetWare minimizes wear and tear on disk drives by retrieving files that are closest to the present location of the heads instead of simply processing retrieval requests in the order in which they are received. This technique is known as:
   a. directory hashing.
   b. disk caching.
   c. rapid file retrieval.
   d. elevator seeking.

4. NetWare workstations need not contain floppy disk drives as long as they have:
   a. a remote system reset prom.
   b. G-Net.
   c. S-Net.
   d. at least 256K of RAM.

5. Workstations using different versions of DOS can coexist on a NetWare network because:
   a. each workstation does not use the file server.
   b. NetWare provides an interpretive shell.
   c. the differences in DOS versions are insignificant.
   d. different machines need different versions of DOS.

6. The QUEUE menu utility is designed to handle:
   a. printing requests.
   b. filing requests.
   c. micro–mainframe communications.
   d. waiting for the mid-morning coffee break.

7. Novell's System Fault Tolerant NetWare automatically places bad sectors in a bad block table using:
   a. a hot fix feature.
   b. elevator seeking.
   c. mirrored disk drives.
   d. the Transaction Tracking System.

8. The automatic rollback feature of the Transaction Tracking System ensures the integrity of a database by:
   a. duplicating each data entry.
   b. rolling back to before the data entry if the entry was disrupted before it was complete.
   c. keeping a log of all data entries.
   d. completing an entry if it is disrupted.

9. The concept of mirrored drives means that:
   a. all drives are the mirror opposites of each other.
   b. a second drive keeps an exact copy of the file server's information.
   c. all hardware and software are duplicated, including disk controllers and interfaces.
   d. if one disk drive becomes cracked, the other drive also is cracked.

10. Duplexed drives increase the speed of a file server by about:
    a. 3 times.
    b. 4 times.
    c. 2 times.
    d. 6 times.

11. System Fault Tolerant NetWare is able to locate potential bad blocks and then avoid them by using the following utility program:
    a. VOLFIX.
    b. QUEUE.
    c. FILER.
    d. NOGOOD.

12. If one workstation fails, the entire G-Net network will go down because it uses which topology?
    a. Star.
    b. Token ring.
    c. Bus.
    d. Distributed star.

13. NetWare enables the file server to quickly locate a file without searching through every directory by use of:
    a. disk caching.
    b. directory hashing.
    c. elevator seeking.
    d. remote system reset proms.

14. Network disk drives are really:
    a. hard disk drives.
    b. floppy disk drives.
    c. network file servers.
    d. logical disk drives.

15. Different networks can be linked using:
    a. a remote PC.
    b. a Bridge PC.
    c. a disk server.
    d. spooled disk files.

16. NetWare's local area networks can communicate with IBM mainframe computers using:
    a. a Bridge PC.
    b. an SNA/Gateway PC.
    c. an Asynchronous Communications Server.
    d. both b and c.

17. Passive and active hubs are found in:
    a. ARCNET.
    b. G-Net.
    c. S-Net.
    d. Proteon networks.

18. Users can shorten the login procedure by:
    a. using the NetWare manuals.
    b. using electronic mail.
    c. using elevator seeking.
    d. using login scripts.

3Com's Local Area Networks

ABOUT THIS CHAPTER

3Com is one of the major local area network manufacturers. It offers file servers as well as very advanced network software. It offers an upwardly compatible migration path for companies that wish to install its Etherseries software and later upgrade to the more sophisticated 3+ series. In this chapter we'll take a close look at the company's hardware and its wide range of software that provides electronic mail, print spooling, bridges to other networks, and communications with mainframe computers.

NETWORK HARDWARE

File Servers

While 3Com supports a variety of file servers, including IBM's PC, XT, and AT, its own 3Server maximizes the network's effectiveness. This 80186-based unit supports up to 420 Mb of storage and 896K of RAM.

3Com's philosophy seems to be to provide very fast, reliable local area networks with varying topologies that are compatible with a variety of industry standards. This philosophy is reflected by the variety of file servers that will work with 3Com network hardware and software. A 3Com network can include virtually all the leading file servers, including IBM's PC, XT, and AT and products by Compaq, AT&T, and Epson. However, the most efficient choice is probably 3Com's own 3Server. The 3Server comes with a choice of built-in 36-Mb or 70-Mb hard disks and can be expanded to a maximum of 420 Mb by daisy chaining five external drives. The 3Servers utilize an Intel 80186 microprocessor running at 8 MHz with no wait states. With a memory expansion board, the 512K of internal memory is expandable to 896K. This expansion is highly desirable in order to utilize the file server's disk-caching ability. One of the keys to this file server's efficiency is its less than 30-millisecond disk-access time. The 896K of RAM is essential if a network needs to have all network services, including file service, print service, electronic mail, remote PC access, and tape backup, on a single server.

To speed up network performance, 3Servers also come with 82586 Ethernet coprocessors. They offer one each of centronics-compatible parallel and asynchronous serial ports as well as a sixteen-character light-emitting diode (LED) for diagnostic messages and time and date displays. *Figure 6-1* illustrates the ports found on the back of a 3Server. Adding a 3Server port expansion board provides another parallel port and four more serial ports. These serial ports offer a number of advantages for companies that will be connecting their networks with other networks and mainframe computers. Two of the serial ports are asynchronous with baud rates from 300 to 230.4K, while the two others are software configurable for asynchronous, bisynchronous, SDLC, and HLDC with baud rates from 300 to 19.2K. The 3Server can support up to seven printers (5 serial and 2 parallel) or up to five modems or a combination of the two.

Figure 6-1.
Back View of a 3Server
(Reprinted with the permission of 3Com Corporation)

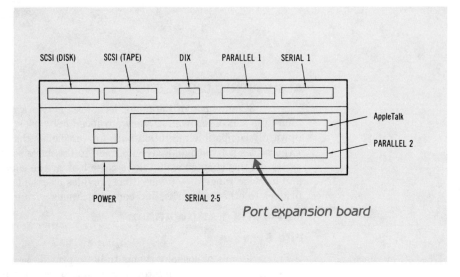

Tape Backup

The 3Backup tape backup unit is able to back up all file servers on a network. The 3+Backup software permits selective backup of those files that have changed.

The 3Servers also come with two Small Computer System Interface (SCSI) ports where tape backup units or additional disk drives can be connected. Since 3Com offers the option of thick (standard) or thin Ethernet cabling, the 3Server comes with BNC (thin Ethernet) and DIX (thick Ethernet) connectors. One major advantage of using a 3Server 60-Mb streaming tape backup unit with the file server is that there is a separate SCSI channel to prevent disk performance degradation during backup. With 3+Backup software, the 3+Backup unit becomes even more valuable. It is capable of backing up all network file servers on a single unit. It can also provide complete backup of an entire server's files as well as incremental backup of files that have changed since the last backup. Full or incremental backup can be scheduled for automatic operation and these processes initiated unattended. Multiple backups can be initiated on the same tape or each backup restricted to a new tape. Finally, it is possible to restore files either on a file-by-file basis for all files below a specified directory or to have a complete restoration of all files.

A network administrator can use 3+Backup to restore files from system-level backup tapes in four ways: restore all files on a server, restore all files on a specific 3Server disk, restore all files within a directory and its subdirectories, or restore one or more specific files. The 3+Backup unit prevents anyone from accessing it to do a backup, restore, erase, or directory while another user is performing one of these operations. In this way it provides some protection against catastrophe.

Network Architecture and Media

3Com offers a baseband 10-Mbit/s bus network that adheres to the IEEE 802.3 standard and a bus with a logical token ring network that adheres to the IEEE 802.5 4-Mbit/s standard.

Historically, 3Com has adhered to the IEEE 803.2 Ethernet standards for a contention bus network. As we saw in Chapter 2, such networks utilize a CSMA/CD protocol, which means that workstations send a signal before sending data on the network. If two workstations utilize the network at exactly the same time, a data collision occurs. Then a jam signal is sent across the network causing workstations to wait a designated period of time (varying from workstation to workstation) before again trying to transmit information. Although 3Com's traditional focus has been on very fast (10 Mbit/s) baseband bus networks, the company has recently added a connection to the IEEE 802.5 token ring standard, specifically IBM's Token Ring Network, and now offers its own token ring architecture as well.

The baseband 10-Mbit/s transmission speed over a bus is achieved using a 3Com network adapter card known as "EtherLink." The EtherLink is inserted in an expansion slot of each network workstation and is capable of 3280-ft (1000-m) transmission using thick Ethernet cable. The cabling, which is .4-inch (1 centimeter) in diameter, utilizes an external transceiver box for each workstation. Network workstations must be a minimum of 7.5 ft (2.25 m) apart.

While the standard cabling permits a larger network, it costs more and is more difficult to install than thin cabling. With the thin Ethernet cabling, which is .2 inch (5 millimeters) in diameter, there is a 1000-ft (300-m) limitation in the total length of a network segment. Network workstations must be a minimum of 3 ft (.9 m) apart. The EtherLink adapter card for a thin cabled network contains its own on-board transceiver. *Figure 6-2* illustrates how a BNC connector links a network's workstations and thin cabling together. One attractive feature of the 3Com local area networks is that it is possible to mix and match thin and thick cabling and file servers to customize the network to meet a company's needs.

**Figure 6-2.
3Com Bus Network with
Thin Cabling**

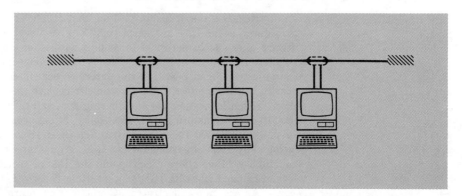

While the type of cabling (thin or thick) determines the length of a particular *segment* of an Ethernet LAN, multiple segments can be linked with *repeaters*, which rebroadcast the signal and prevent data degradation. *Figure 6-3* illustrates the use of repeaters.

Figure 6-3.
Ethernet Network with
Multiple Segments and
Repeaters

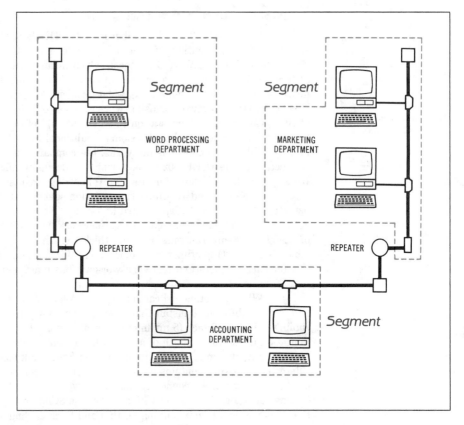

3Com's Token Ring Network Alternatives

Realizing the dominant position that IBM's Token Ring Network
has achieved in the LAN marketplace, 3Com has developed hardware and
software to enable its networks to connect with token ring networks and it
also offers its own token ring alternative. TokenConnection for a 3Server
consists of two circuit boards, a ring interface board, and the processor
interface board. In effect, these components replace the back panel of 3-
Server. TokenConnection has a token ring port and two synchronous serial
ports. In order to assure IBM compatibility, 3Com uses the Texas
Instruments TMS380 Token Ring Chip Set. Since this chip set was jointly
developed by Texas Instruments and IBM, it guarantees IBM
compatibility. 3Com offers RingTap and the TokenPlus cabling system
which are compatible with IBM's Token Ring Network PC Adapter Cables.

As *Figure 6-4* illustrates, 3Com offers an internal ring topology
with an external bus topology. The RingTaps are connected to token ring
adapters in each network workstation. As *Figure 6-5* illustrates, 3Com
offers its own TokenLink Plus adapter cards for IBM PCs, XTs, ATs, and
compatibles that offer IEEE 802.5 and IEEE 802.2 logical link control
interfaces on a 4 Mbit/s baseband token ring network. The 256K RAM

found on each TokenLink Plus adapter card can be used for downloading protocol software with the IBM-compatible NETBIOS interface. The 16K of ROM provides boot and diagnostic firmware.

Figure 6-4.
3Com's RingTap and
TokenPlus Cabling
System *(Reprinted with*
the permission of 3Com
Corporation)

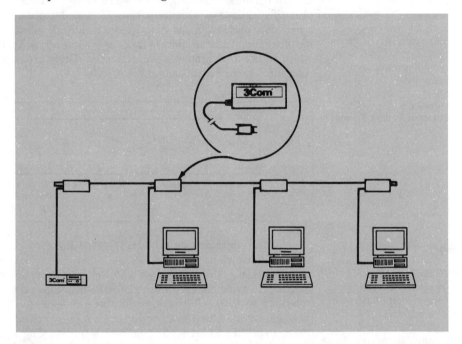

Figure 6-5.
3Com TokenLink Plus
Adapter Card *(Reprinted*
with the permission of
3Com Corporation)

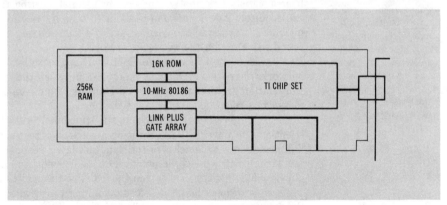

The RingTaps consist of small boxes that connect to the Token Ring Adapter cards with thumb screws. The TokenPlus cabling system links several RingTaps with trunk cables. A Y-MAU cable is used to connect the TokenPlus cabling system with IBM's MultiStation Access Unit. The 3Com cable design for its token ring network uses doubled, shielded, twisted-pair wire.

NETWORK DATA-COLLISION DETECTION AND AVOIDANCE

3Com's local area networks use the standard Ethernet data packet containing information on source and destination addresses, type of protocol used, and error checking.

Under Ethernet the physical layer generates a 64-bit preamble so that all network workstations can synchronize the data stream. The preamble consists of a unique pattern of 1s and 0s that indicate the start of a new data packet. As shown in *Figure 6-6*, the Ethernet packet contains destination and source address fields as well as a type field to indicate which higher-level protocols might be used. There are also fields to hold the data and a cyclic redundancy check (CRC).

Figure 6-6.
Ethernet Packet Format

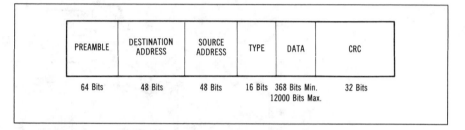

3Com's EtherSeries network software utilizes a CSMA/CD approach to data collisions. The danger occurs during the interval when a workstation sends a transmit signal until the signal returns indicating the workstation may claim the channel. In the event of a data collision, a jam signal is generated, and workstations wait different random intervals before trying again to gain a channel.

In compliance with the IEEE 802.3 standards, 3Com's Ethernet network software delivers the data packets to network workstations using a Carrier Sense, Multiple Access with Collision Detection (CSMA/CD) approach to avoid data collisions along the bus. Since this is a contention (competition) scheme in which workstations compete for the right to send a message, a station that is about to send a message through the network listens to see if another station has sent a transmitting signal. If it doesn't hear a signal, it promptly sends its own signal alerting the network that it has acquired the channel and is about to send a message. Note that this node hasn't acquired the channel until its transmitting signal completes its round trip through the network.

The problem with the CSMA/CD approach is that on very large networks there is a significant time lapse between the time that a workstation acquires a channel and transmits its signal and the time the message is received further down the bus.

If there is a data collision, the transmitting station detects this event and its physical layer turns on a collision-detect signal. The transmit link management elements of the data link layer respond by generating a jam signal that notifies the network of the collision and initiates a hiatus during which no signals are transmitted. The transmitting station then waits an additional interval before beginning to retransmit its message. In the event of another collision, all workstations wait random additional intervals before trying to retransmit.

THE ETHERSERIES vs. THE 3+ SERIES

3Com offers two sets of software that utilize the same Ethernet hardware: the EtherSeries and the far more sophisticated 3+ Series. While the EtherSeries software is based on DOS 2.X, 3+ Series products are based on DOS 3.1. The EtherSeries software provides a disk server with disk- and volume-sharing capabilities while 3+ offers a true file server. The EtherSeries software is ideal for a company that needs a small LAN that will permit peripheral sharing as well as the sharing of already existing DOS 2.X software. It does offer print spooling to two parallel and one serial printer (EtherPrint), security (private volumes as well as public volumes and shared volumes), and economy (inexpensive software and the ability with an EtherStart prom to network a PC workstation without disk drives).

The major distinctions between the EtherSeries and 3+ software are that the more sophisticated 3+ programs permit internetwork connections, remote access, the transparent appearance of all resources on the network, and the use of multiuser software based on PC/MS-DOS 3.1. 3Com's 3+Path permits the upward migration from the EtherSeries to the 3+ Series. Data doesn't need to be retyped. The two operating systems can also coexist on the network as long as they are not on the same file server.

3Com distinguishes its two network options by pointing out that only the more sophisticated 3+ Series offers transparent internetwork communications, transparent access to the network by remote PC's via dialup, minicomputer or mainframe-style file service, and support for multiuser application software that requires PC/MS-DOS 3.1.

Many companies may not need these features immediately, but they certainly may want them in the future. 3Com offers 3+Path for customers who want to purchase EtherSeries software first but later upgrade to the 3+ Series. 3+Path replaces the EtherShare/EtherPrint software with 3+Share (file, print, name, and dial-in remote service). It also upgrades EtherMail software to 3+Mail and 3Server Backup to 3+Backup. 3Com also makes it possible for the EtherSeries and 3+ Series to coexist on the same network although they cannot coexist on the same file server. A 3+ workstation can concurrently access both EtherSeries and 3+ servers. Since the EtherSeries does not provide remote service, 3+Remote doesn't provide access to those EtherSeries servers on the network. *Figure 6-7* illustrates how the two levels of software can coexist on a 3Com network.

Using an EtherShare Network

EtherSeries is the older of the 3Com software series. EtherShare is the key program on an EtherSeries network because it links the other major EtherSeries products such as EtherLink, EtherPrint, EtherMail, and EtherMenu. The program provides disk-server software to divide a hard disk into volumes that may be designated as public, private, or shared. A public volume contains material that can be accessed by several other users at the same time on a Read-only basis. A private volume, on the other hand, can be accessed only by the volume owner on a Read-write basis. Finally, a shared volume can be accessed by several users at a time on a Read-write basis. EtherShare enables users to create passwords for volumes so that only authorized users may access them.

EtherShare's commands allow users to log in and out of an EtherShare server; to create, modify, and delete EtherShare volumes; to link to other EtherShare volumes and create, modify, and delete EtherShare users; and to list a directory of users or volumes. *Figure 6-8* shows the EtherShare menu of commands available to a network user who has logged on to the network by typing ES. The EtherSeries DOS disk contains a LOGIN batch file that can be modified to perform several EtherShare commands without having to go through EtherShare's menus.

Figure 6-7.
3Com Network with
3+Path (*Reprinted with the permission of 3Com Corporation*)

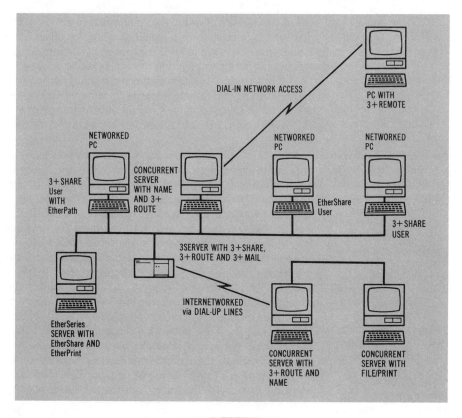

Figure 6-8.
EtherShare Menu

```
EtherShare Commands:
 1 - Login to the Server (LOGIN)
 2 - Logout from the Server (LOGOUT)
 3 - Link to an EtherShare volume (LINK)
 4 - Unlink from a volume (UNLINK)
 5 - List all volumes (DIR)
 6 - Create and format a new volume (CREATE)
 7 - Modify an existing volume (MOD)
 8 - Delete an existing volume (DEL)
 9 - List all users (UDIR)
10 - Create a new user (UCREATE)
11 - Delete an existing user (UDEL)
12 - Modify your user password (UMOD)
13 - List all servers (SDIR)
14 - Receive help (HELP)

Selection?
```

Since the EtherSeries is designed to run programs using DOS 2.X, 3Com was not able to use the record and file locking capabilities of DOS 3.1. 3Com chose to include three *semaphore* operations that provide flags indicating when a shared program's file is being used: LOCK/WAIT, LOCK/RETURN, and UNLOCK. The normal sequence of operations for a program is to lock the semaphore, read the file and/or record, write the new and/or changed data, flush the buffer, and unlock the semaphore. Only programs that have specifically been written to use the EtherSeries semaphores can be used safely in a shared volume. If a network supervisor tries to use single-user programs in this environment, data will be lost as files will be overwritten.

3+ Share

Because of the 3+ Series' ability to run multiuser software written for DOS 3.1, software publishers have developed 3Com LAN versions along with versions for IBM's Token Ring Network and Novell's NetWare. For this reason we'll take a close look at the heart of the 3+ software, 3+Share. This software is the basis for all the advanced features of the 3+ Series, including internetworking (connecting networks together via 3+Route), mainframe/minicomputer gateways (3+3270), configurable menus (3+Menus), remote dial-in access to the network (3+Remote), backup capabilities (3+Backup) and electronic mail (3+Mail). The command structure is remarkably simple. *Table 6-1* is a summary of 3+Share user commands.

The Name Service

The Name Service is a database that requires a user's name, domain, and organization. This information then becomes available to all the other 3+ programs.

A basic function under 3+Share is The Name Service, a database of users and servers. All the 3+ software accesses this information. 3N is the user program that interfaces with the Name Service. It is this program that pulls information from the database to provide user login verification, lists of users, and so on. To login, a user must provide his or her name, followed by the geographic location (domain), followed by company (organization). A typical entry might look like this:

Fred Goodman:Accounting:DeVry

The Name Service has a default domain and organization. Under most circumstances, Fred would not have to retype these default values. In addition to his or her name, a person may have one or more aliases, usually a short form of the user's name. Fred Goodman's alias, for example, might be FredG. Let's assume that for security reasons DeVry wants all employees to logon to the network with a password in addition to their alias. Fred, who selected his childhood nickname "Scrappy" as his password, would type the following each time he logs onto the network:

FredG /PASS=Scrappy

If the network recognizes the password it returns Fred's three-part network name:

Fred Goodman:Accounting:DeVry

**Table 6-1.
3+Share User
Commands**

Command	Function
LOGIN	Login to the network
LOGOUT	Logout from the network
3F User Commands	
3F	Start program file
3F DIR	List names of shared directories
3F HELP	Get help with the File Service
3F LINK	Link to a shared directory
3F LOGIN	Login to the network
3F LOGOUT	Logout from the network
3F MODIFY	Modify a shared directory
3F SHARE	Share a directory
3F STAT	Show 3Share server information
3F UNLINK	Unlink from a shared directory
3F UNSHARE	Delete a shared directory
3N User Commands	
3N	Start program name
3N ASSIGN	Assign a sharename for 3Share
3N DIR	List 3N names
3N HELP	Display helpful information
3N LOGIN	Login to the network
3N LOGOUT	Logout from the network
3N MODIFY	Modify 3N information
3N SET	Set 3N defaults
3N STAT	Display 3N information
3P User Commands	
3P	Start program print
3P DELETE	Delete a file from the print queue
3P DIR	List names of shared printers
3P HELP	Display helpful information
3P LINK	Link to a shared printer
3P LOGIN	Login to the network
3P LOGOUT	Logout from the network
3P SET	St printer options
3P STAT	Show 3Share printer information
3P QSTAT	List a printer queue
3P UNLINK	Unlink from a shared printer

The first time Fred used the network, the administrator added him to the Name Service and assigned him a file server. The 3+Share program assigned Fred a home directory (Fredhome) in which to keep his files. Using the DOS 3.1 hierarchical directory structure, Fred created a number of subdirectories under his home directory. One of these subdirectories (Account) contains an accounts receivable file with customer histories (Cust.his) that Fred frequently accesses.

The pathway to this particular file through DOS 3.1's treelike structure can be written:

C: \ Fredhome \ Account \ Cust.his

Shared Directories

The main reason for using a local area network is to share information. To share files a user needs to tell 3+Share that a particular directory is available to be shared using 3Com's 3F user interface for 3+Share's file service. Let's assume that salespeople want to check on some of Fred's customer histories. Fred shares the file by giving it the sharename "customer" and limiting access to Read-only:

3F SHARE cust.his=E: \ customer /R

If Fred is concerned about security, he can require a password such as "victory":

3F SHARE cust.his=E: \ customer /PASS=victory /R

A variety of access rights may be assigned to a sharename directory, including:

/R	Read
/RW	Read-Write
/RWC	Read-Write-Create
/WC	Write-Create
/W	Write
/SHAR	Read-Write-Create-Share
/PRIV	Private
/PUB	Public

The network's default value is "Private." If network users require differing levels of access for a particular directory, that file can have several sharenames with different passwords for each sharename. All the subdirectories under a particular directory, though, share the same access rights for that directory.

3+Share's Print Service

3Com provides the 3P user interface program for 3+Share's Print Service. The program is started when the user types 3P. With this program it is possible to list or link shared printers and directories, set special printing options for a printer, and examine printing queues. By typing 3P HELP a user can see a complete list of print commands and a brief description of each command.

One of the most powerful yet easy-to-use print commands is 3P SET which enables you to establish special printing options for a printer. The 3Com format for this command is illustrative of its flexibility:

3P SET[prnid:][/HOLD[=OFF]][/COPIES=#][/PRI=#]
[/DEFER[]=OFF]][/RELEASE][/FORM=#][/ SPOOL=#]

The printer identifier can be LPT1, LPT2, or LPT3. The HOLD parameter holds all printing jobs until given the HOLD=OFF or UNLINK command. This command ensures that all files are printed together in batch form.

The COPIES parameter permits you to make multiple copies of the same document—up to 99 copies at a time. The normal default value here is 1. The PRI parameter permits you to assign your files a priority in the print queue from 1 (the lowest priority) to 99 (the highest priority). The default value is 50.

The DEFER parameter allows you to defer the printing of a file no matter what its place is in the print queue. If you defer a file until its place in the queue has already passed, the software automatically moves it to the top of the print queue. The RELEASE command frees deferred files for printing.

The final two print option parameters are FORM and SPOOL. FORM specifies which particular form you want your file to print. The printer will wait until that form is loaded before it begins printing. The default value here is form number 1. Finally, the SPOOL parameter indicates the file's spool identifier, which is assigned by the 3P program. If you specify a spool identifier, only that particular file will be affected by your print specifications. If you do not specify a number here, all the options you have set here will apply to all files you send to the printer.

Since there are default values for all these options, you only list the parameters you wish to set when using the 3P program. To print all your files in the printer's queue on a specific form, for example, you would type:

SET LPT1: /FORM=10

Remote Access

The 3+Remote software permits remote workstations to dial-in to a network and utilize all network services.

Using the 3+Remote software package it is possible for a remote workstation to dial-in to a 3+ local area network. The remote users enjoy all 3+ series services, including 3+Share electronic mail and access to all the file and print functions of the network. The software provides full error checking of transmitted data; if an error is detected, the software automatically retransmits lost data packets. To make it easier and faster for remote users to access a network, the software supports up to nine prioritized telephone numbers that can be up to thirty digits long. The 3Com program supports automatic hang-up for inactivity timeout; this feature is configurable. It also supports automatic, prioritized alternate phone numbers with a user profile to maintain predefined dialing, modem, and port information. *Figure 6-9* shows the 3+Remote software linking three remote users with a 3Com network.

Figure 6-9.
3+Remote Software
Linking Remote Users
with Network *(Reprinted*
with the permission of
3Com Corporation)

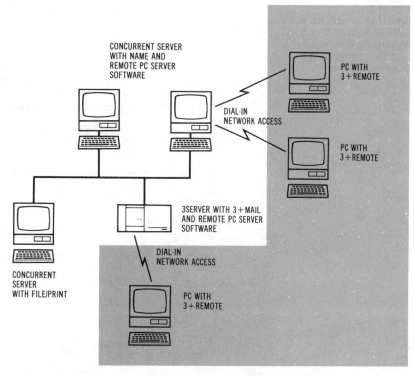

Linking a 3Com LAN to an IBM Mainframe Computer

Network workstations can emulate an IBM 3278 or 3279 terminal and communicate with an IBM mainframe computer with the 3+3270 software and IBM SDLC card.

A 3Com EtherSeries or 3+ network can be linked to an IBM mainframe by using 3Com software that causes network workstations to emulate an IBM 3278 or 3279 terminal. An IBM PC AT with a hard disk is an ideal choice for a dedicated communications server. An IBM SDLC card must be installed in this server. At present, this card does not support an IBM PC XT with a hard disk.

As *Figure 6-10* reveals, it is possible to have two or more dedicated communications servers on a 3Com network. Since only single-host sessions are supported, though, it isn't possible to switch between host and PC sessions. The software supports up to thirty-two LUs that are pooled among fifty users on a first-come first-served basis. While this may sound like quite a few sessions, remember that each terminal and printer in use counts as a session.

The 3+3270 software provides file transfer capability for the workstations on the network. It is necessary, though, to purchase the required host software directly from Forte Communications. The ASCII-to-EBCDIC conversion process is handled at the workstation. The software uses the Microcom MNP protocol, a standard used by Telenet, GEISCO, and The Source. The terminal emulation software can also spool output to any network printer, disk drive, or user workstation. Note that you must first spool files to a local or network storage device before you can spool to a local printer.

**Figure 6-10.
3+3270 Connecting a
LAN to an IBM
Mainframe** *(Reprinted
with the permission of
3Com Corporation)*

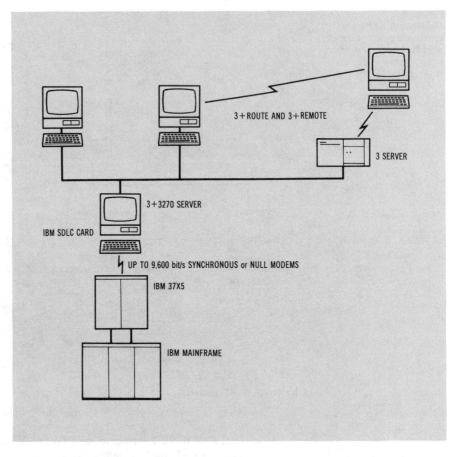

Internetworking (3+Route)

The 3+Route software
provides internetworking
capabilities including
enabling workstations to
access files and resources
on other networks
without knowing their
pathways.

The 3+ network provides true internetworking with 3+Route.
Based on Xerox's XNS internet protocol standards, this program enables
several local area networks to be linked. With the Name Service, all users
can access resources by name without having to define a path from their
workstation to the resource. 3+Route provides (with 3+Mail) full electronic
mail service to the interconnected network users.

The 3+Route software permits a network supervisor to establish
authorized call times in order to reduce telephone costs. It is possible to set
up as many as eight access windows with time schedules for dialing out on
each. For busy internetwork traffic, the program supports up to five ports
on a 3Server with the port expansion board. For dialing other networks, it
automatically looks up telephone numbers. It is possible to specify up to
fifty alternate telephone numbers if a primary number is busy. 3+Route
supports up to 2400-baud dial-in or 9600-baud direct when running
concurrently with 3+Share or 3+Mail. If greater speed is required, 3+

Route's XNS protocol also supports Bridge Communication's high-performance GS/3 and GS/4 Gateway Communication servers. *Figure 6-11* shows a local area network utilizing 3+Route.

**Figure 6-11.
3+Route Providing
Internetwork
Connections** *(Reprinted
with the permission of
3Com Corporation)*

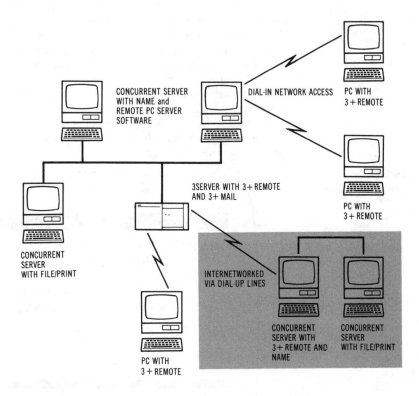

ELECTRONIC MAIL

The 3+Mail program offers a number of features, including automatic internetwork mail service, the ability to send documents appended to messages, the ability to print messages as you receive them, and three levels of mail security.

The 3Com electronic mail program, 3+Mail, has a number of features that distinguish it from its competitors. In addition to its ability to provide automatic internetwork mail between networks and remote PC workstations, it can transfer files along with messages. The program offers three levels of mail security. First, each user logs on with a user name and an optional password. Second, the inbox directories can also be designed to require passwords to access them. Third, messages sent through 3+Mail are encrypted so they cannot be read until their arrival in the designated recipient's inbox folder.

The 3+Mail software is fully integrated with all other 3+ network services and all interconnected networks. In addition to having other networks call at designated times to save money, 3+Mail can keep detailed records of this activity. Virtually all network users will receive and send messages on a daily basis. Let's go through these processes to examine their sophistication and ease of use.

Receiving Mail on 3+Mail

In many ways, having 3+Mail is like having a private postal service. A directory called INBOX serves as a user's personal mail folder. The network server (the post office) sorts all mail, placing each user's in a personal mail folder. A user must perform several initial steps in order to use 3+Mail. These steps are clearly described in the 3+Mail *User's Manual,* so we'll assume that they have been completed, that the user is ready to receive mail, and that the 3+Mail program has created a file called MAIL.DIR in the user's directory to keep track of messages in his or her mail folder. Users may have an unlimited number of message inbox folders, each of which holds up to 110 messages. *Figure 6-12* shows the 3+Mail main display.

Figure 6-12.
3+Mail Main Display

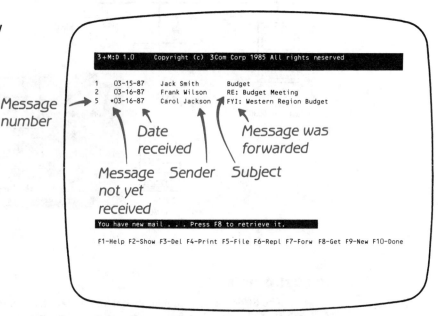

There are several items worth noticing on this display. The asterisk next to message number 5 indicates that it has not been read. After a message is read, the asterisk disappears to designate that it is no longer an unread message. No longer can an employee tell the boss that he missed a meeting because he did not happen to read a particular memo. The 3+Mail service reveals the truth by indicating the date (column 2) that the message was received. The display also notes if a message was forwarded (FYI) or was a reply message (RE). Finally, the status line at the bottom of the screen indicates whether the user has new mail and which function keys to use in order to use the mail service.

For ease of use, 3+Mail uses the same function keys throughout its various menus. It indicates whether messages have been received and if the messages are replies or are forwarded messages .

To display your mail, transfer the mail from the network server to your network server. When you press the <F8> key, the status line displays the message "Connecting to the Mail Server," which is replaced with the message "Message(s) retrieved" when all messages have been transferred. To read a message with 3+Mail, the user moves the cursor down the screen until the message is highlighted and then presses the <F2> key. *Figure 6-13* shows how messages appear on a user's screen. Notice that the user has several options at this point, including printing the message (<F4>), filing the message (<F5>), replying to the message (<F6>), and forwarding the message (<F7>). To return to the main display, the user presses <F10>, the Exit key.

Figure 6-13.
Reading a Message

Sending Mail Using 3+Mail

Use the <F9> key to indicate that you wish to compose a new message. The 3+Mail display contains a message header that has some fields filled in already. The *From:* field is already filled in with your name. The *To:* field is required. The program uses default values for the domain and organization fields if you only enter a person's name. It is also possible to enter distribution lists in the *To:* field. Normally a network supervisor creates such lists and makes them available to all users. By typing "Accounting" in the *To:* field, for example, the message will automatically be sent to all network users in accounting who are on this list.

After the *To:* field is filled in, a *cc:* field appears. While this is an optional field, it is important that you place your own name here if you want to retain a copy of the message. The *Subj:* field is also optional, but for both your own record keeping and that of the person receiving the message it is a good idea to be as explicit as possible when indicating the subject. The optional *Attach:* field permits you to attach a DOS file. The 3+Mail program is particularly impressive in this area because it permits up to twenty-six fields to be attached to a message. The DOS filenames should be separated by commas and should indicate their respective drives, extensions, and pathnames.

When you are replying to a message rather than composing a new message, the 3+Mail program fills in all message header fields except *Attach:* with the information appearing in the original message. The *Subj:* field contains the same subject as the original message except now it is preceded by *RE:* to indicate a reply. An *In Reply To:* field contains the sender and date of the original message. Because there are occasions when it is necessary to send messages back and forth several times the 3+Mail program permits up to six *In Reply To:* fields on the same screen. You may continue to reply to messages after the sixth reply, but the program will simply stop adding to this listing.

The 3+Mail program contains a message editor called MED which is used whenever you edit a message or modify a message header. It can also be run as a separate program to edit programs and text files. MED is a screen-oriented editor: what you see on the screen is what will be sent through electronic mail. It can be used in an insert mode in which typing automatically moves existing text to the right or in a type-over mode in which text replaces (types over) existing text. The MED program utilizes *word wrap* so that it is not necessary to press the <RETURN> key at the end of a line. Text is automatically wrapped around from the right margin to the left margin. The permanent margins for MED are set at 0 for the left and 65 characters for the right. It is possible to use the <Tab> key to set temporary margins. MED uses function keys to perform word-processing tasks such as the deletion of a word <F3>, the deletion of an entire line <F5>, and filing text <F2>. It also enables the user to mark blocks of text and then copy, move, or delete them.

The 3+Mail software consists of three different programs: user software, server software, and administrative software. *Figure 6-14* indicates how the three programs work together to provide complete mail service.

The 3+Mail program contains a message editor (MED) that offers a number of features including word wrap. It may be used independently of 3+Mail to edit programs or text files.

Figure 6-14.
3+Mail Programs
(Reprinted with the permission of 3Com Corporation)

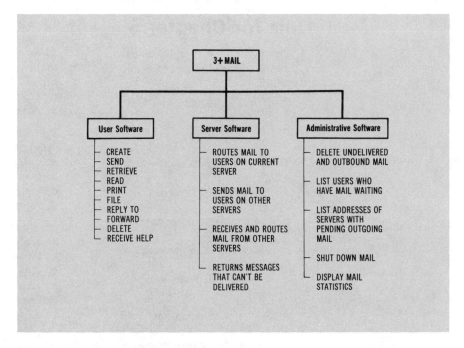

WHAT HAVE WE LEARNED?

1. 3Com offers a high-speed (10 Mbit/s) LAN that utilizes a bus topology following the IEEE 802.3 standards.
2. Both the EtherSeries and 3+Series are contention networks using a CSMA/CD approach.
3. 3Com offers a token ring network (TokenConnection) that follows the 4 Mbit/s IEEE 802.5 standards.
4. The 3+Series is capable of remote access, internetwork connections, and multiuser software record-locking under DOS 3.1.
5. EtherSeries and 3+Series software can coexit on a 3Com network but not on the same file server.
6. Micro–mainframe communication is possible on a 3Com network with 3+3270 software.
7. 3+Mail permits electronic mail between different networks as long as 3+Route is also used.
8. 3+Mail contains a powerful editor (MED) that can be used independently of the electronic mail program to edit programs and text files.

Quiz for Chapter 6

1. The 3Com file server, 3Server, uses a powerful microprocessor, called:
   a. 80186.
   b. 80286.
   c. 80386.
   d. 8088.

2. The 3Server comes standard with:
   a. one serial and two parallel ports.
   b. two parallel and two serial ports.
   c. one parallel and one serial port.
   d. no parallel and one serial port.

3. A 3Server port expansion board adds:
   a. one parallel and two serial ports.
   b. one parallel and three serial ports.
   c. one parallel and four serial ports.
   d. one parallel and five serial ports.

4. The 3Backup unit interfaces with 3Server through a:
   a. parallel interface.
   b. serial interface.
   c. SCSI interface.
   d. synchronous interface.

5. 3Backup is capable of:
   a. incremental backups of data.
   b. automatic unattended backups of data.
   c. backups of all file servers on the network.
   d. all of the above.

6. Thick (standard) Ethernet cabling can support network segments up to:
   a. 1000 feet.
   b. 2550 feet.
   c. 3280 feet.
   d. 5280 feet.

7. It is possible to connect multiple network segments with:
   a. coaxial cable.
   b. t-connectors.
   c. transmitters.
   d. repeaters.

8. An Ethernet packet begins with a 64-bit
   a. introduction field.
   b. data field.
   c. error-checking field.
   d. preamble field.

9. A PC workstation located at another site can communicate with a 3+ Series network by using:
   a. 3+Remote.
   b. 3+Route.
   c. 3+3270.
   d. 3+Path.

10. A company that wishes to upgrade from the EtherSeries to the 3+ Series would use:
    a. 3+Route.
    b. 3+Path.
    c. 3+Remote.
    d. 3+Upgrade.

11. The adapter card that must be installed in an expansion slot of each 3+ Series workstation is called:
    a. Asynchronous Communications Card.
    b. EtherLink Plus.
    c. SerialLink.
    d. 3+3270 Card.

12. The database that is utilized by all 3+ Series programs is called:
    a. the Name Service.
    b. 3+Name.
    c. Name+.
    d. FileManager+.

13. The three types of information needed when creating a user on a 3Com network are:
    a. name, domain, organization.
    b. name, position, title.
    c. name, name of network, machine name.
    d. user name, alias, nickname.

14. People who wish to use a short form of their user profile can use a name known as their:
    a. nickname.
    b. alias.
    c. user name.
    d. company name.

15. 3+Route offers:
    a. automatic hangup.
    b. alternate phone number list.
    c. full error checking.
    d. all of the above.

16. The EtherSeries software avoids file destruction by using:
    a. semaphores.
    b. DOS 3.1 record-locking.
    c. multiuser software.
    d. special warning screens.

17. On an EtherSeries network a data collision is signaled with a(n):
    a. warning alert signal.
    b. jam signal.
    c. early-warning collision signal.
    d. jelley signal.

18. The 3+ Print Service permits the customization of a print job with:
    a. 3+Set.
    b. 3+Print.
    c. 3+Custom.
    d. 3+Option.

19. 3+Mail provides security with:
    a. login passwords.
    b. passwords for inbox directories.
    c. encrypted messages.
    d. all of the above.

20. 3+Mail contains a powerful message editor known as:
    a. MESED.
    b. MED.
    c. ED.
    d. WRITE.

AT&T'S STARLAN and ISN

ABOUT THIS CHAPTER

AT&T's STARLAN is an inexpensive bus network that illustrates the company's open architecture philosophy. In this chapter we'll examine STARLAN's hardware and software and explore why it might be an ideal solution for a small department or for a large company considering departmental networks. Because AT&T is committed to linking its DOS-based STARLAN with its UNIX-based minicomputers, we'll look at what this connection can mean for a company. We will also examine how STARLAN links to AT&T's powerful Information Systems Network (ISN) and how ISN offers true voice and data integration. Finally, we'll see how ISN supports the new Integrated Services Digital Network (ISDN) standards that will become increasingly important.

STARLAN HARDWARE

AT&T designed the STARLAN network to be as simple as possible. Up to ten PC workstations can be linked by installing a network access unit (NAU) in each workstation's expansion bus and then using unshielded twisted-pair telephone wire to daisy-chain the units together. Each NAU has three telephone jacks. The IN jack of one unit is connected to the OUT jack of another unit. The third jack is used for connecting an analog phone to a workstation. One workstation with a hard disk is designated as the file server and each workstation has a copy of the STARLAN software (PC 6300 Network Program). AT&T refers to the workstations that utilize a file server as "clients." *Figure 7-1* shows how a small STARLAN network might look with an AT&T 6300 Plus used as a file server. The maximum distance permitted for a daisy-chained STARLAN network is 400 ft (120 m).

Figure 7-1.
A Small STARLAN
Network

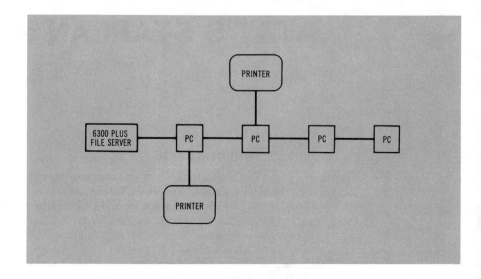

Each network
workstation requires an
NAU circuit card. It is
capable of 1-Mbit/s
transmission speed using
CSMA/CD to avoid data
collisions.

As we just pointed out, the NAU is required in each network workstation. There are actually three kinds of NAUs. STARLANs with a PC or a PC compatible as file server require the Personal Computer 6300 NAU. AT&T's UNIX PC and 3B2 computers require the UNIX PC NAU and 3B2 NAU respectively. Each NAU comes with a 10-ft (3-m) twisted-pair, modular cable, but you can order longer cables from AT&T.

In addition to the three telephone jacks, each NAU contains 8K or 32K of RAM, a network address ROM, and a CSMA/CD controller. STARLAN is a baseband contention network that transmits data at 1 Mbit/s using a CSMA/CD approach. *Figure 7-2* shows how data flows from the NAU to the host computer. The NAU uses a shared-memory system that makes it appear that the memory resides in the host's main memory even though it is actually on the NAU itself. The CSMA/CD coprocessor accesses this memory as do the computer's read-write operations.

An NEU can link 11
workstations in a star
topology or it can be used
as a master unit with 11
secondary NEUs to
create a two-tier network
with up to 1210 units.

An NEU is used to expand a STARLAN network beyond 10 workstations; it enables a network supervisor to link up to 11 workstations up to 800 ft (240 m) from the NEU in a star topology. Or you can use 1 NEU as a master unit and link up to 11 secondary NEUs each with a star topology creating what is known as a "two-tier star." This arrangement can support up to 100 active workstations and as many as 1210 physical connections. An NEU can be mounted in a telephone wiring closet or in the room with the workstations. The NEU has one port labeled OUT that is used to connect it to another NEU or to a network repeater unit (NRU). A connector on the NEU connects to a wall-mounted transformer that provides low-voltage AC. Each NEU must be within 10 ft (3 m) of a commercial power outlet that is not switch-controlled. *Figure 7-3* shows how an NEU creates a star topology.

**Figure 7-2.
AT&T 6300 NAU Block
Diagram** *(Courtesy of
AT&T)*

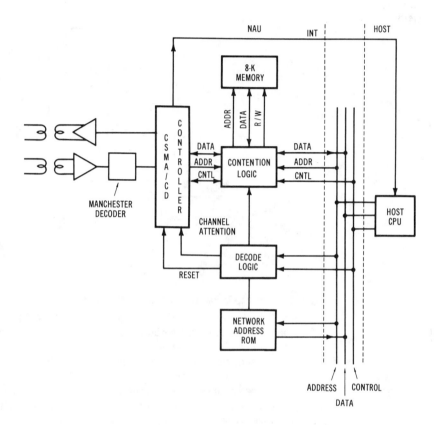

A STARLAN networking several workstations in one room is known as a Room Star. It is also possible to link several workstations in different rooms using a wiring closet. Such an arrangement is called a Closet Star.

The NEU thus serves as a hub around which PC workstations located physically in the same room are clustered in a star-like architecture that AT&T refers to as a "Room Star." A company can also install a STARLAN in departments that are physically separated within a building. AT&T labels this type of arrangement a "Closet Star." AT&T's concept here is to use the building's phone wire that usually is in place as the installing medium and to bring together in wiring closets the cables containing the twisted-pair wire. Since the closets can be locked, this arrangement provides extra network security. Each workstation then has a modular cord going from its NAU to a phone jack. The phone wire carries data to the wiring closet where the NEU is located.

Expanding STARLAN is easy since an additional NEU can always be added at any time. Although as many as eleven NEUs can be connected to a master NEU each one must be directly connected to the master NEU and must be within 10 ft (3 m) of this unit.

**Figure 7-3.
NEU Linking PCs
Together**

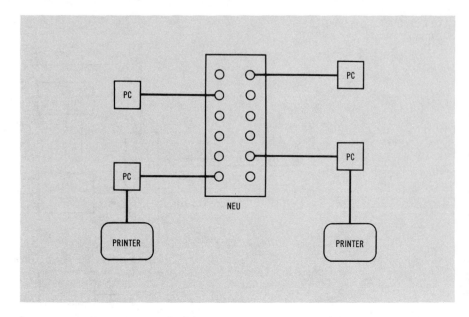

Network Interface Units (NIUs)

To connect peripherals to STARLAN, AT&T offers an NIU that contains two RS-232C serial ports capable of interfacing with asynchronous printers or plotters, asynchronous modems, and asynchronous terminals with speeds up to 19.2 Kbit/s. The NIU contains two digital jacks that can be used to connect peripherals while the third jack permits analog telephone communications when STARLAN is connected to the in-house telephone system. Note that the NIU uses the same NEU ports that network workstations use.

Network Repeater Units (NRUs)

The NRU reconstructs a signal and amplifies it before passing it back to the network. The NRU increases the operational distance of a STARLAN network by permitting multicloset configurations. It functions as both an in-line repeater and a central hub repeater. The NRU contains three interfaces. The IN interface connects to the OUT port on an NEU or NAU while the OUT interface connects to the IN jack on an NEU or NAU. A power interface plugs into a wall-mounted transformer.

File Servers

As we indicated earlier, one version of STARLAN software was designed to run on the AT&T 6300, the AT&T 6300 Plus, and all IBM PC-DOS models with the exception of the PC jr. Since STARLAN uses DOS 3.1 and should handle all software programs written to run on IBM's PC LAN Network, you should be sure that any PC compatible you are considering as a file server has a NETBIOS that can run these programs. In a long-awaited development, AT&T now offers its file-server network software for its UNIX-based UNIX PC and 3B2 computers.

There are several reasons why it might be advantageous to use one of AT&T's UNIX computers as a file server. The 3B2 400, for example, is a supermicro, a true 32-bit machine designed for multiuser, multitasking operations. With it, accounting personnel using inexpensive terminals could utilize sophisticated UNIX-based multiuser accounting programs with record-locking capability and a good deal of security. The same 3B2 400 unit could act as a file server and print server to twelve to fifteen PCs. Since UNIX is a true multitasking operating system, the 3B2 400 would perform these tasks concurrently. Also, a remote user can utilize a terminal and modem to become part of a UNIX-based STARLAN network. *Figure 7-4* depicts some of the differences between MS-DOS–to–MS-DOS machines and UNIX-to-UNIX machines under STARLAN.

Figure 7-4.
MS-DOS and UNIX
Machines on a
STARLAN Network
(Courtesy of AT&T)

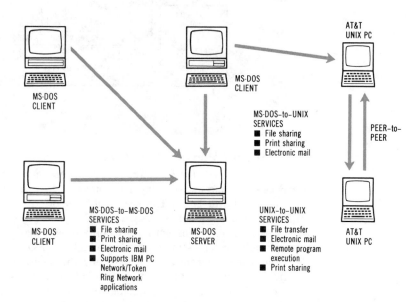

STARLAN SOFTWARE

STARLAN's network software is consistent with the OSI specifications we discussed in Chapter 2. *Figure 7-5* indicates the network's protocol layers. The physical layer is concerned primarily with providing 1-Mbit/s transmission on a baseband network. The medium used is 24-gauge building telephone wiring consisting of two unshielded twisted pairs dedicated to STARLAN. The data link layer regulates this contention network and uses CSMA/CD techniques consistent with IEEE 802.3 standards. The logical link control is consistent with IEEE 802.2 standards and uses LLC Type-1 correctionless protocol.

Between two network endpoints, the network and transport layers create point-to-point connections, including handling flow control. They also control call administration and error handling. Finally, the session layer uses MS-DOS 3.1 protocols to establish sessions with application programs. It has a set of commands enabling it to establish sessions with UNIX-based computers running under STARLAN.

Figure 7-5.
STARLAN Protocol
Layers *(Courtesy of AT&T)*

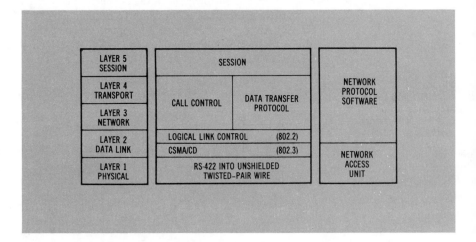

STARLAN Packet Structure

As we noted earlier, in our discussion of the OSI standards, the packet for one network layer becomes part of the information field of the next lower layer. The MAC sublayer of STARLAN follows the IEEE 802.3 standards. As we see in *Figure 7-6,* the media-access control (MAC) frame begins with a preamble to synchronize receiver and transmitter. The start-of-frame Delimiter (SFD) lets the hardware know when the synchronization is over and the message begins. The address field consists of both a destination address and a source address. The length field indicates the number of octets in the LLC data portion of the packet. User data is found in the next field, the LLC data area. The Packet Address Destination (PAD) pads any packets that fall below the acceptable minimum of sixty-four octets of information. Finally, the Frame-Check Sequence (FCS) detects errors so that the MAC layer can discard defective packets.

**Figure 7-6.
MAC Frame**

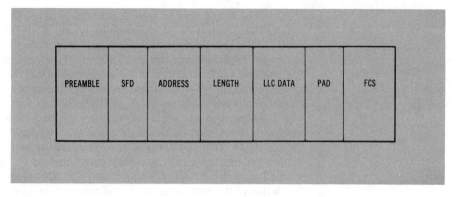

| PREAMBLE | SFD | ADDRESS | LENGTH | LLC DATA | PAD | FCS |

Using STARLAN

STARLAN's network software is similar to IBM's PC Network Program in that both programs are designed to be as easy to use for beginners as possible. Both DOS 3.1-based programs offer experienced network users the opportunity to use DOS commands to access the network and even permit the creation of DOS batch files to customize operations. Both programs also offer beginners the opportunity to perform virtually all major network functions through the use of menus.

All STARLAN commands are classified under administration services, file-sharing services, or printer-sharing services. The login and logout commands along with commands to modify passwords, view statistics, and add and remove users are found under administration (AD). To log on under STARLAN, the user provides the category of command (AD), the actual command, a DOS path, and the password:

LOGIN AD \ \ servername \ username
/PASS=password

To give several consecutive commands for the same command service, the user can use command prompts in order to avoid typing the command service repeatedly. Typing the command service and pressing <ENTER> yields the prompt (AD, FS, or PS) and now the user can enter the commands. For instance, if the user wants to login and then get help on how to use the ADDUSER command, he or she would type the following:

AD> login \ \ servername \ user /pass=password help adduser

Rather than using command prompts, the user can choose to respond to STARLAN's prompts by typing a command prefix and the command name and pressing <RETURN>. For example, a user who types AD LOGIN <RETURN> will be prompted by STARLAN to supply the file-server name, the user name, and a password if needed. By using network prompts a new user can enjoy the faster network operation (rather than going through several menus) without needing to memorize all the network command structure.

All STARLAN commands are classified as administration services, file-sharing services, or printer-sharing services. You can enter commands either by typing a command string, by using command prompts, by responding to network prompts, or by using menus.

The fourth way to enter commands is to use the STARLAN menus. These menus can be accessed by typing MENUS. *Figure 7-7* shows the STARLAN main menu display. Notice that a command bar displays the commands available from this menu (Open, Transfer, Close, Window, Quit). The line below this is known as the subcommand bar and contains subcommands or, when there are none, descriptions of commands. A window indicates the items to be selected. The last line contains the screen label keys that indicate which function key to press for a particular command. Notice that on this main menu only two function keys (F5 and F8) are active. The commands on the command bar and the items in the window can be accessed by using the cursor arrows (<UP>, <DOWN>, <LEFT>, and <RIGHT>). Commands can also be entered by typing the first letter of the command, as seen in the command bar, followed by pressing <RETURN>. To open a highlighted file, for example, a user types O followed by <RETURN>.

Figure 7-7.
STARLAN Menu

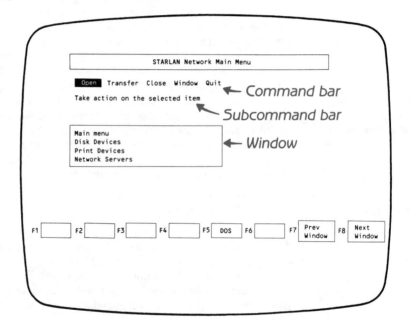

File Sharing

On the file server each user has a personal home directory which may be protected with a password. Upon logging on to STARLAN, a user needs to establish a link between workstation and home directory. Note that a user can only log on to one file server at a time. Use of STARLAN's FS LINK command establishes this connection.

Since one of the major advantages of a network is the ability to share files, STARLAN offers a number of options in this area. You can copy files from your home directory to another user's directory or a subdirectory. To share files, the subdirectory must be shared with other users by using the FS SHARE command. In most cases, you would eliminate use of a password or you'd use a password different from your personal password. The final option for sharing information is to share your home directory. The principal disadvantage of sharing files in your home directory is that other users then have to know your password in order to link their directories with yours; thus, you lose your security.

It is possible to establish various levels of access to files on a file server. The four levels of shared file access under STARLAN are read, write, create, and exclusive. The exclusive option prevents two users from trying simultaneously to update a file and thus wiping out valuable information. The network administrator normally establishes the access level. These options are outlined in *Table 7-1*.

**Table 7-1.
Levels of STARLAN
Shared Access**

Key	Access	Meaning
R	Read	Files in a shared directory can be read
W	Write	Files in a shared directory can be written to
C	Create	Files can be created in a shared directory
E	Exclusive	Only one user at a time can access a shared file

After placing material in a directory or subdirectory so that it may be shared, the user must provide a share name and pathway. Let's assume that Georgia has created a subdirectory called REGMTG in her home directory. This material contains the budget she is developing for a regional meeting. While Georgia wants to share this information with others in her group, she wants to keep her working copy from being changed. The solution is to create a subdirectory called REGPROJT using the DOS command MKDIR (make directory):

```
MKDIR E: \ REGPROJT
```

The next step is to copy the contents of the subdirectory REGMTG over to this new subdirectory using the DOS COPY command:

```
COPY C: REGMTG D: \ REGPROJT
C> FS SHARE \ REGPROJT
```

STARLAN will want to know a sharename—a name by which users will access this shared subdirectory. Georgia decides on BUDGET.

```
Sharename? BUDGET
    \ \ SERVER1 \ GEORGIA \ REGMTG shared as GEORGIA \ BUDGET.
```

At the moment anyone on the STARLAN network can share this file. If Georgia wants to limit access, she could use the FS MOD command and create a password:

```
FS MOD BUDGET/PASS=password
    \ \ SERVER1 \ GEORGIA \ BUDGET modified
```

It is always possible to see a list of shared directories on a network by using the FS DIR command:

```
C> FS DIR
Object list for \ SERVER1 \ *...
GEORGIA C: \ USER /HOME 0 links
TAX C: \ TAX /RWC 0 links
```

File Server Administration Under STARLAN

Perhaps because STARLAN is designed as an inexpensive easy-to-use network, it lacks many of the network management features found in Novell NetWare and IBM's Token Ring Network. STARLAN doesn't come with a program for backing up the file server. But since the program runs under DOS 3.1, it isn't difficult to write batch files, giving them descriptive names (DAILY.BK, WEEKLY.BK, MONTHLY.BK), that can be run to copy files to a tape backup unit.

STARLAN does provide some administrative help for the harried network supervisor. Its NAU Statistics program displays data and verifies connectivity between two workstations. This program is primarily concerned with providing statistics on data collisions and total activity. The program displays a data screen that gives such information as the number of CRC errors, the number of collisions, the number of collision aborts and retransmissions, and the number of total writes compared with the number of writes lost. Helping to compile traffic statistics and to troubleshoot, it can be a valuable tool for the network supervisor. In Chapter 11 we'll look at some more specific backup concerns a network supervisor should consider and the type of additional recordkeeping necessary to ensure effective network operation.

Because STARLAN has been developed primarily as a departmental network solution and not as a network designed to handle a large company's needs, some logistical problems occur that add time to an administrator's network management. To shut down a STARLAN network with several file servers, a network supervisor has to log on to a file server, use an AD STOP command to halt operations, log out, and repeat this procedure on all the other file servers.

Security Under STARLAN

A network supervisor can have STARLAN require a password from each user logging on and can establish passwords using the MOD command for directories and for peripherals such as printers. Finally, STARLAN transmits its information in encrypted form providing one additional measure of security.

Sharing Printers Under STARLAN

STARLAN permits the sharing of two parallel printers (LPT1 and LPT2) and a serial printer (COM1). The printer-sharing services commands are virtually identical to the file-sharing services commands. To share a printer on the network, use the PS SHARE command and to link it to a user's workstation use the PS LINK command:

```
C> PS SHARE PRINTER=LPT2
\ SERVER1 \ LPT2: shared as PRINTER
C> PS LINK PRINTER
PRN: linked to \ \ SERVER \ PRINTER.
C>
```

Use the PS UNLINK command to remove printers from the network. To stop a printer in order to replace a ribbon or repair a paper jam, use the PS STOP command:

```
C> PS STOP PRINTER
\ \ SERVER1 \ PRINTER stopped.
```

As you would expect, to re-start a printer requires the RESUME PRINTER command:

```
C> PS RESUME PRINTER
\ \ SERVER1 \ PRINTER resumed.
```

ELECTRONIC MAIL ON A STARLAN NETWORK

STARLAN doesn't provide electronic mail, but the service is available to users who add the Network Courier program. A network supervisor can install this program easily with the use of an FS ASHARE command to share Courier's subdirectory with the other network users. Each user has a mailbox with a personal password. Courier provides users with the ability to retrieve mail, delete mail, and send mail. Let's observe how a user might use STARLAN's menus to send a message through the Courier program.

We'll assume the program has been installed on drive P (for post office) on a file server named ADMIN. The first step is to link your network workstation with the program:

```
FS LINK P: \ \ ADMIN
\ COURIER
```

Our network user has a mailbox named GEORGIAM and a password FRISKIE (her dog). She types the following:

```
P:MAIL <RETURN>
GEORGIAM <RETURN>
FRISKIE <RETURN>
```

Now Georgia examines the Courier menu and selects (by highlighting) COMPOSE before pressing <RETURN>. Then she selects EDIT and presses <RETURN>. Now Courier needs to know who the recipient of this message will be so it displays a list of current network users. Georgia selects LARRYJ and indicates to Courier that the subject of her message will be Regional meeting on March 15th.

Courier displays a blank window for Georgia to use to write her message. When she finishes, she presses <ESC>, highlights the TRANSMIT option, and presses <RETURN>. Since this is the only electronic mail function Georgia wants to perform, she presses the <ESC> key to exit the program. Courier prompts whether she really wants to exit, she highlights YES, and presses <RETURN>. Georgia unlinks her workstation from the P drive:

```
FS UNLINK P: <RETURN>
```

When you link with the Network Courier program, a beep indicates that you have mail waiting. By highlighting READ and then MESSAGE FROM FRANKP, you'll see Frank's message displayed on your screen. Among the options available to you after reading the message are replying to it, saving the message, and deleting it.

While Network Courier is not as sophisticated as 3Com's 3+Mail and doesn't offer such features as remote access and internetwork mail, it is perfectly adequate for most small companies or departments with under twenty users. It provides fast, inexpensive mail service that can reduce paperwork and improve communication.

STARLAN AND INFORMATION SYSTEMS NETWORK (ISN)

At first glance, STARLAN appears to be an effective, inexpensive network for a department or small business, but of limited value to a larger company. AT&T provides a growth path for companies that need more sophisticated network functions. Information Systems Network (ISN) is a high-speed network capable of providing integrated voice and data transmission as well as providing interfaces to PBXs, IBM mainframes, Ethernet LANs, and its own STARLAN networks. *Figure 7-8* shows the ways that ISN can integrate communications for a large company.

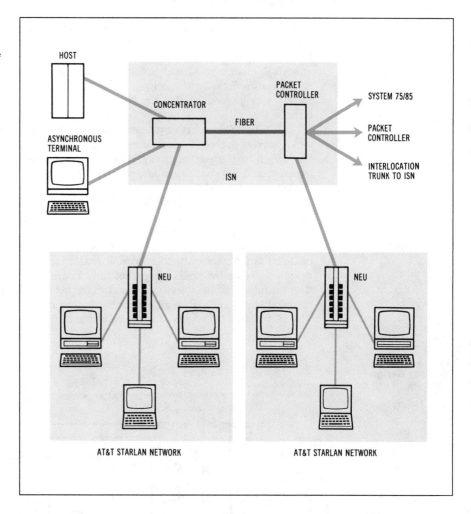

**Figure 7-8.
ISN Links STARLAN
Networks, PBXs, and
Mainframes** *(Courtesy of
AT&T)*

AT&T offers a STARLAN Interface Module (SIM) to connect
STARLAN networks via its ISN. This option increases the effective
distance for a STARLAN from 800 to several thousand feet. Each SIM has
two jacks that can be used to connect workstations on a STARLAN
network or to an NEU located on an ISN concentrator or packet controller.
The SIMs come in two versions. The B version provides a bridge between
multiple STARLAN networks through ISN while the C version provides a
connection between STARLAN nodes and RS232 devices that are not on
the STARLAN network but are on ISN. So an AT&T 6300 workstation on
a STARLAN network, for example, could access a 3B2 computer on ISN.

The heart of ISN is a *packet controller* that acts as a switch and
management center. Concentrators collect data from host computers,
STARLANs, and other devices and pass this data to the packet controller
through multiplexed channels, each composed of a pair of optical fiber. ISN

breaks down messages to very short packets (18 envelopes of 10 bits of data) and interleaves the packets into a sequence of time slots on the transmission bus. The transmission across this short bus is so fast that in effect ISN maintains virtual circuits or direct links between communicating devices with virtually no blocking. An ISN packet controller can support up to 1200 simultaneous virtual circuits, more than enough for most large businesses.

The ISN packet controller contains three buses: the transmit bus, which carries packets from sending modules to the switch; the receiving bus, which carries packets away from the switch to device interface modules; and the contention bus, which determines the order of access to the transmit bus.

As *Figure 7-9* illustrates, under ISN all modules having data packets ready to send compete with each other for access to a time slot on the transmit bus. Each module transmits its own contention code to the contention bus 1 bit at a time. If the module recognizes that another module has a higher contention code, it ceases transmitting. The winning module accesses the next data packet time slot on the transmit bus. The data modules that have lost this round have their contention numbers raised at this point and begin competing for the next available time slot. The ISN switch is capable of a maximum switching rate of 48,000 packets per second.

Figure 7-9.
ISN Bus Design
(Courtesy of AT&T)

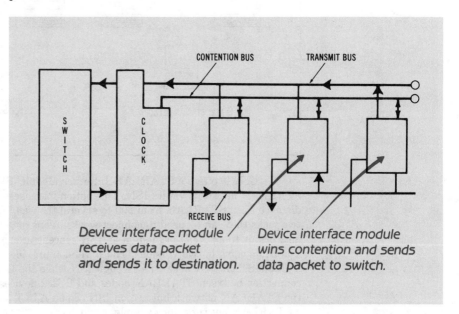

Figure 7-10 illustrates some of the interfaces available through ISN. In addition to linking STARLAN networks, with the proper protocol ISN users can interface directly with asynchronous hosts or IBM 3270 terminals, thus eliminating the need for costly cluster controllers. Users can

establish two sessions per terminal and switch between applications. Each protocol converter on the network contains seven asynchronous ports and one synchronous port. ISN supports Type A coaxial cable at 2.358 Mbit/s as well as IBM 3278/9 and 3178/9 terminals.

Figure 7-10.
ISN Interfaces *(Courtesy of AT&T)*

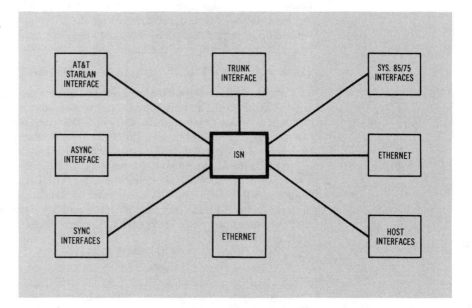

A company with several departments might find it cost effective to tie together several departmental STARLAN networks and use ISN to enable all network users to communicate with distant company IBM mainframes. ISN supports both a BSC and an SNA/SDLC interface. The synchronous traffic can share T1 facilities with an AT&T System 75/85 telephone system, thus eliminating expensive long-distance modems.

ISN also offers an Ethernet bridge consistent with IEEE 802.3 baseband network standards. Companies with Ethernet networks that are too far apart to communicate through direct cabling can communicate through ISN. The ISN Ethernet bridge is a 10-Mbit/s CSMA/CD module that terminates the physical and data link layers of the OSI model. It supports Transmission Control Protocol/Internet Protocol (TCP/IP) as well as Xerox Network System (XNS) devices.

ISN and Network Management

ISN is a star topology just like STARLAN. As we saw earlier, star architecture networks usually provide excellent diagnostic reports and management tools. Because of ISN's star topology it is able to provide detailed traffic and performance statistics. It also makes adding new users easy; the network supervisor simply assigns a new device to an unused port and gives it an address.

The negative side of star topology networks has always been the danger that the entire network will collapse with the collapse of the central processor. ISN provides a measure of protection by utilizing non-volatile memory for its storage of configuration and fault data. In the event of a power failure, it utilizes automatic system recovery when power is restored. It also monitors the functioning of various modules, including the control processor, and reports faulty modules with an indication of the type of module, a description of the faults, and the time they occurred.

ISDN AND AT&T's VOICE/DATA INTEGRATION

In Chapter 3 we examined integrated services digital network (ISDN) architecture and discussed how these standards eventually would result in an office automation revolution. ISDN standards define a digital interface that is divided into B and D channels. B channels are capable of carrying voice, data, and video signals while D channels carry signaling and control information to manage the network. Furthermore, ISDN postulated two types of interface, the basic-rate interface (BRI) and the primary-rate interface (PRI). Although BRI is designed for small-capacity devices such as terminals and PRI is designed for large-capacity devices such as PBXs, both interfaces carry one D channel and several B channels. The B channels transmit at 64 Kbit/s each for both BRI and PRI while the D channels transmit at 16 Kbit/s for BRI and 64 Kbit/s for PRI.

Imagine an office with a STARLAN network and an AT&T System 75 PBX phone system using AT&T's ISN. Let's assume that a network user needs to send a voice message accompanied by a video display and several data files to another user. Using ISDN standards on AT&T's ISN, the user's premises equipment (PBX and data terminal) transmit signals to establish communications with the network. Once the link is established, the video, voice, and data are sent in digital form into the network using its B channels. The network in turn sends this information to the addressee.

As the leader in network integration, AT&T is also a leader in following the ISDN guidelines although its equipment doesn't precisely match all these standards. AT&T's equivalent of PRI is the bit-oriented signaling (BOS) of its digital multiplexed interface (DMI) and its equivalent of BRI is the bit-oriented signaling of its digital communication protocol (DCP). *Figure 7-11* illustrates AT&T's approach to integration of its services following the general ISDN guidelines. An example of ISDN in action, which AT&T likes to cite as an illustration of what we can expect in the future, is its E911 service. When a customer calls the emergency 911 number, the call is routed to an operator who sees the caller's telephone number and address appear automatically on the console screen. A computer has searched a very large database, recovered the key customer information, and transmitted it to the operator's screen while simultaneously routing the voice signal there. In the future, offices will be able to link their networks with several other kinds of networks in a transparent manner to the network user. *Figure 7-12* summarizes how ISN integrates these networks into a coherent system.

**Figure 7-11.
AT&T Premises-
Switched ISDN
Architecture** *(Courtesy of
AT&T)*

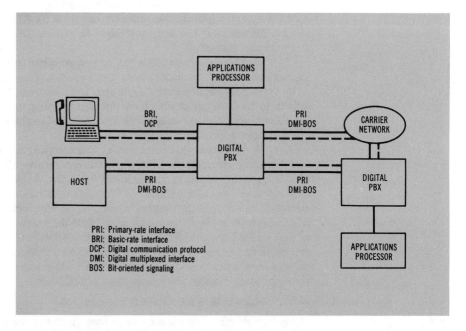

**Figure 7-12.
AT&T Communications
Interexchange Carrier
ISDN Architecture**
(Courtesy of AT&T)

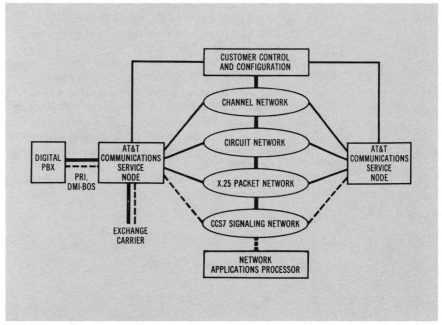

Another example of how AT&T is integrating voice and data applications in the modern office is its use of Unified Messaging Systems (UMS). A company with UMS probably also has a PBX system such as

AT&T's System 75/85. It also probably has AT&T's AUDIX voice-mail service. Managers in this company might use Office Telesystem (OTS) to link with the UMS.

Employees in this office can choose whether to read their messages on their terminals or hear them spoken. They can reply by voice or by typing the replies at the keyboard. Let's assume that an employee calls in to retrieve her or his phone messages. Using such AT&T supplementary products as Mailtalk or Speak-To-Me the employee can hear the messages spoken by a computer.

We indicated that managers at this company utilize OTS. OTS uses the same structure as UMS so that it can receive UMS messages, but it adds a number of handy management functions. Available for up to a hundred users, an AT&T 6300 or AT&T 3B2 user can let OTS provide an electronic calendar with resource scheduling. It also handles the user's telephone management by providing multiple directories and speed dialing as well as enabling the user to write telephone memos. OTS offers a text processor and access to external databases. AT&T hopes to be able to expand services such as these to provide a truly integrated office where voice and data messages are exchanged effortlessly.

WHAT HAVE WE LEARNED?

1. A STARLAN network can daisy-chain up to ten workstations with one node serving as the file server.
2. STARLAN follows the CSMA/CD protocol. It transmits data at 1 Mbit/s.
3. STARLAN networks can handle a single room (Room Star) or several offices in a company (Closet Star).
4. STARLAN software includes three types of commands: administration services, file-sharing services, and printer-sharing services.
5. STARLAN network security consists of a LOGIN password, password requirements for using a directory or subdirectory, and data encryption.
6. Several STARLAN networks can be connected using information systems network (ISN) and the STARLAN interface module (SIM).
7. The ISN packet controller utilizes a transmit bus, a receiving bus, and a contention bus.
8. Under ISDN guidelines, a user can transmit voice, data, and video signals simultaneously.

Quiz for Chapter 7

1. STARLAN permits up to ten workstations to be daisy-chained in what kind of network architecture?
   - **a.** Star.
   - **b.** Bus.
   - **c.** Ring.
   - **d.** Token Ring.

2. The expansion bus of each STARLAN workstation must contain:
   - **a.** at least 640K.
   - **b.** a network expansion unit (NEU).
   - **c.** a network access unit (NAU).
   - **d.** a network interface unit (NIU).

3. STARLAN follows the IEEE 802.3 guidelines for avoiding data collisions using
   - **a.** CSMA/CD.
   - **b.** packets.
   - **c.** tokens.
   - **d.** one-way communications.

4. To connect different offices within the same building, a STARLAN would use:
   - **a.** coaxial cable.
   - **b.** a wiring closet.
   - **c.** network interface units.
   - **d.** an analog phone signal.

5. A network interface unit used with STARLAN contains:
   - **a.** two serial ports.
   - **b.** one serial port and one parallel port.
   - **c.** two parallel ports.
   - **d.** three serial ports and one parallel port.

6. Under STARLAN which of the following can be used as file servers?
   - **a.** AT&T UNIX PC.
   - **b.** AT&T 6300, 6300 Plus, and IBM compatibles.
   - **c.** AT&T 3B2.
   - **d.** All of the above.

7. STARLAN will only work with which version of DOS?
   - **a.** DOS 2.1.
   - **b.** DOS 3.0.
   - **c.** DOS 3.1.
   - **d.** DOS 2.2.

8. To connect more than ten workstations in a STARLAN network it is necessary to use a:
   - **a.** network cable connection (NCC).
   - **b.** network interface unit (NIU).
   - **c.** network repeater unit (NRU).
   - **d.** network expansion unit (NEU).

9. More than a hundred workstations can be connected in a STARLAN network by using a network expansion unit connected to:
   - **a.** other network expansion units.
   - **b.** ten daisy-chained workstations.
   - **c.** network repeater units (NRU).
   - **d.** network interface units (NIU).

10. The practical limit when daisy-chaining workstations under STARLAN is:
    - **a.** 200 ft (60 m).
    - **b.** 400 ft (120 m).
    - **c.** 600 ft (200 m).
    - **d.** 800 ft (240 m).

11. Using a network expansion unit a STARLAN network can extend a maximum of:
   a. 400 ft (120 m).
   b. 800 ft (240 m).
   c. 1000 ft (300 m).
   d. 1200 ft (400 m).

12. STARLAN workstations are connected using:
   a. two twisted unshielded pair of 24-gauge telephone wire.
   b. coaxial cable.
   c. fiber optic cable.
   d. data grade cable.

13. Under STARLAN, a user may log in to:
   a. one file server at a time.
   b. only two file servers at a time.
   c. only three file servers at a time.
   d. an unlimited number of file servers.

14. To protect files from being destroyed by two people trying simultaneously to write to them, STARLAN lets shared files be:
   a. write only.
   b. read only.
   c. create.
   d. exclusive.

15. The electronic mail program that works on STARLAN is known as:
   a. AT&T Mail.
   b. Electronic Messenger.
   c. Network Courier.
   d. Postman.

16. Two STARLAN networks can be connected through ISN by using:
   a. coaxial cable.
   b. STARLAN Interface Module (SIM).
   c. ISN interface.
   d. broadband cabling.

17. Under ISDN, control signals are transmitted using:
   a. the one D channel.
   b. any one of the several B channels.
   c. a special C channel for control.
   d. a token-passing protocol.

18. For limited devices, ISDN has established:
   a. BRI.
   b. PRI.
   c. DRIP.
   d. SIP.

19. For large devices such as PBXs, ISDN has established:
   a. BRI.
   b. PRI.
   c. DRIP.
   d. SIP.

20. The heart of ISN is a:
   a. microprocessor.
   b. packet controller.
   c. analog switch.
   d. cardiac coil.

Corvus's Local Area Network

ABOUT THIS CHAPTER

Corvus has been supplying local area networks for a number of years. The company has developed its own personal computers and workstations designed for optimal network performance. In this chapter we'll survey Corvus network hardware and software and examine some of the features that differentiate these products from the other major networks. Corvus is one of the few companies that makes network products designed for various computers, including Apple, IBM, and IBM compatibles. While our focus will be on PC/MS-DOS networks, we will discuss the mixing of such diverse systems as Apple's Mackintosh and other CP/M machines on a Corvus Omninet network.

CORVUS DISK SERVERS AND FILE SERVERS

The OmniDrive

The Corvus OmniDrive is a Z-80–based disk server that can support a network composed of IBM PCs and compatibles, the Apple IIe, and the Apple Mackintosh, among others.

Corvus offers both disk servers and file servers. The OmniDrive is a disk server that supports volume-level access. It is designed for companies whose major network consists of application programs, such as word processing and spreadsheets, in which users have their own files. OmniDrive is the only Corvus unit that supports a mixed network consisting of such diverse units as IBM PCs and Apple Mackintosh computers. While this Z-80–based drive is slow compared to the Corvus file servers, its ability to support file transfer between unlike computers and its low price make it a desirable option for many companies. The OmniDrive comes in sizes ranging from 11 Mb to 126 Mb and multiple units may be linked on a network. A Corvus OmniDrive is pictured in *Figure 8-1.*

Figure 8-1.
The Corvus OmniDrive
(Courtesy of Corvus Systems, Inc.)

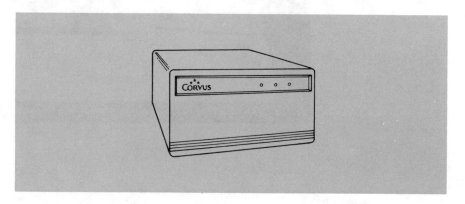

The OmniServer

The Corvus OmniServer is a 80286-based file server that can also function as a stand-alone IBM AT compatible. The OmniServer can serve up to sixty-four network nodes. Its hard disk capacity may be expanded to 126 Mb.

While Corvus permits users to use an IBM PC, XT, AT, or compatible as a file server, network performance increases with the use of its own hardware. The Corvus OmniServer is a high-performance 80286-based file server that includes a built-in 60-Mb streaming tape backup. The unit comes configured with 640K of RAM for network caching and is capable of addressing up to 16 Mb of RAM.

Since the OmniServer is capable of running in both dedicated and non-dedicated modes, it can also be used as a computer. The unit is an IBM PC AT compatible and comes with an AT keyboard, a 5¼-in. floppy disk drive, and a parallel printer port. It also comes standard with a monochrome monitor and high-resolution monochrome display adapter (728 × 348) and eight IBM 16-bit expansion slots, four of which are open. The OmniServer utilizes a 43-Mb hard disk but a 126-Mb drive can be installed. The unit comes with an Omninet interface card designed to handle up to sixty-four nodes on a Corvus network. OmniServers also support Novell software. *Figure 8-2* illustrates the OmniServer's futuristic appearance.

Figure 8-2.
The Corvus OmniServer
(Courtesy of Corvus Systems, Inc.)

The Corvus Series 386

The Corvus Series 386 is an 80386-based file server that can support 32-bit devices as well as emulate an IBM AT. It can run at 16 MHz.

Corvus is the first network manufacturer to offer its own 80386-based file server. The Corvus Series 386 is capable of operating at 6 MHz or 16 MHz. It comes with 512K of RAM with an optional 2-Mb expansion card available. It is capable of handling 16 Mb of 16-bit or 32-bit optional memory. The Series 386 comes with two 8-bit expansion slots, four 16-bit slots, and two 32-bit slots, along with both RS-232 serial and Centronics compatible parallel ports. This file server comes with a standard 70-Mb hard disk drive, a 60-Mb built-in tape unit, and a 1.2-Mb floppy disk drive. The 126-Mb hard disk drive that is available for the OmniServer can be installed in this unit. To increase the speed of this unit even more, it comes with an 80287/80387 numeric coprocessor socket. There are no external physical differences between this unit and the OmniServer in *Figure 8-2*.

Backing Up the Corvus File Servers

Corvus offers an inexpensive tape storage backup unit called "The Bank." This random-access unit, available in 100-Mb and 200-Mb sizes, has a built-in Omninet server and plugs directly into a Corvus network. It is necessary to have an IBM PC or compatible on the network in order to begin the backup program with The Bank. Once the backup has begun, the PC can be used again as a workstation on the network. Corvus has long supported another backup unit called "The Mirror." This device provides video tape backup.

NETWORK WORKSTATIONS

While Corvus supports a variety of computers on its network, it also offers its own network workstations. The 83000 unit is a diskless workstation prepared for network connection. The 84000 workstation resembles an IBM PC XT.

Corvus offers two workstations that are optimized for work on its Omninet network. The Corvus 83000 is a diskless, intelligent workstation utilizing an 8088 microprocessor. It comes with 256K of RAM expandable to a maximum of 640K, and it can utilize an 8087 math coprocessor. Built specifically for distributed processing, this unit comes with five full-length expansion slots and a 55-watt (W) power supply.

Corvus also offers an 84000 model that can function as a stand-alone unit. With eight full-size expansion slots and space for two half-height disk drives (360K floppy, 10-Mb or 20-Mb hard disk), it resembles an IBM PC XT. The unit comes with a 113-W power supply. Users can configure the system with monochrome or RGB color graphics, parallel/serial ports, XT/AT keyboards, and a 60-Mb tape backup unit. What makes these workstations particularly appealing is that they are network efficient and require only an inexpensive Corvus Transporter card to be network ready. *Figure 8-3* illustrates both workstation models.

**Figure 8-3.
The Corvus 80000
Series of Workstations**
*(Courtesy of Corvus
Systems, Inc.)*

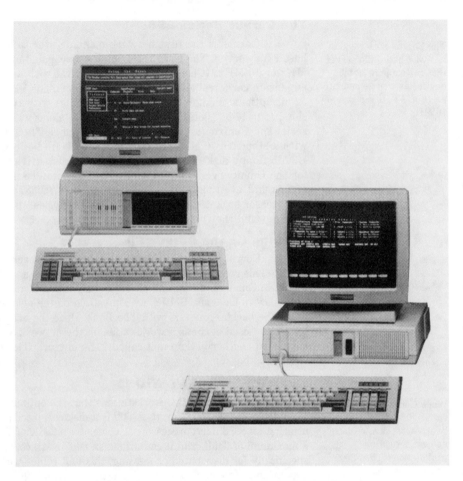

Transporter Cards

A Corvus network
requires that each
workstation have a circuit
card known as a
"Transporter" in its
expansion bus. The
Transporter decodes data
packets, frames data
packets, and transmits
them at 1 Mbit/s along
twisted-pair wire.

Each network workstation must have a Corvus *Transporter* card
installed in one of its expansion ports. Corvus makes a different version of
this circuit card for each computer model that it supports. The circuit card
contains a portion that is host-dependent and provides the interface to the
actual memory bus of the host system. As shown in *Figure 8-4*, Corvus
uses Texas Instruments 75174 and 75175 transceivers to interface the
Transporter to the RS-422 twisted-pair cable. The 75174 translates bits it
receives into differential voltages to be sent through the cable while the
75175 reverses that function and converts the differential voltage from the
cable into bits. The Motorola 6801 functions as the microprocessor for the
Transporter. It contains enough ROM (2K) to hold the instructions that
control the Transporter. The second Motorola chip (6854) functions as the
data link controller. When it receives information packets, the 6854 checks
the CRC and inserts zeros when needed. It also performs packet-framing

tasks when the workstation sends information. The Corvus Monochip provides the synchronization for all data transfers occurring outside of the 6801 microprocessor.

**Figure 8-4.
Transporter Block
Diagram** *(Courtesy of
Corvus Systems, Inc.)*

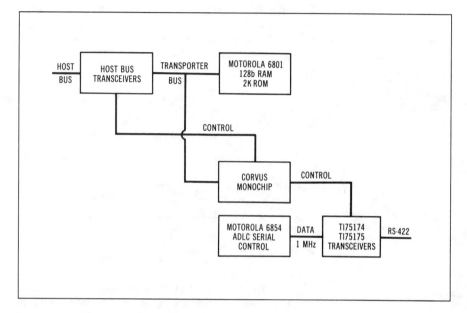

The Transporter Card and CSMA

Omninet doesn't use a single master network controller. Instead, each Transporter uses a carrier-sense multiple access (CSMA) scheme to avoid data collisions. The Transporter first checks the network bus to see if it is idle of traffic. It accomplishes this task by looking for fifteen or more consecutive 1's. If the line is idle, the Transporter begins a 10-microsecond procedure during which it prepares to send its packet. Then it checks once again to see if the line is still idle. It begins transmitting its message if the line is still free, or it generates a random delay count if another Transporter is using the line. Following the delay count, it again checks to see if the line is free. It is unlikely that several Transporters wishing to use a line would generate the same random delay count.

Occasionally, even with these precautions, data collisions will occur because there is a slight delay between the time a Transporter begins sending its message and the time that other Transporters realize that the line is no longer free. When a data collision occurs, the packets that are transmitting at the time are destroyed. We will see shortly how receiving Transporters respond when they realize that a packet has been damaged.

The 6854 chip functioning as a data link controller is responsible for transmitting and interpreting data packets. *Figure 8-5* depicts the standard Omninet packet format. The leading flags enable the receiving Transporter to synchronize its clock with the incoming data. The flag utilizes a pattern of 01111110. As we have seen with other such schemes, the number of consecutive ones here is unique; 0's are inserted in data that might normally require this pattern so that it will not be mistaken for this flag.

Figure 8-5.
Omninet Packet Format
(Courtesy of Corvus Systems, Inc.)

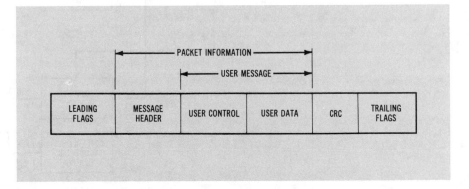

The message header field contains information on the packet's source and destination addresses, the number of times the message has been retransmitted, a parity bit to check for duplicate packets, and information on the length of both the user data and user control fields.

The Transporter doesn't examine the user control portion (0 to 255 bytes as specified in the packet header) or the user data portion (0 to 2047 bytes as specified in the packet header). The 16-bit Cyclic Redundancy Code (CRC) is one of a number of error checks that the Transporter performs. One common algorithm used in Cylic Redundancy Code is to sum all the bits of a message, divide by a specific prime number, and use the remainder for error checking.

The Transporter card also handles such tasks as generation and reception of message acknowledgments, message retransmission, and detection of duplicate messages.

When a Transporter receives a packet, it transmits an acknowledgment packet. If the message has been received successfully, it sends a positive acknowledgment (ACK). It transmits a negative acknowledgment (NAK) if it detects an error. The Transporter then informs the host which signal has been received. If the Transporter receives no reply at all within 20 microseconds, it tries to reacquire the line and retransmit the message. If a Transporter wishes to check to see if another node is functioning, it can send an *echo packet*. If the receiving Transporter is working correctly, it will automatically acknowledge reception of this packet without disturbing the host computer. In effect, the Transporter cards are carrying on their own conversation without any human awareness.

OMNINET ARCHITECTURE AND CABLING

The Corvus Omninet is a bus topology that transmits at 1 Mbit/s. Its maximum length is 1000 ft (300 m) without additional hardware and 4000 ft (1200 m) with Active Junction Boxes.

The Corvus Omninet is a simple bus network transmitting at 1 Mbit/s that can support up to sixty-four nodes for workstations, file servers, and printer servers. It is possible to have multiple file servers on this network. One advantage Omninet offers is that it uses inexpensive unshielded twisted-pair wire that connects through tap cables with each workstation's Transporter card. The bus can extend up to 1000 ft (300 m) without the need for any additional hardware. With the addition of a Corvus *Active Junction Box* it is possible to extend the bus to a maximum of 4000 ft (1200 m). *Figure 8-6* depicts an Omninet network with a variety of computers using Active Junction Boxes to extend beyond 1000 ft (300 m).

Figure 8-6.
An Omninet Network with Active Junction Boxes *(Courtesy of Corvus Systems, Inc.)*

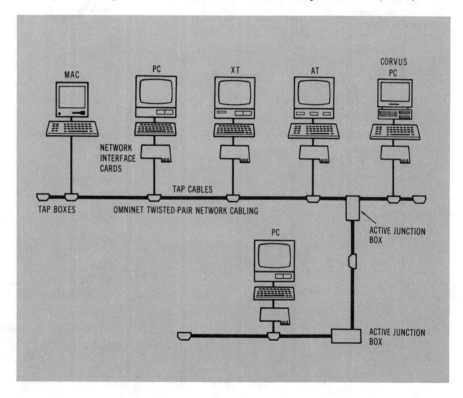

When Is a Bus a Star?

The Omninet Hub is a logical bus that resembles a star architecture. Its star controller can support up to twenty-five branches.

Corvus has developed a way to link workstations in several rooms using telephone cabling. While this approach is still a logical bus, its physical appearance resembles a star. The Corvus Omninet Hub cabling system consists of the hub itself, splitters, and telephone wiring. The hub comes with a Star Controller that can support up to twenty-five network branches, each of which can be up to 1000 ft (300 m) in length. Each branch can have as many as ten workstations as long as the total network doesn't exceed the Corvus maximum of sixty-four workstations. Each workstation is connected to the network through a splitter that is plugged into a standard phone outlet. In effect, the splitter separates the Omninet wire pair from those used for the telephone and provides two outlets, one for the telephone cable and one for the computer cable.

The advantage of the Omninet Hub is that it uses telephone wire already existing within a building to connect workstations that could be separated from each other. Multiple Omninet Hubs can link workstations up to 4000 ft (1200 m) apart. Notice how this approach resembles that taken by IBM with its Token Ring Network wiring closets and AT&T with its STARLAN Closet Star. *Figure 8-7* shows the Omninet Hub.

Figure 8-7.
The Omninet Hub
(Courtesy of Corvus Systems, Inc.)

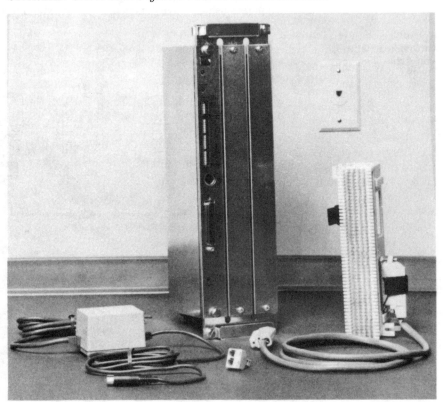

PRINTER SERVERS

A network may dedicate a workstation as a printer server or may select the Utility Server that Corvus offers. Corvus also offers Enhanced Printer-Server software to facilitate network printing.

Up to three printers may be networked with each network file server. While the OmniServer comes with one printer port, additional cards can be installed for a total of one parallel and two serial printer ports. In addition, the network requires a Corvus Utility Server and Enhanced Printer-Server software. The utility software is critical since it provides such network services as automatic queuing of print jobs, multiple copy printing, time stamping of printed documents, and the ability to move a document to the front of the queue if needed.

Corvus offers its own Z-80–based Utility Server, which is designed to share up to three printers with a maximum of sixty-two users. It is possible to add a second Utility Server and share six printers with up to sixty-one workstations. *Figure 8-8* illustrates a Corvus Omninet with different computers sharing printers by means of a Utility Server.

Figure 8-8.
Utility Server on
Omninet *(Courtesy of*
Corvus Systems, Inc.)

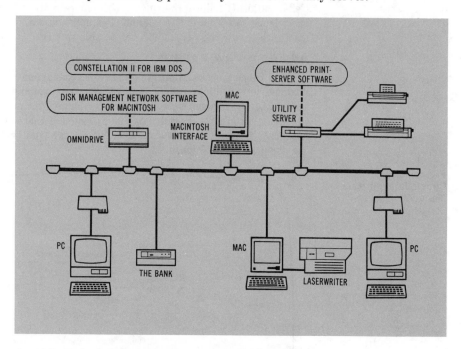

CONSTELLATION NETWORK SOFTWARE

Corvus offers its own network software called "Constellation II." Its major functions are to manage resource sharing of printers and file servers and to facilitate the effective interaction of the various operating systems it supports. It also handles data security, individual workstation management, system maintenance, and system setup. We'll examine how Constellation II handles these tasks.

Storage Management

Just as 3Com's EtherSeries supports older single-user operating systems, Constellation II can also provide this resource-sharing function. It accomplishes this by creating public, private, and shared volumes on its file servers. Private volumes permit individuals to have exclusive read-write use. While all network users are able to read data from a public volume, only one user can write data to such a volume. Shared volumes use a semaphore approach to prevent two users from destroying a common file.

A network administrator must determine how large a volume should be. This usually means counting the number of blocks in each program a user will be storing in the volume and then estimating the amount of data that will be stored. Public volumes save valuable file-server space since several users can share a single program or information file. Constellation II's default value when a volume is created is Read-Write (RW). It is possible to create volumes with a general-access type of Read-Write (RW) and limit a specific user or users to Read-Only (RO) access. Constellation II follows the rule that the more restrictive access type takes precedence. So, if an entire volume is established with Read-Only access, a user with read-write access will not be able to write to the volume.

Adding a New Volume

Since Constellation II is a network management program based on volumes, let's see how easy it is to create a new volume on a Corvus network using this software. We begin by logging on to the network. Constellation II asks for our name and, assuming that the name is a legitimate network user, it then asks for a password. The program displays the menu shown in *Figure 8-9.*

Figure 8-9.
Constellation II Main
Menu *(Courtesy of Corvus Systems, Inc.)*

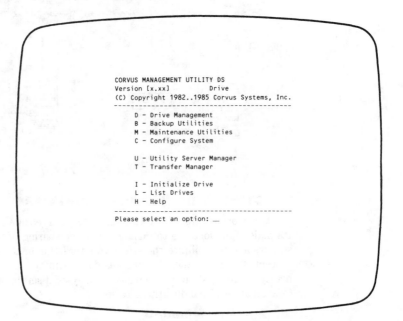

```
CORVUS MANAGEMENT UTILITY DS
Version [x.xx]          Drive
(C) Copyright 1982..1985 Corvus Systems, Inc.
-----------------------------------------------
     D - Drive Management
     B - Backup Utilities
     M - Maintenance Utilities
     C - Configure System

     U - Utility Server Manager
     T - Transfer Manager

     I - Initialize Drive
     L - List Drives
     H - Help
-----------------------------------------------
Please select an option: _
```

From the Main menu display we select D, for Drive Management. We'll now see a Drive Management menu which offers a number of options including U (User/Device Manager), V (Volume Manager), A (Access Manager), B (Boot Manager), S (Select Drive), L (List Drives) and E (Exit). We select V since we wish to create a new volume and should see the Volume Manager menu, shown in *Figure 8-10.*

Figure 8-10.
Volume Manager Menu
(Courtesy of Corvus Systems, Inc.)

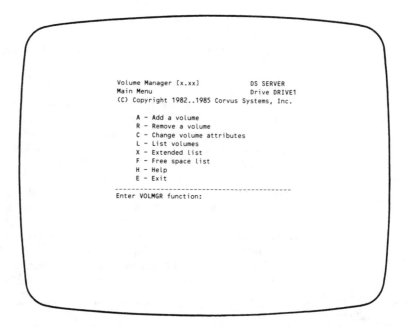

```
Volume Manager [x.xx]          DS SERVER
Main Menu                      Drive DRIVE1
(C) Copyright 1982..1985 Corvus Systems, Inc.

     A - Add a volume
     R - Remove a volume
     C - Change volume attributes
     L - List volumes
     X - Extended list
     F - Free space list
     H - Help
     E - Exit
-------------------------------------------------
Enter VOLMGR function:
```

We want to add a volume. Constellation II asks for the name of the volume (ten characters or fewer). The program assumes that we want an MS-DOS type of file and asks if this choice is acceptable. We're using IBM PCs and compatibles on the network, so we press the <RETURN> key to accept this choice. Constellation II keeps track of the size of its volumes in terms of blocks of 512 bytes. It automatically suggests a volume size of 1024 blocks although the maximum size we may select is 65,000 blocks. For our particular volume, 1024 is large enough, so we press the <RETURN> key to accept Constellation II's suggestion.

Constellation II then suggests a location of a free area on the file server that can serve as the address for our volume. (The program has scanned its drives and determined that this is the first location with enough room to handle the number of blocks in our volume.) We accept the program's suggestion by pressing <RETURN>. A new volume must be initialized in order to be used with the selected operating system (MS-DOS in this case) so Constellation II asks if we wish to initialize the volume (Y/N). When we press <RETURN> the program performs this step. In order to initialize an MS-DOS volume, Constellation II asks us a series of questions about the MS-DOS attributes we wish to have in this volume. In most cases, we can just accept its suggestions for MS-DOS attributes and press <RETURN>. The Corvus *Network Manager's Guide to the IBM PC* offers suggestions for determining which attributes to accept and which to change.

We cannot easily change a volume's size, location, or type once it has been initialized; to effect a change, we must copy all files to floppy disks, create a new volume, and then transfer the old files back to the new volume.

Granting User Access

We have just created a volume, but as of yet no one can use it because we have not granted users access to it. The Access Manager program enables a network administrator to perform this task. As the network administrator, we provide a password, select Grant Volume Access from the Access Manager menu, and the program asks for the volume name. We need to indicate who has access and what type of access they have. For a public volume, we select Read-Only (RO) access. We then *mount* the volume, making it an active network volume. Constellation II responds by assigning the volume a unit number with the default value of 2. The network software mounts the volume on the first drive available after units are assigned for floppy or hard disk drives. Access Manager provides a menu option to list all volumes for which a user has access. *Figure 8-11* illustrates how this information is displayed.

Figure 8-11.
A Listing of Volume Access *(Courtesy of Corvus Systems, Inc.)*

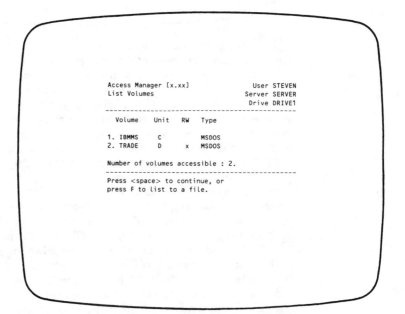

```
Access Manager [x.xx]                    User STEVEN
List Volumes                             Server SERVER
                                         Drive DRIVE1
----------------------------------------------------------
   Volume    Unit   RW   Type

1. IBMMS       C          MSDOS
2. TRADE       D     x    MSDOS

Number of volumes accessible : 2.
----------------------------------------------------------
Press <space> to continue, or
press F to list to a file.
```

The network administrator has a few limited tools for ensuring network security. In addition to the password that can be required upon login, access to volumes can be limited to read-only. Finally, the Access Manager program usually can only be accessed through use of a password by the network administrator, who is called IBMUSER. Without accessing this program, it is impossible to grant users access to the volume.

DATA SHARING ON AN OMNINET NETWORK

Constellation II doesn't offer automatic record-locking or file-locking procedures such as are offered by Novell's NetWare. If two network users try to access a file and both have read-write access, there's a good chance that some information will be destroyed as one user overwrites the other's data. So Corvus offers two ways for users to share information without this danger—semaphores and the PIPES volume. We'll examine both methods since data sharing is one of the major reasons companies install local area networks.

Semaphores

A semaphore is a signal, a flag that is set by an application program to indicate that a user is writing information to a particular volume or file. When a semaphore is set, the volume or file is locked to prevent a second user from writing to it. When the first user completes work, the semaphore is automatically unlocked and the next user may write to the particular volume or file.

On the Corvus Omninet, semaphore locking and unlocking amounts to a programming job for the network administrator. Information on this subject is found only in the *Network Manager's Guide* and not in the *Network User's Guide* that Corvus supplies. After writing a program that contains semaphores, the network administrator can select the Maintenance Utilities program and the menu shown in *Figure 8-12* will be displayed.

Figure 8-12.
Constellation II Utilities
Menu *(Courtesy of*
Corvus Systems, Inc.)

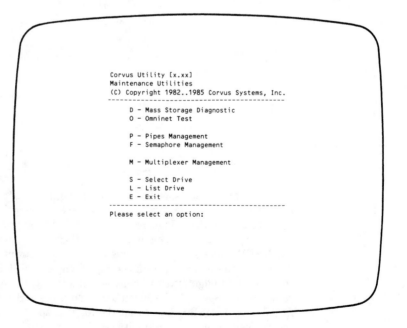

```
Corvus Utility [x.xx]
Maintenance Utilities
(C) Copyright 1982..1985 Corvus Systems, Inc.
---------------------------------------------
       D - Mass Storage Diagnostic
       O - Omninet Test

       P - Pipes Management
       F - Semaphore Management

       M - Multiplexer Management

       S - Select Drive
       L - List Drive
       E - Exit
---------------------------------------------
Please select an option:
```

The semaphore management options include Display Active Semaphores, Lock a Semaphore, Unlock a Semaphore, Clear All Semaphores, and Exit. Locked semaphores remain so until they are unlocked using that option. This process does require programming skills, a burden on the network administrator that network software such as 3Com's EtherSeries shelters users from.

Pipes

Constellation II enables the network administrator to set up a special area on the OmniDrive, a volume labeled PIPES, to act as a holding area for files before they are sent to a network printer or to another computer. Constellation II has a spooling program that can be used in conjunction with a *pipe name* for the file being sent. By typing d:SPOOL and pressing <RETURN> a network user can see the menu pictured in *Figure 8-13*.

Figure 8-13.
Spool Utility Menu
(Courtesy of Corvus Systems, Inc.)

```
Corvus Spool Utility [x.xx]
Main Menu
---------------------------
S - Spool A File

C - Change Spool Parameters

D - Display Pipes

H - Help

E - Exit
---------------------------
Please select an option _
```

In effect we spool a file so that another user can receive it just as a file would be spooled to a printer. We select Change Spool Parameters in order to change the default pipe-name setting. *Figure 8-14* displays the Change Spool Parameters menu. Notice that the current pipe name is PRINTER. Unless we change this name to a non-printer name, the file will be spooled to the printer with the pipe name PRINTER. If we want to send the file Budget.Txt to Sue, we would give it the pipe name Sue and return to the Spool Utility menu and then press <S> in order to send the file. We would let Sue know that the file was spooled under the pipe name Sue so that she could retrieve it.

**Figure 8-14.
Change Spool
Parameters Menu**
*(Courtesy of Corvus
Systems, Inc.)*

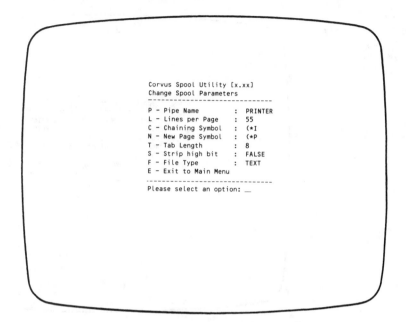

```
Corvus Spool Utility [x.xx]
Change Spool Parameters
--------------------------------
P - Pipe Name          : PRINTER
L - Lines per Page     : 55
C - Chaining Symbol    : (*I
N - New Page Symbol    : (*P
T - Tab Length         : 8
S - Strip high bit     : FALSE
F - File Type          : TEXT
E - Exit to Main Menu
--------------------------------
Please select an option: _
```

In order to retrieve a spooled file a user needs to use the despooling program. First the user selects the Display Pipes option from the Spool Utility menu to see if the file is already there and ready; a file that has finished spooling is shown to be "closed." To enter the despool program, the user types d:DESPOOL, where d represents the drive letter for the IBMMS utility program, and presses <RETURN>. The Constellation Despool Utility menu offers the options to Despool a File, Change Despool Parameters, Help, and Exit. The user selects C for Change Despool Parameters.

The Change Despool Utility Menu shown in *Figure 8-15* shows that the pipe name is PRINTER. The user needs to press P and <RETURN> in order to change the name to that under which the file was spooled. The user then indicates where to despool the file. He or she selects the Output Device option and is then asked to select Printer, File, or Console. The printer indicated here is a local printer attached directly to the user's computer. File is the normal selection since a file that has been despooled to a printer or console cannot be despooled later to a file. Constellation II displays the information shown in *Figure 8-16*. Here we have used the same despooled filename (BUDGET.TXT) as the spooled filename. We could have selected a different name. We now can exit the program since the despooling has taken place.

**Figure 8-15.
Change Despool Utility
Menu** *(Courtesy of
Corvus Systems,
Inc.)*

```
Corvus Despool Utility [x.xx]
Change Despool Parameters
--------------------------------------------
P - Pipe name                     : PRINTER
O - Output device                 : PRINTER
L - Do you want <LF> after <CR>   : YES
T - Transparent despool of data   : NO
S - Single page printing          : NO
E - Exit to main menu
--------------------------------------------
Please select an option: _
```

**Figure 8-16.
Verifying Despooling
Pipe Name** *(Courtesy of
Corvus Systems, Inc.)*

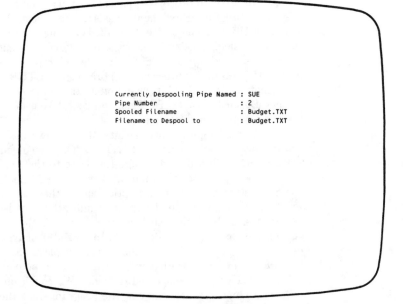

```
Currently Despooling Pipe Named : SUE
Pipe Number                     : 2
Spooled Filename                : Budget.TXT
Filename to Despool to          : Budget.TXT
```

Printing Files on a Corvus Network

The spooling program we just described is an ideal way to send
files from one user to another, but it is far too complex to use for routine
printing. Most application programs that have printing options will send

their print files to a network printer under Constellation II software. Some programs, though, take liberties with MS-DOS and BIOS system calls and bypass normal software channels to go directly to a local printer. On a Corvus network, such programs can be handled by spooling the print files to files in the pipes area where they can be printed on a network printer.

NOVELL SOFTWARE ON A CORVUS NETWORK

Corvus Constellation II software offers adequate network management for many companies. For users that require more elaborate security or file server functions. Novell's Advanced NetWare can be installed on a Corvus Omninet network. The Corvus/Novell hardware/software combination offers a number of features. An on-line tutorial helps novice users become competent users. It offers network bridging, linking two to four Omninet networks or Omninet networks with Token Ring or Ethernet networks.

Unlike the Constellation II software, the Advanced NetWare offers automatic print spooling. A truly distributed network, NetWare permits up to eight file servers to be linked together on a network. Since the software is DOS 3.1 and NETBIOS compatible, most programs written to run on an IBM network will also run on this hybrid Corvus/Novell system.

WHAT HAVE WE LEARNED?

1. The Corvus Omninet is a 1-Mbit/s local area network that transmits over unshielded twisted-pair wire.
2. Intelligent Transporter Cards use a CSMA approach to avoid data collisions.
3. Corvus has its own line of disk servers, file servers, and network workstations. Its 386 series offers a state-of-the-art 80386 file server.
4. Up to sixty-four nodes may be connected within a Corvus Omninet.
5. Corvus permits mixed networks linking various computer manufacturers' products.
6. The Omninet Hub consists of a star controller, splitters, and unshielded twisted-pair wire. It is capable of linking a maximum of twenty-five network branches.
7. The Corvus Constellation II software divides a file server into volumes with read-write and read-only access.
8. Files may be placed in private volumes, public volumes, and shared volumes.

Quiz for Chapter 8

1. In order to link a mixed network consisting of different kinds of computers, a Corvus Omninet must use a(n):
   a. Series 386.
   b. Omninet Hub.
   c. OmniDrive.
   d. OmniServer.

2. The OmniDrive is based on which microprocessor?
   a. 6502.
   b. 8088.
   c. 8086.
   d. Z-80.

3. The Corvus Series 386 uses an 8386 microprocessor and is capable of a processing speed of:
   a. 12 MHz.
   b. 16 MHz.
   c. 4 MHz.
   d. 8 MHz.

4. The Omninet is which kind of network topology?
   a. Star.
   b. Token Ring.
   c. Bus.
   d. Hub.

5. Over unshielded twisted-pair wire without additional hardware, Omninet is capable of sending a signal a maximum of:
   a. 2500 ft (750 m).
   b. 1000 ft (300 m).
   c. 500 ft (150 m).
   d. 5000 ft (1500 m).

6. With the use of Active Junction Boxes, an Omninet network can extend a maximum of:
   a. 1000 ft (300 m).
   b. 2000 ft (600 m).
   c. 3000 ft (900 m).
   d. 4000 ft (1200 m).

7. The Omninet Hub is a device that has a maximum of:
   a. five branches.
   b. ten branches.
   c. twenty-five branches.
   d. fifty branches.

8. Instead of dedicating a PC workstation as a printer server, Corvus recommends the use of its own:
   a. OmniServer.
   b. Utility Server.
   c. Network Server.
   d. OmniDrive.

9. Files that users do not want viewed or altered by others should be placed in:
   a. public volumes.
   b. private volumes.
   c. shared volumes.
   d. hidden volumes.

10. The default value for files placed on a Corvus network Under Constellation II software is:
    a. read-write.
    b. read-only.
    c. read-write-create.
    d. write-only.

11. The holding area for files waiting to be sent to another user or to a printer is known as:
    a. spooler central station.
    b. despooler volume.
    c. pipes volume.
    d. cigar volume.

12. A special flag that locks a file is known as a:
    a. semaphore.
    b. pipe.
    c. nibble lock.
    d. bit lock.

13. Users who wish others to view certain files but not change the results would place them in a:
    a. private volume.
    b. shared volume.
    c. public volume.
    d. read volume.

14. When a new file is placed on a volume, it cannot be read until it is:
    a. decoded.
    b. spooled.
    c. mounted.
    d. despooled.

15. Users who need such features as automatic spooling and network bridging should use:
    a. Constellation II.
    b. Constellation III.
    c. Novell Advanced Netware.
    d. Omninet software.

16. Performing such tasks as granting user access to a newly created file is the job of the:
    a. volume manager.
    b. file-server manager.
    c. access manager.
    d. disk-server manager.

17. IBMUSER is a designation normally used by:
    a. the network administrator.
    b. IBM's service administrator.
    c. the Omninet network user with an IBM PC AT.
    d. the CEO of the company.

18. When a Transporter Card successfully receives a message, it responds by sending a signal known as a(n):
    a. ACK.
    b. NAK.
    c. YEP.
    d. NOPE.

19. On the other hand, if a Transporter Card receives a garbled message, it send a signal known as a(n):
    a. ACK.
    b. NAK.
    c. YEP.
    d. NOPE.

20. If a Transporter Card wishes to check to see if another node is functioning, it can send a(n):
    a. ACK.
    b. NAK.
    c. echo packet.
    d. jam signal.

Other Networks and Pseudo-Networks

ABOUT THIS CHAPTER

While we have focused on the major local area networks, a number of other local area networks offer specific features that might be advantageous for some companies. In this chapter we'll examine LANs offered by Fox Research, Ungermann-Bass, and AST Research. We'll also look at the phenomenon of multiuser systems running under DOS. These pseudo-networks feature software linking as many as thirty-one terminals to a single IBM PC AT or compatible.

FOX RESEARCH'S 10-NET

Fox Research's 10-Net local area network is an IEEE 802.3 bus network that provides micro-mainframe communications as well as effective electronic mail at a reasonable cost.

Fox Research offers an efficient, inexpensive local area network known as "10-Net." This network, which already has 50,000 installations, follows the IEEE 802.3 standards for a 1-Mbit/s bus topology with CSMA/CA protocol. Like AT&T's STARLAN, 10-Net uses twisted-pair wire, but, unlike most local area networks, 10-Net does not *require* a file server even though it offers one of its own: 10-Server.

10-Net Hardware

Each workstation in a 10-Net network requires an interface card in one of its short expansion slots. Because it fits into a short slot as well as a long slot, 10-Net works with portable computers as well as desktop models. A cable connects each interface card to a tap box which in turn connects the workstation to the rest of the network along the network bus of twisted-pair wire.

The 2000-ft (600-m) maximum length and the bus topology of 10-Net might not be acceptable for some installations. For these Fox Research offers the 10-Net Repeater, shown in *Figure 9-1*. Four of these devices permit network expansion up to 10,000 ft (3000 m). This repeater also makes it possible to use a T configuration for greater network functionality. The 10-Net Repeater also allows users to exceed the 32 standard workstation maximum for one network.

Figure 9-1.
10-Net Repeater
*(Courtesy of Fox
Research, Inc.)*

Users on 10-Net may install diskless workstations with the 10-Net "Boot" ROM chip. This chip is installed on a 10-Net circuit board where it loads DOS and 10-Net software from a network "Superstation" to the diskless workstation. As with Novell's "boot" ROM chip, the diskless workstation represents both a considerable cost saving and greater security for a company since users cannot download network information.

Even though 10-Net is a moderate-speed local area network, it offers some features not found on faster, more expensive networks. Fox Research offers a 10-Net SNA Gateway package which includes a circuit card and emulation software. With this circuit card, a workstation becomes the Gateway PC and emulates an IBM Cluster Controller. Other network workstations load the 10-Net SNA software and then can access an IBM mainframe by emulating a 3278/3279 terminal. The 10-Net SNA Gateway allows one to four simultaneous active SNA sessions from each workstation that emulates a 3278/9 terminal. A "hot key" enables a workstation to switch between DOS and active SNA sessions.

10-Net also permits remote users. Fox offers a 10-Net RS-232 PC Remote software package which enables remote users to dial-in to the network using an asynchronous Hayes 1200-baud or 2400-baud Smartmodem. Remote users can share data, programs, and network printers. They also can use other 10-Net services including all the utilities.

While 10-Net doesn't require a lot of hardware, any network faces the possibility that a component might fail. Fox offers a 10-Net Diagnostic Module to test 10-Net hardware integrity, including the boards, tap boxes, and twisted-pair network wiring. Because all boards are on the same bus, this device makes it relatively easy to isolate a board that is malfunctioning.

10-Net Software

Included among the network utilities 10-Net offers are three different electronic mail programs. The first, 10Mail, functions as a standard menu-driven electronic mail system that can broadcast messages to all users as well as deliver correspondence to a single recipient. Fox Research also offers a program called CHAT which is a real-time conversation program. Two users who wish to "talk" can use CHAT to type a conversation rather than leave their desks to visit each other. The third electronic mail program found on 10Net is CB. This program functions much like a series of citizen's band radio channels; the forty CB channels can be used by a company for conferencing by various groups.

In addition to electronic mail programs, 10Net also includes 10CAL, a network calendar program that enables users to keep their own calendars but also permits the scheduling of meetings based on several users' calendars. In effect, this program searches a committee's calendars and selects the first meeting time that all users are free.

Fox Research offers a database called 10-BASE which includes an SQL query language as well as an applications language interface. SQL databases utilize certain key verbs and nouns when constructing commands to *query* the database about a specific record. The 3.1 version of 10-Net will be compatible with IBM's NETBIOS which means that most major network software designed for the IBM PC should run on this network.

UNGERMANN-BASS'S NET/ONE NETWORKS

Baseband Networks

Ungermann-Buss offers Ethernet local area networks using broadband, coaxial, or optic-fiber cable.

Ungermann-Bass has long been one of the most knowledgeable network companies. Its Net/One networks offer tremendous flexibility because they can be configured as baseband, broadband, and even as fiber-optic networks. As a baseband network, Net/One functions as a 10-Mbit/s Ethernet network consistent with IEEE 802.3 standards, including CSMA/CD. Each workstation contains a network adapter card, known as a "Network Interface Unit," which formats data into packets and routes them to their destinations. Network transceivers transmit and receive at 10 Mbit/s and detect collisions. Ungermann-Bass uses NRU to extend the length of its baseband networks by regenerating the signal and extending the maximum end-to-end channel length to 7800 ft (2600 m). Ungermann-Bass offers local bridges to connect compatible baseband networks to Net/One networks on other media such as broadband and fiber optics. Figure 9-2 illustrates how Ungermann-Bass utilizes fiber-optic links for point-to-point connections in a multiple-segment Ethernet network.

Figure 9-2.
Multiple Ethernet Cable
Segment Configuration
*(Courtesy of Ungermann-
Bass, Inc.)*

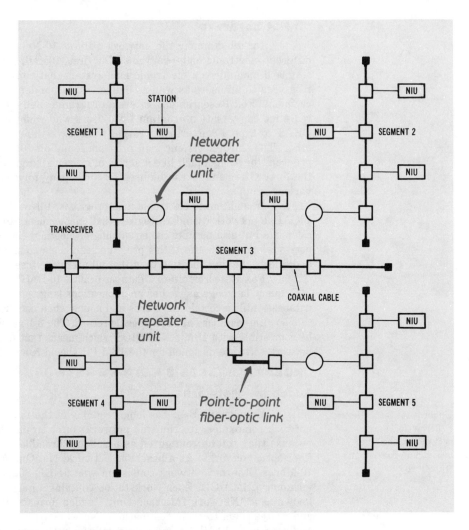

Broadband Networks

Net/One can operate on broadband CATV coaxial cable using up to
five channels, each operating at 5 Mbit/s. Net/One uses modems to provide
the RF interface to the broadband cable with a channel translator at the
head end to provide frequency translation for each CATV channel. This is a
contention network using CSMA/CD to avoid data collisions. As with
Ungermann-Bass's baseband networks, the broadband networks may be
connected by local bridges to other networks on different channels and to
baseband and fiber-optic networks. In addition to data transmissions, the
CATV channels can carry other signals such as video and voice. *Figure 9-3*
illustrates how this broadband network functions.

**Figure 9-3.
Net/One Broadband
Network** *(Courtesy of
Ungermann-Bass, Inc.)*

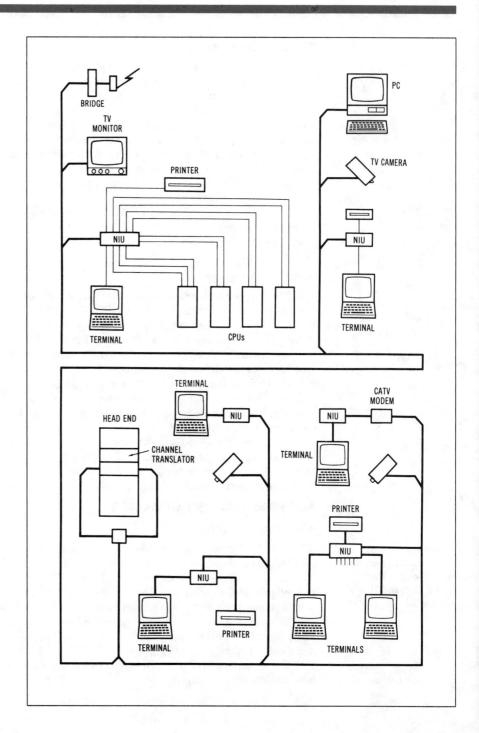

Fiber-Optic Networks

There are several reasons why a company might need a fiber-optic network. Such a network doesn't create interference with other company equipment; it is virtually immune to environmental noise and interference. Equally important, such a network is secure from illegal tapping, even when installation goes between buildings. Ungermann-Bass offers optical transceivers to provide the transmission interface to the optical fiber on its Net/One network. Data is converted by the transceiver into an optical signal that is coupled to an optical fiber. The data then is sent to a star coupler from which the signal is sent onto the fibers. The data travels until it is received by a transceiver.

Network repeaters can be used to boost these signals. Since the repeaters can regenerate signals from one segment to another, several star couplers can be connected so that one has several cable segments, as shown in *Figure 9-4*.

Net/One Software

The network administrator runs network software on Net/One from a management console, an IBM PC XT with a personal NIU circuit board. Downloader Server software permits the administrator to download requests from NIUs. The Data Link Monitor is a program that lets the network administrator collect and evaluate network statistics. In effect, the administrator can use this program to evaluate an NIU's effectiveness. Other network software enables the administrator to transfer files between two host systems running different operating systems, broadcast messages to all network users, and monitor and debug network software.

Ungermann-Bass supports the X.25 standards for packet switched networks. Net/One also supports X.25 Gateways, remote bridges, and local bridges. Net/One remote bridges connect with such public networks as telephone systems, satellite links, and point-to-point microwave radio.

AST RESEARCH'S NETWORKS

AST Star System

AST Research offers local area networks that closely resemble AT&T's STARLAN and IBM's PC Network.

AST Research offers a number of cost-effective networks. Its AST Star System is designed to meet the IEEE 802.3 STARLAN draft specifications. It closely resembles AT&T's STARLAN network, using twisted-pair wire to achieve 1-Mbit/s speed and handle up to sixty-four workstations. Each workstation must have an AST Star System adapter card in its expansion bus. AST makes an AST-NETBIOS option available, providing adapters that appear to its software as IBM PC LAN Network Adapters. In addition to running the IBM PC LAN Network Program, with this option an AST network will run virtually all NETBIOS-compatible software.

**Figure 9-4.
Net/One Fiber-Optic
Network** *(Courtesy of
Ungermann-Bass, Inc.)*

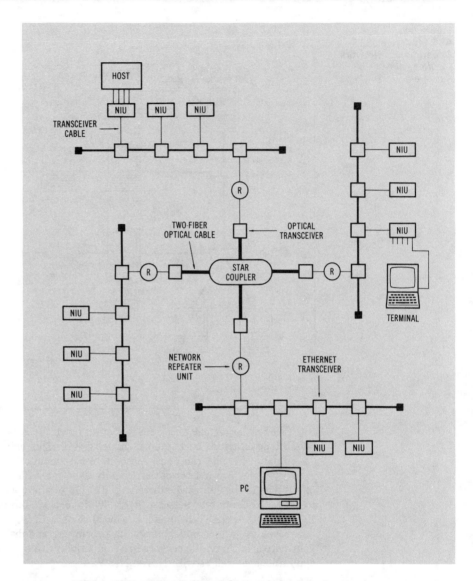

AST suggests daisy chaining up to ten workstations as long as
they are within 400 ft (130 m) of each other. For networks with more than
ten workstations, AST offers a StarHub/8 or StarHub/16. The StarHub/8
connects up to eight PCs and/or StarHubs, each of which can be up to 800
ft (260 m) from the hub. The StarHub/16 links up to sixteen workstations
and/or StarHubs with a maximum distance of 400 ft between the hub and
farthest removed PC on the chain. *Figure 9-5* is AST's conception of a
departmental network using this hardware.

Figure 9-5.
AST StarSystem
Departmental Network
(Courtesy of AST
Research)

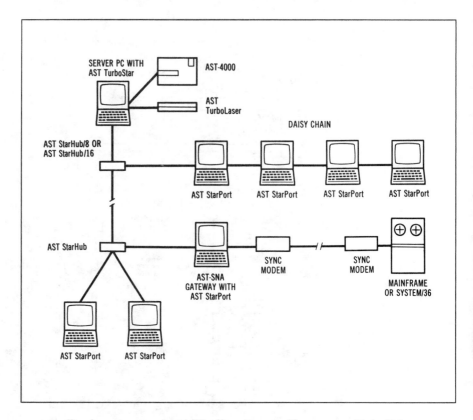

For larger networks, AST offers its own file server with built-in 60-Mb tape cartridge backup unit, the AST-4000. This unit comes with a 74-Mb hard disk that can be increased to a maximum of 370 Mb with plug-in subsystems. For networks that require even more file server space, AST offers the AST-5000, which starts with 120 Mb of storage and is expandable to 2240 Mb. Users may select either a 60-Mb or a 125-Mb tape backup. Because both the AST-4000 and AST-5000 come with SCSI expansion buses, you can attach optical disks, laser printers, and disk subsystems to your network. These file servers are compatible with all PC-DOS applications as well as with Novell NetWare.

AST-Resource Sharing Network

In addition to offering a version of AT&T's STARLAN, AST offers its own version of IBM's PC LAN Network. Its AST-RSN is a twisted-pair bus topology utilizing CSMA/CA data-access techniques. This 800-Kbit/s network has a 5000-ft (1500-m) maximum length using RG-11/U 75-ohm coaxial cable and a 2000-ft (600-m) maximum length using RG-59/U 75-ohm coaxial cable. Up to 32 PCs may be linked per 500-ft (150-m) bus segment. AST sets a practical limit of 160 PCs linked over 2500 ft (750 m) from end-to-end using repeaters to boost the network signals. *Figure 9-6* illustrates an AST-RSN network.

Figure 9-6.
AST-RSN Network
*(Courtesy of AST
Research)*

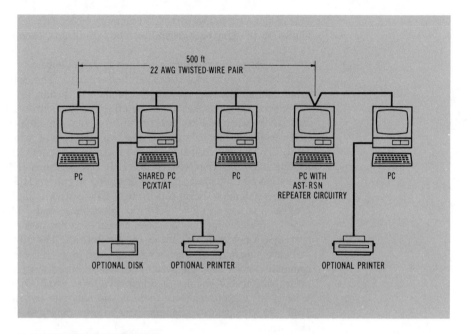

PSEUDO-NETWORKS

The local area networks we have examined by Fox, Ungermann-Bass, and AST are full-featured networks although less expensive than comparable products from IBM, AT&T, and 3Com. Several companies offer connectivity products that combine the best features of local area networks and multiuser operating systems. These pseudo-networks are often able to utilize the growing volume of LAN DOS 3.X software and still reduce costs by substituting inexpensive terminals for PC workstations. Since these solutions involve sharing the processing power of a single file server, a limited number of active users can be supported. Relatively small departments, however, can realize considerable savings with adequate resource sharing. We'll examine the two major examples of this approach to resource sharing—The Software Link's MultiLink and Alloy Computer Products' PC-PLUS.

MultiLink Advanced

MultiLink Advanced is an inexpensive way to link several terminals to a PC or an AT. These terminals can then be linked to a local area network using LANLink.

The Software Link's Multilink Advanced is based on the premise that a company has an IBM AT and wishes to link several terminals to it, each emulating an IBM-PC having up to 640K of RAM. The Software Link offers a multiported serial board that can support up to eight terminals. The secret of this multiuser system under DOS 3.1 is effective memory management. The Software Link offers a RAMLink 2-Mb board that can be used in conjunction with a memory management board (The AT Gizmo) to address up to 16 Mb of memory. This circuit card remaps addresses used to access memory so that extended memory becomes addressable memory. It allows up to eight background memory partitions, each of which can be up to 600K.

Since the memory cards contain the allocated memory for each workstation, the workstations can be terminals. The Software Link and other companies, such as Kimtron, make PC terminals that use the IBM PC special character set and even offer AT keyboards. Theoretically, MultiLink Advanced can support up to seventeen such terminals, but The Software Link suggests supporting from six to nine workstations with an IBM AT. The MultiLink Advanced software supports file- and record-locking in conjunction with DOS 3.1. It also provides IBM NETBIOS emulation so that most software designed to run on IBM's PC LAN Network should work on this system. The software supports such leading programs as Lotus 1-2-3, WordStar, MultiMate, and dBASE III.

The distinctions between a local area network and this multiuser system are not as significant as the similarities. The MultiLink Advanced software supports print spooling, password-protected remote communications with the system, a bulletin board system, and task prioritization that enables an administrator to establish up to eight levels of priority for each user. Since there is still only one central processor (the IBM AT), this prioritization amounts to providing specific time slices for each user.

What makes this MultiLink Advanced system intriguing is that The Software Link offers a simple local area network (LANLink) built around data transmission through RS-232 ports that can be linked to it. *Figure 9-7* illustrates how a company could utilize several MultiLink clusters linking them with simple RS-232 cabling and LANLink software. While such a network would not be fast, it would communicate information and cut costs considerably.

PC-PLUS

Alloy's PC-PLUS has assumed a dominant role in the multiuser DOS market. It offers some significant advantages over the lower-priced MultiLink system, including the ability to use local area network software designed to run under Novell's NetWare. The principal difference between PC-PLUS and MultiLink Advanced is that Alloy's product provides each network workstation with its own microprocessor.

Each user under PC-PLUS requires a PC-Slave/16 circuit board containing an NEC V20 operating at 8 MHz. This chip executes all 8088 instructions approximately 30 percent faster than an 8088 processor. The PC-Slave/16 comes with 256K of RAM that can be expanded to a maximum of 1024K partitioned into 64K banks switched by the host PC. This approach is much faster than the normal DMA approach. The boards also come with two serial ports that can send data at speeds up to 19.2K to a terminal, printer, or modem. Alloy offers PC-MATH/16, an 8087 math coprocessor that can be placed on the PC-SLAVE/16 for those workstations that require this feature.

Figure 9-7.
MultiLink Clusters
Linked Using LANLink
*(Courtesy of The Software
Link)*

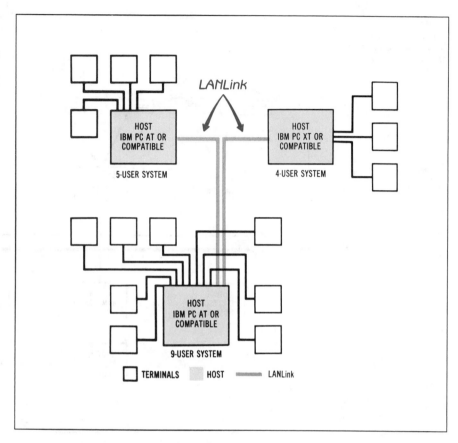

At first glance, the natural limitation of such a system would be the number of available expansion slots within an IBM AT, but this is not the case. Alloy offers PC-XBUS, a cabinet containing twelve additional PC bus slots and a separate power supply. It is connected to a PC with a controller that occupies a PC short slot. In effect, Alloy's system will support up to thirty-one workstations using these expansion units.

Alloy also offers the QICSTOR-PLUS unit, which can support additional hard disk storage as well as tape backup as a supplement to the IBM AT's storage capabilities. QICSTOR-PLUS comes with formatted hard disks ranging in size from 30 to 110 Mb, and it contains both disk and tape controllers. *Figure 9-8* illustrates a typical PC-PLUS configuration.

Figure 9-8.
Typical PC-PLUS
Configuration *(Courtesy of Alloy Computer Products)*

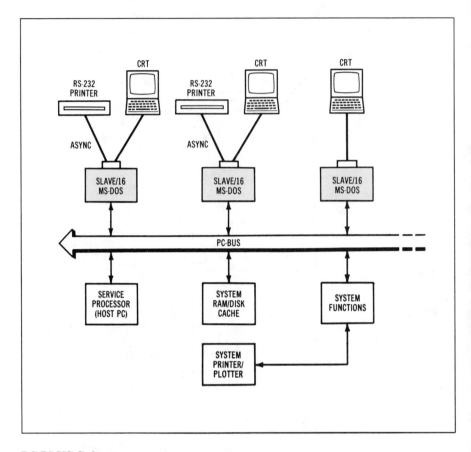

PC-PLUS Software

Alloy's Network Executive software runs with MS-DOS on the host computer. It controls disk access and printer spooling for each PC-SLAVE/16 card and emulates the IBM PC monochrome display and keyboard on each user terminal. For companies that require color or graphics, Alloy offers its own bit-mapped graphics terminal emulation. The PCST/G graphics terminal emulates the Hercules GB 101 graphics card. *Figure 9-9* shows the Alloy graphics terminal.

**Figure 9-8
Cont.**

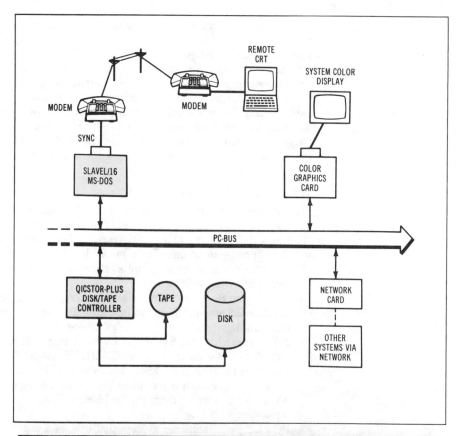

**Figure 9-9.
The Alloy Terminal**
*(Courtesy of Alloy
Computer Products)*

Alloy multiuser software allows programs to access files directly, yet it also provides file- and record-locking while managing file access. There are three versions of Network Executive software available: RTNX software is designed for software running DOS 2.x; ATNX supports software running DOS 3.x; and NTNX software supports software designed to run under Novell's NetWare software. The development of NTNX is most exciting. Since virtually all major network software has a Novell NetWare version, a company could couple the advantage of having the largest collection of network software to select from with the low cost of the multiuser workstation comprising a terminal with a corresponding PC-SLAVE/16 card for the host computer.

WHAT HAVE WE LEARNED?

1. Fox Research's 10-Net is an unusual network that offers CHAT, a program that permits real-time conversations among users.
2. Fox's 10-Net is also able to utilize portable computers that use their short slots in order to be linked to a network.
3. The 10-Net CB program permits companies to hold conferences with up to forty different participants.
4. Ungermann-Bass's Net/One is a 10-Mbit/s local area network that follows IEEE 802.3 standards. It can be configured with a variety of media, including baseband, broadband, and fiber-optic cabling.
5. AST Research's Star System is a twisted-pair, 1-Mbit/s local area network that closely resembles AT&T's STARLAN. Its AST-RSN is an 800 Kbit/s local area network that closely resembles IBM's PC Net.
6. MultiLink Advanced is a multiuser software package that enables an IBM AT to use its own memory (up to 16 Mb of RAM) to support up to nine terminals.
7. PC-PLUS is a multiuser system that utilizes a separate circuit card with its own microprocessor for its terminal user.
8. NTNX is software available for PC-PLUS that enables users to run local area network software designed for Novell's NetWare.

Quiz for Chapter 9

1. An inexpensive local area network, 10-Net utilizes:
   a. baseband cabling.
   b. broadband cabling.
   c. fiber-optic cabling.
   d. twisted-pair wire.

2. Users of 10-Net can communicate on-line by using:
   a. EMS.
   b. CHAT.
   c. TALK.
   d. Electronic Mail.

3. Users of 10-Net who wish to participate in a conference with up to forty people can use:
   a. CHAT.
   b. CB.
   c. Electronic Mail.
   d. FOX PACK TALK.

4. Each workstation in an Ungermann-Bass local area network must have a(n):
   a. repeater.
   b. NIU.
   c. BASS card.
   d. RF interface.

5. A fiber-optic network would use all of the following except:
   a. transceiver.
   b. repeater.
   c. optical fibers.
   d. RF interfaces.

6. For networks of more than ten workstations, AST Research's Star System requires a(n):
   a. cluster controller.
   b. StarHub.
   c. wire concentrator.
   d. interface unit.

7. The AST-NETBIOS option is important because it means compatibility for AST with:
   a. software designed to run under UNIX.
   b. software designed to run under DOS 3.1.
   c. software designed to run under Xenix.
   d. software designed for Novell's NetWare.

8. MultiLink software enables a company to connect several terminals to an IBM AT and utilize its processor by use of:
   a. time slices.
   b. extra RAM within the IBM AT.
   c. cabling via serial ports within the IBM AT.
   d. all of the above.

9. It is possible to link terminals running MultiLink Advanced with other IBM PC units via:
   a. LANLink.
   b. coaxial cabling.
   c. gateway PCs.
   d. 3270 emulation.

10. Each workstation in an Alloy PC-PLUS configuration must have its own:
    a. PC-Card.
    b. network interface card.
    c. PC-SLAVE/16 card.
    d. PC-LINK card.

11. A major advantage of NTNX software is that it permits PC-Plus workstations to use software designed for:
    a. PC Net.
    b. AT&T STARLAN.
    c. Novell NetWare.
    d. MultiLink.

12. Each workstation running under PC-PLUS is utilizing an:
    a. 8088 chip.
    b. 8086 chip.
    c. 80286 chip.
    d. 8087 chip.

A Guide to Networkable Software

ABOUT THIS CHAPTER

Many companies have found that installing a local area network also meant selecting new software written specifically for their network. The development of MS-DOS 3.1 has provided some uniformity in network software. Since the network hardware and software offered by IBM, 3Com, Novell, and AT&T all adhere to DOS 3.1 standards, it has made it much easier for software publishers to write generic network editions.

In this chapter we will examine how MS-DOS 3.1 provides network features such as record locking and what options companies have if their single-user software cannot be upgraded to DOS 3.1 standards. We'll survey the most desirable features found in word processing, spreadsheet, database managers, and accounting programs and see how they function in a network environment.

MS-DOS 3.1

MS-DOS 3.1 has provided true multiuser operations with its Share program that provides different levels of access and its "byte-locking" function.

As *Figure 10-1* shows, MS-DOS 3.1 resides in the presentation layer of the OSI model along with the Redirector program. It acts as an interface between the application programs and the NETBIOS which resides between the presentation and session layers. It provides multiuser access to files under network conditions by use of its Share program. Share enables the programmer to specify that the first workstation to use a file has certain levels of access while subsequent users have different levels of access. A key accounting data file used by several different workstations could be designated as read-write for the first user to request it. While this user continues to write to this file, other users will be only able to read the file under Share's Read-Write with deny-write sharing mode. MS-DOS 3.1 has a "byte-locking" function which enables a programmer to write a program so that a range of bytes is locked and other users cannot write to this area until the first user "unlocks" the area. The result of the Share program's different access rights and MS-DOS 3.1's byte-locking is that a file will not be destroyed by two users simultaneously writing over each other's data.

**Figure 10-1.
MS-DOS 3.1 Role in the
OSI Model**

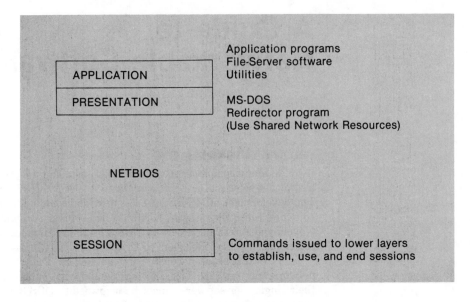

Programs written before the release of MS-DOS 3.1 are unable to utilize this multiuser feature. They can be installed on a network so that one user has the ability to write while other users can only read a file, but such manipulation is of limited value in most office environments.

The Redirector program acts as a "traffic cop."

In addition to MS-DOS 3.1's multiuser capabilities, programmers have begun to utilize its ability to use the Redirector program. This program acts as a "traffic cop" directing requests for shared network resources. Because of the way the program works, future network software will be file-server–oriented rather than disk-server–oriented. For companies that have large quantities of MS-DOS 2.X software and have flourished in a disk-server environment, the most viable solution might be a 3Com Etherseries network since they will be able to add 3+Path in the future to create a network in which both MS-DOS environments can coexist.

NETWORK SOFTWARE AND THE LAW

Most single-user software is licensed for one user and/or one machine. To use software on a network it is necessary to buy a network version of the program, sign a site licensing agreement, or negotiate a volume purchase from the software manufacturer.

Most single-user software packages specify that the program may only be used on a single machine and/or by one user at a time. Clearly use of such programs under network conditions is illegal.

So a major consideration in selecting network software is the software vendor's policy toward network use of its product. Many companies have developed special network versions of their products that are licensed for specific sizes of user groups. A network supervisor might select SSI's Word Perfect, for example, and then license a certain number of copies to run on its network. The customer pays for the initial package and then a per/user fee. Beyond the basic program, SSI supplies extra network features such as some laser-printing utilities that make it advantageous for a customer to purchase this version.

For a negotiated fee, other companies provide a site licensing agreement that specifies that the product may be used at that site by an unlimited number of users. Unfortunately, many major software companies simply offer discounts if their single-user products are purchased in large volumes. This solution is not acceptable for most companies.

WORD PROCESSING SOFTWARE

Why Use a Network Version of a Word Processing Program?

Most network users have already developed a fondness for a particular word processing program and prefer to continue using it. One problem with everyone using his or her own word processing program and then using the network file server simply as a storage area for documents is that not all word processing files are completely compatible. Also, since different programs have differing formatting capabilities it is difficult to provide uniformity in a company. Bill's proposals might look completely different from Mary's, and when they work on a document together and try to exchange data files it might be impossible for either of them to determine what the final document will look like.

Another limitation to single-user word processing software is that various program versions offer varying features. If two employees are using two versions of WordStar only one of them might be able to perform a mail merge with a customer file to create customized form letters. Different versions of the same program might contain slightly different printer drivers that could create some unpleasant printing surprises. Finally, single-user word processing programs do not offer file-locking capabilities. This feature is extremely important on a network because it means that several individuals can use the same word processing program without worrying about inadvertently destroying a particular document file.

Word Processing Features

While there are hundreds of word processing features available on some of the major network versions, we'll concentrate on those features of particular value to network users. We'll assume that a company with a local area network prints dozens of types of documents, including some material on pre-existing forms. Further, the company has several hundred customers that it wishes to communicate with on a regular basis. To achieve these word processing objectives, a company would have to examine programs that offer certain formatting, editing, and file-managing features and a number of utility programs. Let's look at some key formatting features.

Page-Oriented and Document-Oriented Word Processing

Perhaps the single most significant word processing program feature is whether the program is page-oriented or document-oriented. A *page-oriented* program displays one page of a file at a time much as a secretary would edit a typed manuscript by working on one page at a time. Page-oriented programs such as MultiMate, Display Write III, and the Leading Edge Word Processor do not display page breaks on a screen. If you add new material to the bottom of a page, a line count shows that you have added the material displayed on the screen, but

Network versions of word processing programs provide some assurance of file compatibility, printer compatibility, and the standardized appearance of company documents.

Page-oriented word processing programs display one page at a time while document-oriented word processing programs can display a page break and paragraphs on both sides of the page break.

you will not see a page break. With some of these programs, after adding material you need to repaginate to see which material will appear on a particular page. Since dedicated word processors are page-oriented, software writers emulated this when developing many MS-DOS word processing programs.

As *Figure 10-2* illustrates, a *document-oriented* word processing program enables users to see the end of one page and the beginning lines of the next page on their screens simultaneously. Usually these programs enable users to move from one page to another by using cursor keys to scroll up or down across the screen. Since a great deal of editing is based on such issues as how a paragraph looks in the context of the paragraphs that have come before it and the paragraph following it, how consistent verb tense usage is, and how effective transitions are in linking paragraphs, a document-oriented program makes it much easier to edit longer documents.

**Figure 10-2.
Document-Oriented
Word Processing
Program**

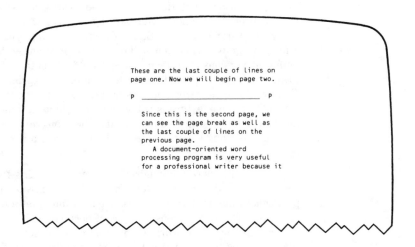

```
These are the last couple of lines on
page one. Now we will begin page two.

P _____ P

Since this is the second page, we
can see the page break as well as
the last couple of lines on the
previous page.
    A document-oriented word
processing program is very useful
for a professional writer because it
```

For network users who write memos and letters that rarely exceed one page there is little difference between a page-oriented program and a document-oriented program. There is a significant difference, however, for those writers who need to produce long reports or multipaged memos.

Seeing Is Believing

A second major formatting feature that distinguishes some word processing programs is their ability to display information exactly as it will appear when printed. This "what you see is what you get" feature is particularly important in a network program since networks frequently use the economy of scale gained from the sharing of resources to share laser printers. Microsoft's Word has a network version that takes advantage of IBM's Enhanced Graphics Adapter to display a number of fonts as they will appear when printed. The network version is specifically designed to work with a laser printer to produce typeset-like quality. For those network users who need actual typesetting, Microsoft offers the Linoword interface between Word and the Linotron laser typesetting machine. While few programs can match Word's ability to display different fonts, the minimum acceptable functionality for most network users is the ability to see boldface, underlining, and strikeovers displayed on the screen. Word Perfect performs these features admirably.

Style Sheets

Style sheets enable word processing users to format documents after writing them by linking the document to a particular style sheet's set of specifications.

Companies large enough to support a local area network usually require specific formats for their various types of documents. A company might stipulate, for example, that all top-level headings in its proposals be uppercase and boldface and all subheadings be lowercase and underlined. Company policy might also dictate that all memos use a specific font with the headings in boldface. Research reports might require still another company-dictated format with footnotes placed at the bottom of the relevant page. Microsoft Word offers several styles for creating footnotes, headings, and subheadings. A network user writing a letter, memo, report, or proposal selects the appropriate style sheet and Word automatically formats it correctly. This feature is especially valuable on a network since it ensures that all company correspondence and reports are uniform in style and format.

Forms Processing

Certain word processing programs can design forms and then place information into these forms.

One frustrating aspect of using a word processing program rather than a typewriter is that it is difficult to print information within the computer precisely where a standard form requires it. This ability to define and print fields anywhere on a pre-existing form is known as "forms processing", and it is particularly valuable on a company network in which several different forms are used on a regular basis. Samna's Word IV is a program that has this capability.

Editing Multiple Documents

A LAN user might need to view two documents simultaneously in order to compare certain passages. Some network word processing programs such as WordStar 2000 and Word enable users to view and edit different documents in this fashion. WordStar 2000 enables users to view up to three documents simultaneously as they are displayed in screen windows and Word enables viewing up to a maximum of eight windows.

Mail Merge

Some word processing programs can merge names, addresses, and other information found in a database program with a letter to produce individualized form letters.

One of the major word processing functions on a local area network is the *mail merge*. Companies frequently merge customer information (name, address, etc.) contained in database files with a form letter produced on the word processing program. Beyond that, the merge often permits key individualized information to be inserted within the letter *if* certain conditions are met. Widget company might write a form letter to all its customers, for instance, but it might include a paragraph about an upcoming megawidget seminar only in those letters addressed to customers who recently purchased this product.

One of the key questions a network administrator must address if mail merging will be a major network function is what form the customer data will take and how easily this information can be merged with a particular word processing program. Some word processing programs offer the capability to merge with several types of files, including dBASE, ASCII, and SYLK formats.

Word Processing Program File Formats

While it is critical to ensure complete compatibility between word processing program and database customer files for effective mail merging, it is equally important to determine the file formats a word processor produces if data communication is a major network concern. A company might have its local area network connected through a gateway PC with its mainframe computer. It also might have its LAN connected with remote branch locations. Since PC communications programs are usually designed to transmit ASCII files without word processing control codes, it is important to consider which kinds of word processing file formats are available. Word Star 2000 and Word Perfect are two of several major programs that are capable both of producing standard ASCII files and of importing ASCII files on the network that were produced by other word processing programs. For network users who wish to incorporate Lotus 1-2-3 worksheets within their word processing documents, WordStar 2000 offers the rare capability of directly reading Lotus files.

Printer Support

To utilize all the features of a laser printer, a word processing program should have a printer driver specifically written for that printer.

A principal advantage offered by a local area network is the ability to share valuable resources, such as laser printers. A network administrator might discover that proliferation of microcomputers and accessories in the company has resulted in some serious incompatibility problems. Since software programs require *printer drivers* in order to print documents, a company with incompatible printers offers a real challenge for a network administrator. Perhaps the administrator's key question when selecting network word processing software is "Does the program support *all* of our printers?" Programs such as Word Perfect, Word, and WordStar 2000 are particularly strong in this area. Because network programs normally are installed to run with a specific printer, the administrator usually writes batch files under DOS that enable a user to access the word processing program with the specific printer driver needed. In other words, a novice network user will normally access the network version of Word or Word Perfect already installed with the printer needed for a specific application and won't have to worry about specifying the printer.

Because laser printers have assumed such a major role on most local area networks, a major consideration in selecting word processing programs is whether or not the program supports proportional spacing fonts on the laser printer. Proportional spacing eliminates those gaping spaces found in most documents when a word processing program justifies the left and right margins.

A second word processing program consideration for global companies with local area networks is whether or not they must write in other languages. Word Perfect offers editions in French, German, Spanish, Finnish, Swedish, Norwegian, Dutch, and Danish. Perhaps the most specialized such foreign language-oriented word processing program is Computers Anyware's Arabic/English/French Interword. The program comes with an EPROM chip that when installed in the motherboard of a PC permits the use of multiple languages. Interword also includes keyboard overlays identifying the letters in each language. The program permits the simultaneous display of the three languages in multiple side-by-side columns. Computers Anyware also offers word processing programs in several other languages, including Russian, Dutch, and Icelandic.

If network users need to print in any foreign language, it is imperative that the administrator select a laser printer, such as the Hewlett Packard LaserJet Plus, that can download fonts. A printer's ability to download fonts is also necessary on a network if users wish to print special mathematical and scientific symbols.

Technical Report Considerations

There are several levels of word processing, ranging from the typing of short memos to the writing of technical manuals. Network administrators often find that the best response to this wide range of software needs is to select two word processing programs that have compatible data file structures. Secretaries whose responsibilities include typing short letters and memos and executives whose word processing needs are similarly limited might be best served with a simple word processing program. Technical writers might require programs with more elaborate features. Technical writers producing a software manual, for example, might require a program that can produce a table of contents and an index. WordStar 2000 and Microsoft Word both are capable of performing these tasks and both programs offer menus for novices while enabling more experienced users to use shortcuts.

Other Desirable Word Processing Features

Among the more advanced word processing features are macros, mathematical functions, multiple columns, and graphics capabilities.

All the major networkable word processing programs offer the standard, expected features, such as the ability to search and replace text, the ability to move and replace block paragraphs, and the ability to format text. Other word processing features are not standard, yet might be desirable on a local area network: macros, glossaries, mathematical functions, dictionaries, and searches of documents by key words.

Some programs, such as Word Perfect, are able to produce macros, a list of instructions that the program will perform when a specific combination of keys is pressed. If a company required that certain documents be formatted in ways that required several complicated steps, a network administrator could write a macro that incorporated these steps and enabled the novice user to accomplish the formatting by pressing two keys.

Many companies use what are called "boiler plate" letters consisting of a series of form paragraphs that are organized based on a customer's individual request. For example, a customer who wanted to know about the availability of a Superwidget and the training classes offered might receive a letter with paragraphs describing the company, the Superwidget, and the training classes available, as well as a stock concluding paragraph offering immediate service. Some programs, such as Microsoft's Word, provide glossaries that can be written and then stored. A network user who needs to insert a paragraph about the Superwidget's specifications checks the list of glossaries and selects the appropriate Superwidget glossary. This material, which can range from one paragraph to several pages, would then be inserted into the letter at the desired location.

Using mathematical functions can also save network users valuable time. A salesperson can draw up a contract and have the word processing program line up the numbers in appropriate columns and perform all the mathematical operations before providing the final cost to the customer on the appropriate contract line.

As valuable as a program's ability to perform mathematical operations is its inclusion of a dictionary and even a thesaurus. Programs such as Microsoft's Word and Word Perfect offer sophisticated dictionaries that help guide spelling accuracy. If a word processing program does not offer an internal dictionary, the administrator should determine whether the program's files can be read by one of the major dictionary programs on the market, such as the Random House Dictionary and Thesaurus programs.

Because of the sheer number of document files found on many local area networks, a word processing feature that proves just as advantageous as a dictionary or thesaurus is the ability to identify documents by certain key words. A company routinely uses its word processing document summary screen to list the document's recipient (ABC Supply Company), the type of correspondence (sales order confirmation), and the salesperson involved (Frank Wilson). With a program such as

Ashton-Tate's network version of MultiMate Advantage it is possible to create a document library and search it for a list of correspondence that matches specified criteria. This particular program also offers other special network features, including enabling each user to create a customized dictionary and create public and private document files.

Many of the significant word processing features we have not discussed, such as the ability to produce columns side-by-side and to incorporate text and graphics on the same page, are related to desktop publishing. The network administrator needs to be aware of this aspect of word processing because it is becoming a major network function for many companies.

Desktop Publishing

Desktop publishing refers primarily to the ability to perform a series of closely related functions, including combining text and graphics on a single page and designing a page with multiple columns and multiple typefaces. The MultiMate Advantage program, for example, has a network version that comes with GraphLink, a program that enables users to integrate graphics and text. It can also produce columns side-by-side. With a laser printer attached to the network, users can construct a newsletter with graphics and multiple columns and then produce typeset-quality copies. Few of the current desktop publishing programs have been released in network versions, but publishers are bound to offer these soon.

SPREADSHEET PROGRAMS

At this time there are no spreadsheet programs with network versions, although it is relatively simple for a network administrator to satisfy network users' spreadsheet needs. Since there are no specific network versions of the major spreadsheet programs, the administrator's first concern should be to provide a legal way of implementing such a program, whether this takes the form of a site licensing agreement, volume purchase, or other alternative. Before we look at spreadsheet features that might make one spreadsheet more advantageous than another for a network, let's examine the limitations on network use imposed by implementation of a spreadsheet program designed for a single user.

Potential Network Problems with Single-User Spreadsheet Programs

Using single-user spreadsheet programs on a local area network requires certain precautions, including placing them in read-only directories and keeping key driver files in users' own directories.

Copy protection schemes, such as that used by Lotus on its 1-2-3 program, pose a problem for network administrators. Because the program requires that a key disk be inserted by the user, network Lotus users cannot use workstations without disk drives. Another problem for the network is that single-user programs such as Lotus 1-2-3 and SuperCalc do not provide for file locking since the software companies are assuming only one user.

Both programs can be used effectively on a network, however, with certain administrative precautions. Normally, the programs should be placed in a public file area with read-only restrictions. Each user creates a private directory where the actual data files are kept secure from other users who might inadvertently write over them and destroy the information.

A third network concern when using single-user spreadsheet programs involves the various individual workstation configurations and needs. Users need to keep key driver files in their own directories so that Lotus can provide them with a display consistent with their monitor and video card and output for the appropriate printer. In effect, users must install Lotus for their own workstations and keep these key files in their own directory area from which to start the program. SuperCalc, on the other hand, maintains these key driver files in its master file and doesn't permit such manipulation. Network users can temporarily change the default settings each time they enter the program, but they cannot permanently customize their own workstation settings. An unattractive alternative is to simply provide each user with a copy of SuperCalc in his or her own directory. This option is usually unacceptable because it is not a cost-effective use of file-server memory.

Generally most network administrators will create templates for types of users. Salespeople, for example, might have a bid form while financial analysts have a budget form. These templates can be in a public area of the file server so that everyone can use them; network users who need to share information generally place a copy of their completed spreadsheet data in the public area.

Key Spreadsheet Features For Network Use

Key spreadsheet features include macros, graphic interfaces, and the ability to perform goal seeking.

While all DOS spreadsheets are currently designed for single users, there are certain normal network usage patterns that when coupled with a company's needs should help the network administrator decide which program is most appropriate. Among the key features we will consider are macros, graphic interface, size, RAM/Disk based, and special financial/mathematical considerations.

Macros

Because network users' levels of sophistication vary so widely, macros provide an easy way for network administrators to enable novices to use complicated spreadsheets such as SuperCalc or Lotus 1-2-3.

Graphic Interface

Programs such as Lotus 1-2-3 and SuperCalc come with their own graphic capabilities. Programs such as Multiplan have links to sister graphics programs such as Chart. If a network uses certain plotters or color printers, a primary consideration might be whether a program provides appropriate device drivers. Since Lotus 1-2-3 has become a spreadsheet standard, virtually all graphics programs will read its files if Lotus's own graphics prove to be inadequate.

RAM/Disk Based

Generally, spreadsheet programs are RAM based now, but some still are disk based. RAM-based programs, such as Javelin and Lotus, are faster, but there are inherent limitations on the size of the spreadsheet based on the amount of available RAM. Multiplan offers an interesting alternative because it requires a minimum of RAM and yet also permits the direct linking of several spreadsheets. Since these individual spreadsheets are smaller, they will recalculate values faster than one massive spreadsheet.

Special Financial/Mathematical Considerations

Some companies select a spreadsheet because of particular financial or mathematical functions. One such feature is "goal seeking," which allows a user to name a target value and have the program calculate the required variable value to reach that goal. If a company wants to achieve a certain profit level, for example, the spreadsheet will indicate the sales volume necessary to achieve this level. SuperCalc offers this highly desirable feature. Some programs have built-in functions to handle amortization and depreciation. A network of financial analysts would be pleased that SuperCalc offers built-in functions for net present value, internal rate of return, payment, future value, and present value.

DATABASE MANAGEMENT

Database programs on a network must have record locking as well as the ability to provide customized reports to meet the range of needs of network users.

While word processing might be the function used most often on a local area network, the LAN's very heart and cost justification is likely to be its database management program. An insurance office might have several agents accessing a central database to identify customers whose policies are about to come due. Similarly a mail order business might have several people processing phone orders, checking current inventory, and determining customer credit history, all dependent upon a central database program on a local area network.

Because many network users will need to use the database program simultaneously it is essential to select a program that has a network version so that it will have *record locking,* so that several people may use the same file (such as a list of customers) as long as they don't try to view the same record (a customer's history) simultaneously. The program permits only one user to revise a specific record at a time. Most of the major network programs are *relational database* programs. This means that it is possible to create a number of files or tables and then produce reports that reveal the relationships among various fields. Microrim's R:BASE System V network database, for example, can hold data in up to eighty distinct tables that forms and reports both can access in one-to-many relationships. While today's database management programs have hundreds of features, we'll examine only the few key ones for a network.

Key Disk Required

Some database management programs such as dBASE III Plus require a key disk at each workstation. As we saw in our discussion of spreadsheet program features, this requirement raises the hardware cost for each workstation since it eliminates the possibility of workstations without disk drives. It also creates a network housekeeping problem since one advantage of a LAN is the elimination of floppy disks. R:BASE System V, on the other hand, does not require a key disk, allowing unlimited users per server at no extra software cost.

Customized Reports

Since a network must serve many different user needs it is essential that the database management program have a sophisticated report generator that can create customized reports. Network administrators with unusual reporting needs might want to consider such issues as whether the program can create reports that are column or row oriented, is capable of time and date stamping, and can provide custom borders and footers.

Record and Field Limitations

Because of the scope of many network database management files, it is imperative that the network administrator determine the maximum number of records and fields that might be needed and determine unusual field requirements so that the company will not outgrow the program. While dBASE III Plus's maximum of 128 columns (fields) might seem almost infinite, some companies could require more.

Procedural, Programming, and Query Languages

Some companies might find even the most sophisticated database program cannot meet its unique needs. In such cases, it is essential that the program offer programming interfaces so that database information can be manipulated by a customized program. MicroData Base Systems' KnowledgeMan's data tables can be manipulated from C programs. Many of the network version programs such as R:BASE offer *procedural language* capabilities. This means that they permit the writing of short programs within the database itself. Finally, many network users do not need a programming or procedural language so much as they need the ability to ask (*query*) complicated questions based upon data relationships. A police department with a network database program containing the characteristics of thousands of criminals might ask to see a list of all the red-headed male burglars between 20 and 35 who are left-handed and walk with a limp. A query language would permit the user to phrase this question in English. R:BASE's Clout program is designed to let users query about any possible combination of relationships. Microrim's FileGateway program enables users with Multiplan, Lotus 1-2-3, or dBASE files to convert their files to R:BASE form so that they can use the Clout program.

IBM has made it clear that it supports its SQL (Structured Query Language) as the future standard for relational database programs. Companies that wish to install network software consistent with this language and that want their future minicomputer and microcomputer network software to have file compatibility would be wise to look at Informix-SQL, a program that supports SQL.

File Formats

Because a network might be linked to a mainframe computer or another LAN it is advantageous to have a database program that is capable of importing and exporting data files in a variety of formats. In addition to the dBASE format that has become a standard at some companies, other formats that are useful include ASCII, DIF, and SYLK.

A second major consideration is whether the company already has a multiuser computer system and wishes to move database information back and forth between the network and the operating system. Informix-SQL is an example of a powerful database management program available under both DOS and UNIX. Since the file structure is identical under both operating systems, data can be imported and exported quickly.

Application Generators

A network administrator might know exactly the kind of format and the kinds of data relationships the company needs to establish but lack the technical expertise and knowledge of programming to design such an application. R:BASE 5000 offers a program called "Application Express." This program enables a user to progress through a series of menus answering questions about the nature of the application. The program then automatically creates the application and lets the user modify it to meet special needs. Other database programs offering applications generators range from DataFlex's sophisticated language to dBASE III Plus's very limited Advanced Applications Generator program.

NETWORK ACCOUNTING SOFTWARE

Network accounting programs must have record-locking capabilities as well as a set of integrated modules that provide adequate network security.

Just as a database program would lose most of its value on a network without record-locking capability, an accounting program must also enable several users to access the same module simultaneously. A large company with hundreds of payments arriving the first week of each month might need several accounts receivable clerks to update its accounting program. While these clerks wouldn't need to examine the same customer record simultaneously, they all would need to be able to use the accounts receivable module. Similarly, a computerized retail store must have an accounting program that enables several clerks to perform order entry or point-of-sale processing as the program instantly updates the store's inventory information.

In addition to record-locking capabilities, the network administrator and company accountant should consider a number of other accounting program features. We'll examine some of the more pressing issues that must be addressed.

The Scope of Integrated Accounting Modules

Network accounting programs offer a variety of *integrated modules*. This means that a customer chooses whether such program modules as Order Entry, Point-of-Sale, Fixed Assets, and Job Costing are needed to supplement the standard General Ledger, Accounts Receivable, Accounts Payable, and Payroll modules. Many network programs offer integrated modules for specific industries. PROLOGIC, for example, links its financial modules with its distribution modules through Accounts Receivable and Accounts Payable. As *Figure 10-3* shows, the relationships between integrated modules can be quite complex. A wholesale distributor might have several different prices for various customers. The Customer Order Processing module creates an invoice using information from the Bill of Materials and Inventory modules and sends the invoice to the Accounts Receivable module where a record of the customer's invoice amount is maintained along with any payments made. A network administrator who needs specialized accounting modules may have to compromise some basic accounting program features in order to enjoy the advantages of integrating specialized information into the General Ledger.

Figure 10-3.
Data Flow Within a
Financial and
Distribution System
(Courtesy of PROLOGIC
Management Systems,
Inc.)

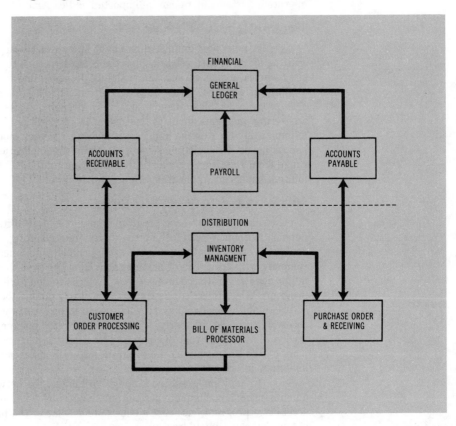

Program Security

Because of the nature of accounting, simple network security such as a logon password is not sufficient. Most Accounting departments need different security levels within a module. A payroll clerk might need security access to produce a payroll, but definitely not to change pay rates or view confidential salary information. Many of the more sophisticated network accounting packages such as PROLOGIC enable the network administrator to limit access to portions of a particular module. An employee might be able to enter inventory when it is received but not see the screen listing the actual cost of the items; some companies don't want their employees to know what their profit margin is.

Closely related to this security issue is the accounting program's ability to produce a clear *audit trail* of all transactions. Most of the better programs will produce a report listing all inventory transactions, for example. An employee cannot simply reduce an item's inventory total by one and then take the item home. The audit trail report will identify the employee from the password used when he or she logged on to the system, and it will indicate that on a certain date at a certain time the employee reduced the inventory value by the specified amount.

Specific Requirements

While many companies keep track of their inventories using a FIFO approach (first in, first out) or a LIFO approach (last in, first out), most accounting programs don't compute inventory in this fashion, using instead a weighted average approach. Some powerful programs such as Solomon III let the network administrator and accountant specify which type of cost method to use: LIFO, FIFO, average cost, specific identification, standard, or a user-defined approach.

Companies often have specific field requirements. They may need a twelve-digit general ledger account number or inventory part numbers of fourteen digits, for example. The network administrator and accountant should use their present accounting reports as a model and ask prospective software vendors to provide a demonstration that proves their programs can meet these requirements. The demonstration should also provide evidence of how easy it is to enter information and move from one menu screen to another. *Figure 10-4* illustrates the amount of information provided on typical menu screens in the Solomon III program.

Report Capabilities

Many accounting programs offer dozens of standard reports, but what happens if a company needs a certain report that doesn't follow the conventional pattern? Some companies, such as MBA, offer built-in financial report writers that permit some choice in selecting which lines will be printed in a balance sheet.

What if a company needs a report comprising information from two or three modules?

**Figure 10-4.
Solomon III Inventory
Menus** *(Portions of this
work have been
copyrighted by TLB, Inc.,
and have been used in
this work with the
consent of TLB, Inc.)*

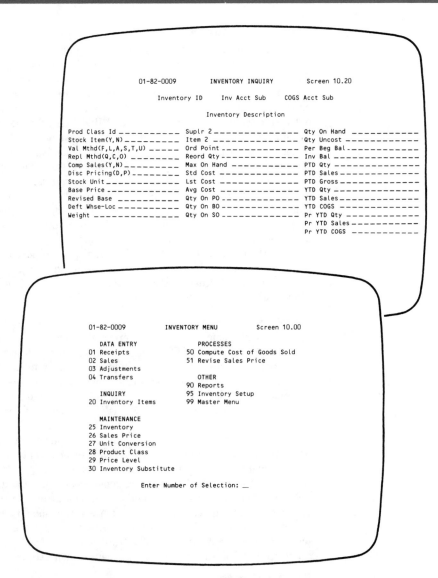

What if a company needs a report comprising information from two or three modules?

There are two possible solutions to this dilemma. One solution is to pay thousands of dollars for a customized program. Or, if the accounting program is written in COBOL, Snow Software's qPLEX IV might be a viable solution. This program is capable of generating reports from various files and then performing mathematical operations within the reports. The program works with accounting programs such as Real World and PROLOGIC and database management programs such as DataFlex and dBASE III.

Customization

It's unlikely that one program will satisfy all the accounting needs of a company. Some programs permit user customization while others require the purchase of a source code or provide customization to users at standard programming rates. Open Systems Accounting Software permits users to customize menus, including the rewriting of menu entries and the changing of the order of a menu. If more elaborate programming changes are needed, Open Systems makes the source code available. The company also publishes a list of software developers familiar with its source code.

Other Major Accounting Features Worth Considering

Since the implementation of an accounting program on a network is supposed to make the accounting more efficient, a number of program features that can help achieve this goal are worth considering. One such feature is the ability to handle recurring entries automatically, rather than manually. Another feature is the ability to provide help screens. Since a network frequently adds users, on-line help screens reduce training time and make new users more productive. Finally, networks are as prone to power failure as single user systems. Some accounting programs provide frequent backups. A program such as PROLOGIC's Financial Accounting updates its master file with each transaction. This approach ensures accurate on-line data queries and minimizes data loss in the event of power failure.

WHAT HAVE WE LEARNED?

1. PC/MS-DOS 3.1 permits multiuser operations on a local area network because it enables byte locking.
2. Single-user software lacks the record-locking feature desirable on a local area network. Using such a program on a network also violates its licensing agreement.
3. Document-oriented word processing programs offer many advantages over page-oriented programs.
4. While some single user programs may be used in a network, they rarely provide a way to configure the program to work on different types of workstations.
5. A query language can make it much easier to use a powerful database management program.
6. Database management programs can create new applications with an application generator.
7. Network accounting programs often consist of a number of sophisticated integrated modules.
8. Some software vendors encourage customers to customize their packages in order to meet individual needs.

Quiz for Chapter 10

1. The version of PC/MS-DOS that permits multiuser operations is:
   a. 3.0.
   b. 2.1.
   c. 3.1.
   d. 1.1.

2. The program that acts as a "traffic cop" to direct requests for shared network resources is called:
   a. Master Manager.
   b. IBM PC Traffic Manager.
   c. The Director.
   d. The Redirector.

3. A word processing program that only displays one page at a time is:
   a. page-oriented.
   b. document-oriented.
   c. paragraph-oriented.
   d. style sheet-oriented.

4. Writing a customized form letter using a list of names and addresses is a function known as:
   a. the "Dear John" letter.
   b. boilerplate special.
   c. mail merge.
   d. "Shopping List" processing.

5. A series of form paragraphs linked together is a word processing function known as:
   a. mail merge.
   b. boiler plate.
   c. mail link.
   d. paragraph meld.

6. A feature that enables an electronic spreadsheet user to program several spreadsheet functions so that they may be performed with a simple keystroke is known as a:
   a. micro.
   b. macro.
   c. BASIC interface.
   d. firmware chip.

7. A spreadsheet feature that allows a user to name a target value and have the program calculate the required variable value to reach that goal is known as:
   a. circular reasoning.
   b. target variables.
   c. micro justification.
   d. goal seeking.

8. As a query language, IBM supports:
   a. Clout.
   b. SQL.
   c. ADL.
   d. QUESTION.

Local Area Network Selection and Management

ABOUT THIS CHAPTER

A company must make many decisions before it purchases a local area network. We'll examine how a company can do its initial needs analysis, factoring in company information needs, existing resources, and plans for future growth. While most companies will still need to talk with data communications and telecommunications consultants, this analysis provides a basis for discussion and prevents the consultants from selecting a system that meets *their* needs while not solving the company's major problems.

We'll look at the steps necessary to develop a request for proposal (RFP) and follow-up procedures. We will also consider the problem of multiple vendors and hardware and software maintenance and training.

Local area network management is a major responsibility. We will examine some of the duties of a network administrator and the type of recordkeeping required to prevent network downtime. In this section we'll address network access and security and software integration, and survey the types of information and reports necessary for effective network management.

SOLVING PROBLEMS WITH LOCAL AREA NETWORKS

Once problems are identified, the question to ask is, "Will a local area network help solve these problems?"

For companies that already have data communication and telecommunication equipment, the first question generally asked in a LAN needs assessment is "What problems do we have that might be solved if we implement a network?" Often after interviewing employees from several departments, you will have heard similar problems described. These might include:

Too much duplication of effort (several salespeople typing the form letters, for example)

Too much paperwork (Why can't we eliminate most of the memos and use electronic mail?)

Loss of data integrity because people working on the same project need to swap disks frequently

Mounting hardware and software expenses since departments don't share resources but build "kingdoms"

Inability to obtain data from other departments

Security concerns over use of computerized information

Growing hardware and line expenses for departments that need to use public information networks

Problems such as these suggest a need for a local area network. The next step is to inventory existing hardware and software resources to determine if they are compatible with a local area network solution.

SURVEYING YOUR DATA COMMUNICATIONS AND TELECOMMUNICATION RESOURCES

Telecommunications Equipment

In some small companies the survey might take one minute and consist of looking around the office to conclude that the company has a simple telephone system with four lines and eight telephones and two IBM PCs that are used for word processing and accounting respectively.

Companies need to survey their data communications and telecommunications equipment to learn the most effective way to improve the flow of information.

In larger companies, with much more equipment, the survey must be formalized and an instrument developed to ensure that all answers are standardized. Assuming the company has a PBX telephone system, some of the questions that should be asked include:

1. Has a traffic study been done to determine peak periods of phone system usage?
2. If the PBX were to be used for data as well as telecommunications, how much surplus capacity does the system have at present? People are used to a brief delay when accessing a computer, but they expect instant telephone response. It is necessary to estimate the degree of degradation that would result if telecommunications and data communications were combined. Since some older PBX systems require two dedicated data lines for a single voice line, it is essential to estimate the number of terminals that the company will need for the future.
3. Would some of the PBX functions such as its ability to record each call and keep track of the expense resulting from this transaction (a call accounting system) be cost-effective if the company's data communications were linked to these functions? In other words, if the company currently now uses modems to transmit data over telephone lines, would it save money if these transactions could be tracked and perhaps recharged to the departments using these services?
4. Is there significant interest in or need to integrate voice and data communications?
5. If the PBX represents a possible local area network, is there any redundancy built into this switch? What happens if the PBX fails?
6. Is a mainframe computer located at the same location? Is it feasible or even desirable for the microcomputers composing a local area network to communicate with the mainframe computer through the PBX?
7. What kinds of private networks must be accessed by the local area network? Do these networks require speeds that are possible with a PBX?

8. Does the company need to tie a number of asynchronous PC terminals to its synchronous mainframe? (Since a PBX is an excellent way of linking synchronous and asynchronous devices and providing protocol conversion, a company that already has a PBX should consider this question very carefully.)
9. Perhaps the most critical question of all is what kind of information needs to be shared and transmitted through a network. If the information consists of lengthy files, it might well be that the PBX isn't fast enough to accommodate the network. Also, some of the major networkable programs are designed to work only with specific LAN software. Many of the major accounting programs, for example, only work with Novell, 3Com, and IBM software. So, while the PBX might be acceptable for a network that utilizes short bursts of file transfers, it might prove completely unacceptable if the major purpose of the network is to share these specific application programs.

In most cases a PBX will prove to be inadequate to handle all data communications because its speed cannot approach that of a dedicated computer system with data grade cabling. Since IBM and AT&T both offer local area network interfaces to their digital PBX systems, a company with a PBX might well consider the advantages of using the interface in order to utilize such features as modem pooling and automatic route selection while handling heavy data communication over a computer-based local area network.

Surveying Present Hardware and Software and Desirable Additions

It is essential that a company inventory available hardware and software and information needs that would be shared within the local area network. A Marketing department's inventory of current hardware and software might look like this:

1 IBM PC AT with 640K and a 30-Mb hard disk
2 IBM PCs with 256K and dual floppy disk drives
1 Leading Edge PC Model D with 256K and dual floppy disk drives
1 Epson Equity II with 640K and dual floppy disk drives
1 AT&T 6300 with 256K and dual floppy disk drives
1 Hewlett-Packard Laser Jet Plus printer
3 Epson FX 286 wide carriage dot matrix printers

The department currently uses a word processor, a spreadsheet, and a database manager program. Its list of present computer activity as well as what it would like to be able to do in the future with a local area network might look something like this:

Lotus 1-2-3 worksheets for forecasting future sales
dBASE III customer list that everyone could access
dBASE III customer sales histories
Word Perfect sales form letters

Ability to merge form letters with customer lists
Ability to print sales contracts
Lotus 1-2-3 commission worksheets
Ability to access MRP manufacturing information (from mainframe)
Electronic mail
Remote ability to inquire on product availability
Ability to inquire on customer's accounts receivable
Ability to input an order on-line
Ability to track salespeople's phone expenses
Ability to switch salespeople to least expensive long-distance carrier
Ability to share resources such as laser printer and dot matrix printers
Ability to print envelopes as well as letters
Ability to track salespeople's performance and produce graphs available only to
the salesperson involved

After having each department make a "wish list" that includes
present activity as well as these future capabilities, it is necessary to look
at whether the present software can be networked. If the Accounting
department has a single-user program that is not upgradable to a
networkable version with record locking, buying a new program might be
prohibitively expensive. Even if the present accounting program uses
ASCII data files, extensive programming is needed to format this data so
that it corresponds to a new program's field and record parameters. And
this assumes that it is possible to obtain the source code of the new
accounting program.

The Marketing department's desire to have remote access to the
local area network is understandable. Salespeople would like to be able to
view current inventory levels and perhaps even place their orders over
phone lines. If the company decides that this capability is essential in its
LAN implementation, it must include this requirement in its request for
proposals. Not all major local area network software can support remote
entry. Even those networks that do may have their own requirements.
Novell, for example, requires a gateway PC that is not used for any other
function while it serves to connect the remote user with the file server.

The Marketing department also expressed an interest in being able
to access (or at least view) manufacturing data currently residing on a
mainframe computer. Before deciding that a micro-mainframe network
connection is desirable, the network administrator must determine whether
or not this mainframe information is important enough to Marketing's
performance to justify its access. Also, what programming would be
necessary to download the information directly into one of the network's
programs? Do departments that will be linked by the local area network
have sufficient reason to view mainframe information to warrant the
security problems that could result from establishing the link?

A major concern in many companies is the variety of computer
models within departments. Not all IBM compatibles are actually
compatible enough to use network adapter circuit cards. The first release of
the Epson Equity, for example, was not compatible with Novell's network

hardware because its NETBIOS was not close enough to that of IBM. Subsequent releases have eliminated this problem, but the threat of incompatibility is still a major problem with clones. As we will see shortly, the request for proposal needs to address this issue and place the burden of proof on the network vendor to guarantee that its network will work with all present equipment. *Table 11-1* illustrates how a company might gather this information in a form to present to a vendor when soliciting proposals.

**Table 11-1.
Computer Resource
Inventory**

Department	User	Company	Software	Printer	Product
Marketing	Frank	IBM PC	Lotus	FX 286	Commissions Sales Forecasts
	Susan	PC AT(30)	WordPerfect dBASE III	Laser+	Sales Solicitations MailMerges
	Bill	Leading Edge	WordPerfect dBASE III	FX 286	SalesProposals Invoices
	Carol	Epson Equity II	WordPerfect dBASE III Lotus	FX286	Marketing Reports Demographics Sales Reports
	Larry	AT&T 6300	WordPerfect dBASE III		Sales Reports Sales Histories
	Laura	IBM PC	dBASE III Lotus		Sales Reports Sales Histories Demographics

Nature of Data Transmission

When contemplating installing a LAN, a company must consider what type of data will be transmitted and address geographic and security concerns.

Before selecting the media and network hardware and software, it is necessary to examine the work that will be done on the network. We just saw what the Marketing department has in mind, but we need to know how large the dBASE III customer lists and Lotus 1-2-3 worksheets are. Very large dBASE III file transfers will consume valuable network time and may suggest that the company eliminate from consideration some of the slower LANs (1–2 Mbit/s) in favor of a faster network (6–10 Mbit/s). Once this determination has been made, the company can look at related issues such as geographic considerations and security requirements.

Geographic Considerations

Once a company has an idea of the software it plans to use in its network and a clear picture of its present resources, the next step in a needs analysis is to determine the geographic parameters of the network. Will it encompass several departments, a single building, or multiple buildings? Since many of the local area networks use a bus topology that is limited to 1000 ft (300 m), a network administrator might have to look at another architecture such as a token ring for a larger building.

Media Selection

The network medium might be directly related to the company's geographic requirements. If the network will be installed in an environment where there is a good deal of interference, fiber optics might be required. If the building already has twisted-pair unshielded telephone wire installed, it might be cost effective to determine whether a network could handle the data transmission requirements using this medium. If the company wants simultaneous voice and data transmission, then a medium capable of such transmission must be selected.

Security Considerations

Local area networks vary in the degree of security they offer. As a rule, star topology networks offer the means to monitor all workstations and record the files and programs that they access. Software such as Novell's NetWare establishes several levels of network beyond simple password protection including the ability to set file attributes. It is also important to consider whether it is possible to change user access quickly. Novell's conception of user groups is beneficial in situations where people's assignments change frequently, requiring changes in network access. Finally, there needs to be some concern for the security and integrity of data. What happens if a user turns off the workstation without properly closing his or her files? Sophisticated network software will prevent files from being damaged in such situations.

Another security consideration is the ease with which the network topology and media allow unauthorized entry. It is relatively easy to connect a tap via a small isolation transformer hidden behind a termination panel. It is then child's play to connect this transformer to another line and dial-in from another location to access the network. Fiber-optic cabling offers the optimal protection against such intrusions.

If security is a great concern, the network administrator should consider incorporating additional security measures in the request for proposals. One such measure is the purchase of terminal locks to protect unattended workstations from unauthorized entry. Another safeguard is the use of *callback modems*. In this system, a remote user must provide a password which the network checks against its list of authorized passwords. If there is a match, the network hangs up and calls the remote user back using a telephone number that is stored next to the authorized password. This practice ensures that only authorized users can access sensitive network files, and, with the use of inexpensive WATS lines, offers substantial savings. Unhappily, not all networks permit this security measure. IBM's Asynchronous Communications Server, for example, is not designed to handle callback modems.

DEVELOPING A REQUEST FOR PROPOSALS (RFP)

A request for proposals to implement a local area network must solicit vendor information on network hardware, software, and applications programs.

We have seen that before a company can begin the process of inviting vendor proposals, the company must take several steps in order to analyze needs. In our example, the company first determined which software was currently being used and then which software it planned to use under network conditions. To ensure complete compatibility, the company also surveyed its present computer workstations and printers.

Because of the limitations inherent in many networks, the company also determined the maximum size of the network, the potential for expansion, and the type of information and size of files that it wanted to transmit over a network. It also examined the security measures it might want to require to ensure only authorized access. Now the company can develop a formal Request for Proposal.

In aid of viable vendor proposals, we must provide information in a logical order. Here is an outline for the heart of the RFP:

I. Hardware
   A. Microcomputers
      1. Currently on hand (brand, configuration)
      2. Additional workstations required for network
         a. IBM compatibility to be able to run which programs?
         b. How much RAM is required?
         c. Number of disk drives required
            1. For security reasons, do you prefer no disk drives and an auto-boot ROM chip?
            2. If disk drives are required, half height or full height?
            3. 360K or 1.2 Mb?
         d. If hard disk is required
            1. Size (megabytes)
            2. Mounted in what kind of microcomputer?
            3. Formatted in which version of DOS?
         e. Monitors and Monitor Adapter Cards required
            1. Color or monochrome
            2. Resolution
            3. Size
            4. Other features required
            5. Dual mode
            6. Ability to run certain graphic programs
         f. Other I/O Cards required
            1. Parallel or serial cards and cables
            2. Additional RAM cards
            3. Multifunction cards
            4. Accelerator cards
            5. Others
   B. File servers
      1. Size required (Note: Most networkable integrated accounting packages have sizing charts that estimate the minimum file server required based on such variables as the number of open accounts, the

size of the chart of accounts, the number of open files at any given time, etc.) A network administrator may have to work with a systems analyst to configure the minimum file-server size based on the maximum number of database records (in bytes) as well as the number of word processing documents that will reside on the file server. For many companies it makes very good sense, both for security and for increased network efficiency, to contemplate a network with several distributed file servers.

   2. Processing speed of file server
   3. System fault tolerance (if required)
   4. Other features required
   5. Number of Tape Backup Units (size in megabytes). This decision depends on whether the company will use distributed file servers.

C. Bridges to other networks
   1. Other networks to be connected
   2. Adapter cards and cabling required

D. Backbone network required to connect multiple bridges
   1. Description of bridges to be connected
   2. Processing speed required

E. Gateways to mini/mainframe environments
   1. Local or remote connections
   2. Protocols required
   3. Number of concurrent sessions required
   4. Terminal emulation required
   5. Local printer emulation required
   6. Amount of activity to be handled

F. Minicomputers
   1. Currently on hand (brand, configuration)
   2. Need to integrate information with LAN

G. Mainframe Computer
   1. Currently installed (brand, configuration)
   2. Need to integrate information with LAN

H. Printers
   1. Currently on hand (brands, buffers, accessories)
   2. Additional printers need for the LAN
      a. Speed required
      b. Type (letter quality, daisy, etc.)
      c. Compatibility with which major printer drivers?
      d. Type of connection (parallel, serial)
      e. Length of distance from workstations
      f. Other special printer features
   1. Special language fonts or downloadable fonts
   2. Near letter quality and fast dot matrix modes
   3. Which workstations/areas will need to access which printers?
   4. Any unusual printing requirements (color, multiple copy, specific accounting forms, etc.)?
   5. Do any software packages that will be on the network require a specific printer?

I. Modems
1. Currently on hand (brand, speed, special features, etc.)
2. Needs for additional units with the LAN
3. Transmission mode required (simplex, half duplex, full duplex)
4. Interconnections required (point-to-point, multiple drops)
5. Special features needed
   a. auto-dial
   b. auto-logon
   c. auto-answer
   d. other
J. Plotters
1. Presently on hand (brands, configuration)
2. Additional units required
   a. Speed
   b. Number of colors
   c. Compatibility with which major brand?
   d. Programs to drive plotters?
K. Optical scanners
1. Currently on hand
2. Additional units required
   a. Speed
   b. Which fonts will be scanned?
   c. Which programs will need to access this data?
L. Other hardware required
1. Cash registers (for retail environment)
   a. Type of connection (serial, parallel)
   b. Compatibility with which point of sale accounting program?
2. Badge readers (for manufacturing environment)
   a. Will employees clock in and out of several jobs the same day?
   b. Does this information have to be interfaced with an accounting program's payroll module?
3. Multiplexers
   a. Devices to be attached
   b. Location of these devices
   c. Type of transmission required
   d. Speed required
4. Protocol converters
   a. Devices to be attached
   b. Protocols involved (SNA, BSC, ASCII, etc.)?
5. Power protection required
   a. Voltage regulation
   b. Limits sags, surges
   c. Prevents common-mode noise
   d. Provides battery backup
II. Software
A. Operating system and utility programs
1. DOS
   a. Which version for the root directory?

        b. Are there multiple versions of DOS (2.1, 3.1, etc.) to be found on the network?

  2. Electronic mail

    a. Menu driven

    b. Help screens

    c. Display messages

    d. Distribution lists possible

    e. Notification when a message arrives

    f. Ability to forward messages to a different workstation

    g. Ability to define multiple user groups for broadcasting

    h. Ability to file messages

    i. Ability to print messages

    j. Other features desirable

  3. Network calendar

    a. All workstations access to calendar features

    b. Ability to schedule rooms, hardware resources, etc.

B. Network management

  1. Ability to perform diagnostics

  2. Ability to add and delete user groups

  3. Password protection

  4. Maintain user statistics

  5. Ability to handle remote dial-in users

  6. Ability to handle multiple operating systems

  7. Ability to handle bridges to other networks

  8. Ability to add and delete printers easily

  9. Security provided

    a. Log-in level (password required)

    b. Directory level

    c. File level

    d. File attributes

  10. Menu driven with ability for sophisticated users to bypass the menu

  11. Log-in scripts or other facilities such as batch files permitted to make it easier for novice users to log-on

  12. Printer-server software

    a. Number of printers permitted on the network

    b. Number of shared devices

    c. Printer queues

      1. Size

      2. Ability to change printing priority

    d. Commands available to network users

      1. For setting parameters for specific printing jobs

      2. For disabling printers for routine servicing

      3. For changing printers from shared to local

    e. Print spooling software

    f. Types of printers supported

      1. Parallel

      2. Serial

      3. Laser

4. Line printers
13. File-server software
    a. Size of volumes permitted
    b. Access speed
    c. Network drives (logical drives) permitted
    d. Virtual drives (transparent to user)
    e. Restore tape to disk capability
    f. Directory hashing
14. Network communications server software
    a. Protocols supported
        1. ASCII asynchronous
        2. 3270 BSC
        3. 3270 SNA
        4. X25
    b. Speed supported
    c. Ability to handle call-back modems
    d. Automatic dial-out
    e. User statistics provided
C. Current software that the network must support
    1. Word processing
    2. Spreadsheets
    3. Database management
    4. Accounting

Trying to Avoid Starting Over Again

It is unlikely that the company's current software will be supported by a new local area network. Your request for proposals should detail which programs are currently being used and the nature of their current file structure. If the word processing program permits files to be saved in ASCII form, it probably will be possible to use the data files with the new network program. Many of the most popular programs (Word Perfect, for example) have network versions of their programs. Selecting a networkable upgrade would ensure that there would be no training necessary for this portion of network activity.

Accounting is a far more complex area. Some programs such as (BPI and PROLOGIC, for example) have networkable upgrades. A company fortunate enough to be using a single-user version can upgrade to a network version without having to worry about file transfers or training. In most cases, however, as we saw earlier, moving from a single-user accounting program to a network accounting program means starting over. In this case, the company probably will choose to run the single-user program until the fiscal year's accounting cycle is complete while gradually adding more and more customer information to the network software. After running at least a couple of months concurrently to ensure the accuracy of the new program, a company can switch to the new system. In Chapter 10 we examined many of the issues associated with selecting an accounting program. Because of the complexity of such software, training is critical for all employees who will need to access this information. It should be a major provision of your RFP.

Software Licenses

Virtually all software packages restrict their usage, sometimes to one user and sometimes to one machine. The RFP should include provision for software licensing for the network site ("site licensing") or a network version licensed for a specific number of users (for example, SSI's Word Perfect network version).

    D. New application software required
        1. Word processing
            a. Compatibility with current software
            b. Features required
            c. Training to be provided
        2. Spreadsheet/financial analysis
            a. Compatibility with current software
            b. Features required
            c. Training to be provided
        3. Database management
            a. Compatibility with current software
            b. Features required
            c. Training to be provided
        4. Accounting
            a. Compatibility with current software
            b. Features required
            c. Training to be provided
        5. Custom software required
            a. Compatibility with current software
            b. Features required
            c. Training to be provided

VENDOR REQUIREMENTS

Vendors replying to an RFP must match benchmarks for hardware and software.

In order to complete this outline of information in our RFP, we need to examine the relationship between company and LAN vendor(s). A number of questions need to be asked of prospective vendors before a network is purchased and installed. It is an excellent idea, for example, to require that vendors demonstrate their networks' ability to run the software your company plans to install. Often companies will require a benchmark showdown of sorts in which competing vendors are asked to perform under similar conditions.

Even if a vendor's equipment is capable of providing a LAN that meets your company's speed and compatibility requirements at a reasonable cost, the equipment may not prove to be sufficiently reliable. As you will see in our outline for an RFP, it is imperative to request references to vendor customers with installations similar to yours. It is also essential to secure information about the equipment's reliability, including a mean time before failure (MTBF), maintenance contracts, and response time.

Frequently network vendors will offer a variety of maintenance options, including a guaranteed response time, a repair or replace designation, or even a guarantee to provide a file-server loaner if unable to repair the network within a given length of time. Before issuing an RFP your company must determine how long it can afford to be without network services and then require vendors to meet a response time requirement that suits your needs.

Because a local area network includes computer hardware, network hardware and software, and third-party software, it is common for vendors to "pass the buck" and not accept responsibility when a network problem arises. Part of the RFP should require the principal vendor to take overall responsibility for the network's maintenance. If a software problem suddenly develops, for example, the principal vendor should act as a liaison with the software company to solve your problem.

Often you may discover to your horror that none of the vendors has practical installation experience with the precise network configuration that your company requires. At that point, you may insist on serving as a "beta" site for the vendor (and perhaps the manufacturer). For so doing, you should receive a substantial discount in price in exchange for the experience and referral you may later provide.

Other safeguards that your company might want to insist on include a performance bond to be posted by the vendor and a payment schedule phased to correspond to the completion level of the network (including software and hardware). Your safeguards should be linked to a minimum level of performance that you specify in your RFP. If you fear serious degradation in response time with heavy activity, you might require a minimum response time for each of a certain number of workstations when all are involved simultaneously in a certain procedure. Several major network software companies including Novell and 3Com provide benchmark test reports that provide excellent "tests" that you can require your vendors to duplicate.

Since local area networks' maximum distance is directly related to their topology and media, be sure to include in the RFP a diagram indicating where workstations will be placed and their approximate distances from each other. Also—and this is essential—indicate where future growth will take place and whether these future workstations will require additional file servers and other peripherals.

III. Vendor Requirements
    A. Experience
        1. Company history. How long at present location?
        2. Experience installing local area networks
        3. Customer references for similar installations
    B. Service
        1. Number of factory-trained service technicians

   2. Ability to provide on-site service
      a. Repair or replace service within twenty-four hours
      b. Respond twenty-four hours/day
      c. Ability to respond within 2 hours
      d. Maintains a sufficient inventory of parts to provide adequate service
C. Ability to provide a LAN demonstration
   1. Software to be identical with ordered software
   2. Hardware to be identical with ordered hardware
   3. Benchmark tests to be conducted
D. Training
   1. Ability to provide basic user training
   2. Ability to provide training on all purchased software
   3. How much training is provided with network installation?
   4. What is the charge for additional network training?
   5. Is phone support included in the purchase price?
   6. What kind of training does the network administrator receive? How many people may take this training?
E. If multiple vendors are required for this network, who will assume responsibility for:
   1. Hardware training and network familiarization
   2. Hardware service
   3. Software training
   4. Software service

NETWORK MANAGEMENT

After a network has been installed and the network supervisor has been trained, he or she assumes full responsibility for network management. There are three major areas of responsibility when managing a local area network: security, efficiency, and maintenance. Network security responsibilities include providing user passwords, setting up user groups, and developing a set of reports on network usage. This last task is essential because supervisors need to be able to identify who has been accessing a directory. Since some network software permits "hidden" files and directories, network supervisors often use this technique to remove potential temptations from employees. Network software that permits remote dial-in workstations, such as Novell's NetWare, presents many opportunities for security breaches. One way to minimize security risks after hours at a remote network link is to restrict access from that workstation to certain file servers. If the network communications software permits them, modem callbacks are useful.

Network Efficiency

Network management also includes maximizing the system's overall efficiency. Since new and occasional users may have trouble with such routine network functions as the login, network supervisors must help them by establishing routines to follow. In the case of IBM's network software, these are customized batch files that need be written only once.

Novell's NetWare includes login scripts that may take a supervisor only a few minutes to write but that can save novices hours and eliminate a good deal of frustration.

Another area of network efficiency is software and hardware compatibility. The network supervisor assumes responsibility for installing new software requested by a user. This responsibility includes determining the program's compatibility with the network software, its compatibility with network printer drivers and default printers, and its compatibility with the version of DOS on the network. (Some network software such as Novell's NetWare permits different versions of DOS to reside in separate directories with their accompanying programs.)

Still another area of network efficiency that needs to be monitored by the network supervisor is network traffic statistics. By examining printer usage statistics, for example, the supervisor might determine that certain long reports need to be spooled and printed after peak hours. Heavy usage of certain accounting programs that place a premium on file-server access can slow the entire network. The supervisor might decide to add a separate file server for the accounting department in order to speed up the rest of the network.

A network supervisor can use certain tools to help monitor the system and maximize efficiency. IBM, Novell, and Corvus all offer network management software. Other companies such as J. A. Lomax Associates offer packages such as "Network Management Report Utilities" to provide detailed reports on file and volume usage and offer the capability of spooling to a printer from within an application program, of monitoring the number of open files, and of determining the degree of system degradation that would result with the addition of another workstation. Since network performance will grow sluggish as files become fragmented across the file server, most supervisors periodically back up all files and reformat the file server.

A major issue for all network supervisors is the development of a carefully planned schedule for network backups. Some network areas, such as accounting, might require backups twice a day. The entire system, of course, should be backed up on a daily basis. Most software will time stamp files, requiring backup only of those files that have been modified since the last backup. The supervisor should perform backups of all files every two weeks and place the six-week old backup in a safe off-site location.

Network Maintenance

Network management includes maintaining network efficiency, making regular backups of files, and keeping accurate maintenance records.

The third major management responsibility of a network supervisor is network maintenance. This doesn't necessarily mean physically repairing defective network components, although most supervisors of large systems do keep an inventory of basic components such as network adapter cards. Since many network software packages include diagnostics, a defective adapter card can often be identified and replaced immediately.

The network supervisor must keep accurate records of equipment serial numbers, service records and warranty ranges. *Figure 11-2* shows a workstation log that the supervisor should keep up-to-date. Notice that at a glance it is easy to see what the unit's service history has been and whether it is currently under warranty.

**Figure 11-1.
Network Workstation
Log**

Network Workstation

Location _____
Phone # _____
Contact _____
Model _____

Serial # _____
Vendor _____ Phone # _____
Users _____
_____

Date Installed _____
Service Contract Date _____ Expires _____ Contract # _____

Expansion Cards Installed

Card   Vendor   Serial #   Date

Service Record

Date   Service Required   Performed By

Finally, network supervisors need to keep logbooks that provide clear audit trails of all network changes. Password changes, alterations in user access, software updates that have been installed, and program additions or deletions should be noted and dated. Such a logbook should be kept under lock and key when not being used. Without such an administrative tool, the network represents a disaster waiting to happen.

WHAT HAVE WE LEARNED?

1. The first step in developing an RFP is to analyze the company's needs.
2. The geography of a company's proposed local area network will determine what kind of network topology and media are feasible.
3. Some network workstations should use auto-boot ROM chips and not have any floppy disk drives in order to ensure network security.
4. Most software generally is licensed for one user. Network applications require special network versions designated for a certain number of users or software "site licensing."
5. The three major network management responsibilities of a network supervisor are network security, efficiency, and maintenance.
6. To maintain network efficiency it is essential to monitor traffic statistics.

Quiz for Chapter 11

1. The first step of a company LAN needs analysis is to:
   a. examine the problems that currently exist that could be solved with a local area network.
   b. inventory all current software.
   c. inventory all current computer hardware.
   d. write a request for proposal (RFP).

2. The variety of microcomputers found in most companies creates a potential LAN problem because of:
   a. different costs for different components.
   b. service needs.
   c. NETBIOS incompatibility.
   d. different disk drive speed.

3. If a needs analysis reveals that several programs on the network will include large databases, this could mean:
   a. you will need a disk server rather than a file server.
   b. there might be a problem with file-server access speed.
   c. the database software better be able to handle long field names.
   d. the operating system cannot be DOS.

4. The geography of the company's building including where it will need workstations has a direct effect on:
   a. the network topology.
   b. the network's medium.
   c. the network's cost.
   d. all of the above.

5. For security purposes, a network workstation might include:
   a. a lock.
   b. an auto-boot ROM.
   c. no disk drives.
   d. all of the above.

6. In order to have the entire network use a specific software program, the company must obtain permission from the software company. This is known as:
   a. site licensing.
   b. software permission.
   c. multiple network copies (MNC).
   d. workstation access to software help (WASH).

7. The major problem with multiple vendors in a network environment is:
   a. the expense.
   b. the lack of quality.
   c. the lack of clear responsibility.
   d. network efficiency .

8. To help novice users, network supervisors often provide:
   a. their own set of manuals.
   b. a keyboard template.
   c. training at the manufacturer's home plant.
   d. login scripts and batch files.

9. Network supervisors use traffic statistics in order to:
   a. monitor network efficiency.
   b. avoid network data collisions.
   c. prevent network users from having accidents.
   d. produce reports that will improve automobile traffic safety.

10. In order to maintain control of a
network, network supervisors
must:

    a. keep a logbook.

    b. have excellent memories.

    c. be excellent politicians.

    d. have advanced degrees in
computer science.

Directory of Local Area Network Vendors

Alloy Computer Products
100 Pennsylvania Avenue
Framingham, Massachusetts 01701

AST Research
2121 Alton Avenue
Irvine, California 92714

AT&T Information Systems
1 Speedway Avenue
Morristown, New Jersey 07960

Banyan Systems
135 Flanders Road
Westboro, Massachusetts 01581

Corvus Systems
2100 Corvus Drive
San Jose, California 95124

Datapoint Corporation
9725 Datapoint Drive
San Antonio, Texas 78784

DCA
1000 Aldermann Drive
Alpharetta, Georgia 30201

Fox Research
7005 Corporate Way
Dayton, Ohio 45459

International Business Machines
P. O. Box 1328
Boca Raton, Florida 33432

IEEE*
10662 Los Vaqueros Circle
Los Alamitos, California 90720

Novell
748 North 1340 West
Orem, Utah 84057

PROLOGIC Management Systems
(Accounting software)
2020 East Speedway Boulevard
Tucson, Arizona 85719

Proteon
4 Tech Circle
Natick, Massachusetts 01700

The Software Link
8601 Dunwoody Place Suite 632
Atlanta, Georgia 30338

3Com
1365 Shorebird Way
Mountainview, California 94039

TLB (Solomon III)
1218 Commerce Parkway
Findley, Ohio 45839

Ungermann-Bass
2560 Mission College Boulevard
Santa Clara, California 95050

* Source of information on IEEE standards

Glossary

ACK: A positive acknowledgment sent from a transporter card when it successfully receives a signal.

Active Junction Box: A repeater used by Corvus networks.

Active Token Monitor: The workstation that assumes responsibility for network management in IBM's Token Ring Network.

Application Layer: The layer of the OSI LAN model concerned with application programs such as electronic mail, database managers, and file-server software.

ARM: Asynchronous Response Mode. Stations send messages whenever they desire to transmit without waiting for a poll bit.

ASCII: American Standard Code for Information Interchange. A character code used by microcomputers.

Asynchronous Communications Server: Provides the capability for network workstations to access ASCII applications via switched communications lines.

Automatic Rollback: Under TTS, when a system fails, the database is reconstructed at the point just prior to the transaction during which the failure took place.

Backbone: A high-speed link joining together several network bridges.

Background Tasks: The tasks performed by other network users under PC Network.

Baseband: Single-channel coaxial cable.

Batch File: A file containing commands that can cause several different programs to execute automatically.

Beacon: A special network signal indicating the address of a node immediately upstream from a defective node.

BIOS: Basic Input/Output System. ROM software.

Bit Stuffing: The insertion of a 0-bit to ensure that no data contains more than five straight 0s.

BRI: Basic Rate Interface. Under ISDN, used to service small-capacity devices such as terminals.

Bridge: A connection between two networks.

Broadband: Coaxial cable capable of carrying several signals simultaneously on different channels.

Broadcast Messages: Messages sent to all computers on a network.

BSC: Binary Synchronous Communication. A synchronous protocol used on some older IBM mainframe computers.

Bus: A data highway. This term is also used to designate a simple linear-shaped local area network.

Callback Modems: Modems designed to call back a remote caller to verify identity for security purposes.

CCIT: Consultative Committee for International Telephone and Telegraph.

CCITT X.25: An X.25 standard for data packets sent to public switched networks. This standard corresponds to the OSI's first three layers.

CCITT X.25: Protocol for interface between DTE and DCE for terminals operating in the packet mode on a public data network.

CCITT X.28: Protocol for DTE/DCE interface for a start-stop mode DTE accessing the packet assembly/disassembly facility (PAD) on a public data network situated in the same country.

CCITT X.29: Procedures for the exchange of control information and user data between a packet assembly/disassembly facility (PAD) and a packet model DTE or another PAD.

CCITT X.3: Protocol for the packet assembly/disassembly facility in a public data network.

CCITT X.75: Terminal and transmit call control procedures and data transfer system on international circuits between packet-switched networks.

Centralized File Server: A single file server that serves a local area network.

Cladding: A layer of glass that surrounds optic fibers in fiber-optic cables.

Closet Star: Rooms connected under STARLAN using several NEUs and a wiring closet.

Contention Network: Workstations compete for the right to send a message.

CSMA/CD: Carrier Sense Multiple Access with Collision Detection. A method of avoiding data collisions on a local area network.

DCE: Data Communication Equipment; generally refers to modems.

Dedicated File Server: A file server that performs only that function and performs no computing functions.

Directory Hashing: File-server software that maps all directory files and keeps this information in RAM.

Disk Caching: File server keeps often-requested files in RAM for rapid response to workstation requests.

Disk Server: A hard disk used to share files with several users. Usually programs are single user (only one user may use them at a time).

Distributed File Serving: Multiple file servers that speed up operations on a local area network.

Distributed Processing: Distributing data processing to several computers rather than one central computer.

DTE: Data Terminal Equipment; generally consists of terminals or computers.

Duplexed Drives: A system fault tolerant technique in which virtually all hardware is duplicated, including disk controller, interface, and power supply.

EBCDIC: The Extended Binary Coded Decimal Interchange Code. A character code used by IBM's larger computers.

Echo Packet: A packet sent from a Transporter Card to see if another node is functioning.

Elevator Seeking: A file server determines in which order to execute file requests based upon the current location of the disk heads.

EtherLink: A circuit card required in each workstation's expansion bus on a 3Com local area network.

EtherSeries: 3Com software designed primarily for a local area network utilizing single-user software running under DOS 2.XX.

FAT: File Allocation Table. A table that helps a disk server or file server keep track of where particular files are located.

FDDI: The fiber data distributed interface of fiber-optic cabling.

File Locking: Software that locks a file so that only one user may use it at a time.

File Server: A hard disk with software that permits it to maintain its own FAT and provide files to nodes while appearing transparent to these users.

Foreground Tasks: The tasks a user performs under PC Net.

FSK: Frequency Shift Keying. A technique to modulate ones and zeroes and speed up transmission by shifting between two close frequencies.

Gateway PC: A PC emulating an IBM cluster controller and permitting communication between network nodes and an IBM mainframe computer.

HLDC: High-Level Data Link Control Procedures. This protocol defines standards for linking a DTE and a DCE.

IEEE: The Institute for Electrical and Electronic Engineers.

IEEE 802.3: The industry standard for a bus local area network using CSMA/CD.

IEEE 802.4: The industry standard for a token bus local area network.

IEEE 802.5: The industry standard for a token ring local area network.

IEEE 802.6: The industry standard for metropolitan area networks.

Inbound Band: Carries data from a LAN node to the head end.

ISDN: Integrated Services Digital Network. A CCITT model for the eventual integration of voice and data and a universal interface for networks.

ISN: Information Systems Network. AT&T's high-speed network featuring integrated voice and data transmission.

ISO: International Standards Organization.

Jam: A signal sent through a network indicating that there has been a data collision.

LLC: The logical link sublayer of the data link layer of the OSI model.

Local Printer: A printer attached to a microcomputer that prints this computer's documents only and performs no network printing functions.

Login Script: A predetermined set of steps performed to customize a network environment whenever a user logs on.

LU: Logical units. These can represent end users, application programs, or other devices. Communication under SNA is among LUs.

LU 6.2: A protocol that will make it possible to have peer-to-peer communications under SNA.

MAC: The media access control sublayer of the data link layer of the OSI model.

Mirrored Drives: A system fault tolerant technique in which a hard disk mirrors everything on the file server.

MSAU: Multistation Access Unit. A wiring concentrator permitting up to eight network workstations on an IBM local area network.

MTBF: Mean time before failure. A standard used to evaluate a product's reliability.

Multimode Fiber: Fiber-optic cabling consisting of several fibers.

NAK: A negative acknowledgment signal sent from a Transporter Card when it detects an error.

NAU: Network Addressable Unit. Logical units, physical units, and system services control points under SNA.

Network Adapter Card: Circuit card required in the expansion bus of workstation under IBM's PC Network.

Network Layer: The layer of the OSI LAN model that establishes protocols for packets, message priorities, and network traffic control.

NEU: Network Expansion Unit. A STARLAN expansion unit can link eleven workstations in a star topology.

NIU: A Network Interface Unit containing two RS-232C ports. Used in a STARLAN network.

Node: An individual local area network workstation.

Non-dedicated File Server: A file server that also functions as an independent microcomputer.

NRM: Normal Response Mode. When a central computer receives a message that a station wishes to send it sends it a poll bit.

NRU: A Network Repeater Unit used under STARLAN to prevent signal degradation.

NTU: Network Translator Unit. Performs frequency translation on an IBM PC Network.

OSI Model: Open Systems Interconnection protocols for establishing a local area network.

Outbound Band: Carries data from the head end to LAN nodes.

Partitioning: Dividing a hard disk into several user volumes or areas.

Path Control Network: Responsible under SNA for identifying addresses of devices that wish to converse and then establishing a network path for them.

PBX: Private Branch Exchange. A sophisticated telephone system.

Physical Layer: The layer of the OSI LAN model that establishes protocols for voltage, data transmission timing, and rules for "handshaking."

Pipes: A volume used in a Corvus network as a holding area for files before they are sent to a network printer or another workstation.

PMD: The physical media-dependent layer of the fiber data distributed interface found in fiber-optic cabling.

Presentation Layer: The layer of the OSI LAN model concerned with protocols for network security, file transfers, and format functions.

PRI: Primary Rate Interface. Used under ISDN to service large-capacity devices such as PBXs.

Print Spooler: Software that creates a buffer where files to be printed can be stored while they wait their turn.

Protocol: A set of rules or procedures commonly agreed upon by industry-wide committees such as the IEEE.

PU: A physical unit. This represents something tangible such as a terminal or intelligent controller under SNA.

Public Volume: An area of a hard disk that contains information that may be shared by several users.

Read-Only: Files that can be read but cannot be changed.

Record Locking: Software that locks a record so that several users can share the same file but cannot share the same record.

Repeaters: Devices on local area networks that rebroadcast a signal to prevent its degradation.

RFP: Request for Proposals.

RJE: Remote Job Entry. The sending of information in batch form from a remote site often unattended by a user to an IBM mainframe.

Rollforward Recovery: Under TTS, a complete log is kept of all transactions to ensure that everything can be recovered.

Room Star: A star-like topology clustered around an NEU under STARLAN.

SCSI: Small Computer System Interface. An interface used to connect additional disk drives or tape backup units to a local area network.

SDLC: Synchronous Data Link Control. A subset of HDLC protocol used by IBM computers running under SNA.

Semaphore: A flag that is set in order to make a file local and prevent two users from using the file simultaneously, thereby destroying it.

Session: Under SNA a logical and physical path connecting two NAUs for data transmission.

Session Layer: The layer of the OSI LAN model concerned with network management functions including passwords and network monitoring and reporting.

Site Licensing: Software that is licensed to be used only at a particular location.

SMDR: Station Message Detail Reporting.

SNA: System Network Architecture. The architecture used by IBM's minicomputers and mainframe computers.

Split Seeks: With duplexed drives the system checks to see which disk system can respond more quickly.

Splitter: A device that divides a signal into two different paths.

SRPI: Under SNA, the Server/Requester Programming Interface allows PC applications to request services from IBM mainframes.

SSCP: System Services Control Point. An SNA network manager for a single SNA domain.

Star: A network topology physically resembling a star. This network built around a central computer fails completely if the main computer fails.

Synchronous Transmission: The sending of information continuously in packet form rather than one byte at a time.

System Fault Tolerant: Duplication of hardware and data to ensure that failure of part of a network will not result in network downtime.

Token: A data packet used to transmit information on a token ring network.

Topology: The physical arrangement or shape of a network.

Transient Error: A "soft" network transmission error that is often intermittent and easily corrected by retransmission.

Transport Layer: The layer of the OSI LAN model concerned with protocols for error recognition and recovery as well as regulation of information flow.

Transporter Card: The network adapter card required in each Corvus network workstation.

TSI: Time Slice Intervals. The way a file server divides its time.

TTS: Transaction Tracking System. A way to ensure data integrity on multiuser databases.

Twisted-Pair Wire: Two insulated wires twisted together so that each wire faces the same amount of interference from the environment.

Wire Center: Connections that enable network administrators to add and remove network workstations without disrupting network operations.

Workstation: A network node. Often such nodes do not contain disk drives.

Bibliography

An Introduction to Local Area Networks, IBM Publication GC 20-8203-1.

AT&T STARLAN Network Custom Guide, AT&T Information Systems Publication 999-350-00115.

Bartee, Thomas C., editor, *Data Communications, Networks, and Systems,* Howard W. Sams, 1985.

Dixon, R. C., Strole, N. C., and Markov, J. D., A Token Ring Network for Local Data Communications, *IBM Systems Journal,* Vol 22, Nos. 1&2 (1983), pp. 47–62.

EtherSeries User's Guide, 3Com Publication 0659-03.

General Technical Information Omninet Local Area Network, Corvus Publication 7100-0661401.

Green, James Harry, *Local Area Networks: A User's Guide for Business Professionals,* Scott, Foresman and Company, 1985.

IBM PC Network Program User's Guide, IBM Publication 6361559.

IBM Token Ring Network: A Functional Perspective, IBM Publication G520-6062-1.

IBM Token Ring Network Decision, IBM Publication G320-9438-1.

IBM Token Ring Network: Introduction and Planning Guide, IBM Publication GA27-3677-01.

IBM Token Ring Network PC Products Description and Installation, IBM Publication GG 24-173900.

Introduction to Information Systems Network (ISN), AT&T Information Systems Publication 999-740-1011S.

Network Manager's Guide for the IBM PC, Corvus Publication 7100-06074-02.

Network User's Guide for the IBM PC, Corvus Publication 7100-06072-02.

O'Brien, Bill. Network Management: Tips & Traps, *PC World* (September 1986), pp. 228–237.

Stamper, David. *Business Data Communications,*Benjamin/Cummings, 1986.

STARLAN Network Application Programmer's Reference Manual, AT&T Information Systems Publication 999-802-215IS.

STARLAN Network Design Guide, AT&T Information Systems Publication 999-809-101-IS.

STARLAN Network Introduction, AT&T Information Systems Publication 999-809-100IS.

STARLAN Network Technical Reference Manual, AT&T Information Systems Publication 999-300-208IS.

STARLAN 6300 Training Package, AT&T Information Systems Publication 999-809-117IS.

Strole, Norman C. A Local Communications Network Based on Interconnected Token-Access Rings: A Tutorial, *IBM Journal of Research Development,* Vol 27, No. 5 (September 1983), pp. 481–496.

3+Backup User Guide, 3Com Publication 1912-00.

3+Mail User Guide, 3Com Publication 1911-00.

3+Share User Guide, 3Com Publication 1694-00.

Index

Answers to Quizzes

Chapter 1

1. a
2. b
3. a
4. b
5. d
6. a
7. c
8. b

Chapter 2

1. c
2. c
3. b
4. b
5. b
6. b
7. d
8. a
9. b
10. c
11. a
12. c
13. a
14. b
15. c
16. b
17. b
18. b
19. d
20. a

Chapter 3

1. b
2. b
3. d
4. c
5. b
6. c
7. a
8. c
9. d
10. c
11. c

12. b
13. b
14. c
15. b
16. b
17. d
18. a
19. a
20. a

Chapter 4

1. b
2. b
3. b
4. a
5. b
6. b
7. a
8. c
9. a
10 b
11. c
12. c
13. b
14. a
15. c
16. b
17. a
18. c

Chapter 5

1. c
2. b
3. d
4. a
5. b
6. a
7. a
8. b
9. b
10. c
11. a
12. c
13. b
14. d

15. b
16. b
17. a
18. d

Chapter 6

1. a
2. c
3. c
4. c
5. d
6. c
7. d
8. d
9. a
10. b
11. b
12. a
13. a
14. b
15. d
16. a
17. b
18. a
19. d
20. b

Chapter 7

1. b
2. c
3. a
4. b
5. a
6. d
7. c
8. d
9. a
10. b
11. b
12. a
13. a
14. b
15. c
16. b
17. a

18. a
19. b
20. b

Chapter 8

1. c
2. d
3. b
4. c
5. b
6. d
7. c
8. b
9. b
10. a
11. c
12. a
13. c
14. c
15. c
16. c
17. a
18. a
19. b
20. c

Chapter 9

1. d
2. b
3. b
4. b
5. d
6. b
7. b
8. d
9. a
10. c
11. c
12. a

Chapter 10

1. c
2. d
3. a
4. c

5. **b**
6. **b**
7. **d**
8. **b**

Chapter 11

1. **a**
2. **c**
3. **b**
4. **d**
5. **d**
6. **a**
7. **c**
8. **d**
9. **a**
10. **a**

HOWARD W. SAMS & COMPANY
HAYDEN BOOKS

Related Titles

Understanding Expert Systems
Louis E. Frenzel, Jr.

Understanding Advanced Solid State Electronics
Don L. Cannon

Understanding Artificial Intelligence, Second Edition
Dan Shafer

Understanding Automation Systems, Second Edition
Robert F. Farwell and Neil M. Schmitt

Understanding Automotive Electronics, Third Edition
William B. Ribbens

Understanding C
Carl Townsend

Understanding Communications Systems, Second Edition
Don L. Cannon and Gerald Luecke

Understanding CAD/CAM
Daniel J. Bowman and Annette C. Bowman

Understanding Computer Science, Second Edition
Roger S. Walker

Understanding Computer Science Applications
Roger S. Walker

Understanding Data Communications, Second Edition
Revised by Gil Held

Understanding Digital Electronics, Second Edition
Gene W. McWhorter

Understanding Digital Troubleshooting, Second Edition
Don L. Cannon

Understanding Electricity and Electronics Circuits
David L. Heiserman

Understanding Electricity and Electronics Principles
David L. Heiserman

Understanding Fiber Optics
Jeff Hecht

Understanding Microprocessors, Second Edition
Don L. Cannon and Gerald Luecke

Understanding MS-DOS®
Kate O'Day and John Angermeyer, The Waite Group

Understanding Security Electronics
Joseph J. Carr

Understanding Solid State Electronics, Fourth Edition
William E. Hafford and Gene W. McWhorter

Understanding Telephone Electronics, Second Edition
John L. Fike and George E. Friend

For the retailer nearest you, or to order directly from the publisher, call 800-428-SAMS. In Indiana, Alaska, and Hawaii call 317-298-5699.

Understanding Expert Systems
Louis E. Frenzel, Jr.

This book explains how an expert system can function like an expert or intelligent consultant and answer questions, solve problems, and help make decisions.

This new Understanding Series title is suited for the technically inclined professional or manager interested in artificial intelligence and its subset, expert systems.

With the self-instructional format, readers can gain an understanding of expert systems, how they work, where they are used, and how to develop them. The material is completely illustrated, clear, concise, and application oriented. It also has marginal notes and review questions and answers.

Topics covered include:

- Expert Systems: The Big Picture
- Types of Expert Systems
- Applications of Expert Systems
- Knowledge Representation and Search
- How Expert Systems Work
- Expert System Development Tools
- How to Develop an Expert System
- References: Expert System Tool Vendors, AI Language Vendors, Publications, Glossary, and Quiz Answers

288 Pages, 7 x 9, Softbound
ISBN: 0-672-27065-X
No. 27065, $17.95

Understanding Advanced Solid State Electronics
Don L. Cannon

No single invention has influenced the electronics industry more than the integrated circuit. This volume covers all the major benefits of IC technology for the experimenter, serious hobbyist, and electronics technician in an easily-understood, fully-illustrated text for individualized learning.

It covers the advances in integrated circuits including the latest logic devices, standard cells, gate arrays, and microprocessors.

Basic concepts, progress review of IC fabrication technology, and an update of modern design approaches and IC performance (both digital and linear) are presented in ten chapters.

Topics covered include:

- Integrated Circuit Technology
- Logic Circuits
- Logic Cells and Arrays
- Microprocessors
- Digital Signal Processing
- Graphics Processors
- Communications Processors
- Bit-Slice Systems
- Linear Integrated Circuits
- Interface Integrated Circuits

272 Pages, 7 x 9, Softbound
ISBN: 0-672-27058-7
No. 27058, $17.95

Understanding Artificial Intelligence
Henry C. Mishkoff

Artificial intelligence (AI) provides the potential to model and simulate human intelligence in reasoning and decision-making. The potential impact AI could have on productivity and efficiency is staggering.

This book provides an introduction and basic understanding of this new technology. The book covers definitions, history, expert systems, natural language processing, and LISP machines. You'll also learn the specific requirements of AI hardware and the thrust of AI research.

Topics covered include:

- An Introduction to Artificial Intelligence
- History of Artificial Intelligence
- Expert Systems
- Natural Language Processing
- Amplifying Human Capabilities
- Artificial Intelligence Applications
- Symbolic Processing
- Expert System Development Tools
- LISP Machines
- Continuing Efforts in Artificial Intelligence

258 Pages, 7 x 9, Softbound
ISBN: 0-672-27021-8
No. 27021, $17.95

Understanding Automation Systems, Second Edition
Farwell and Schmitt

For the newcomer, here is an in-depth look at the functions that make up automation systems—open loop, closed loop, continuous and semi-continuous process, and discrete parts. This book explains programmable systems and how to use microcomputers and programmable controllers. It surveys the types of robots available and their typical applications.

This is a book for anyone interested in the subject of automation systems, rich with insight and facts, yet written in everyday language that the non-engineer can easily understand.

Topics covered include:

- History and Importance of Industrial Control
- Industrial Control Fundamentals
- Basic Control System Hardware
- Basic Electronic Functions
- Software/Programming Languages
- Continuous Process Control
- Examples of Semi-Continuous (Job Shop) System Control
- Discrete Parts Manufacture Using Programmable Controllers
- A New Dimension—Robots
- Automation Example
- Future Trends and Reliability

280 Pages, 7 x 9, Softbound
ISBN: 0-672-27014-5
No. 27014, $17.95

Visit your local book retailer, use the order form provided, or call 800-428-SAMS.

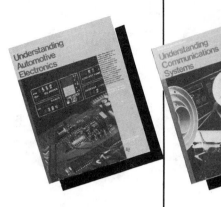

Understanding Automotive Electronics, Third Edition
William B. Ribbens

A step-by-step guide to the latest electronic instrumentation and control devices for automobiles, this tutorial clearly explains how electronics technology functions in today's environment. Using this self-paced, individualized learning approach, the reader soon understands the complexity and breadth of automotive electronics.

The book is ideal for the beginning-intermediate level automotive mechanic, industrial training student, or "backyard" automotive repair hobbyist. Providing the necessary background in electronics and automotive basics, the book details electronic instrumentation and explains the microprocessor and its pivotal role in automobile performance. It includes scores of detailed illustrations for such functions as diagnostics, sensors, engine control, and motion control—all presented in an easily understood, easy-to-learn format.

Topics covered include:

■ Automotive Fundamentals
■ The Systems Approach to Control and Instrumentation
■ Electronics Fundamentals
■ Microcomputer Instrumentation and Control
■ Computer-Aided Diagnostics
■ Sensors and Actuators
■ Electronic Engine Control Basics
■ Typical Digital Engine Control System
■ Vehicle Motion Control
■ Automotive Instrumentation
■ Future of Automotive Electronics Systems
■ Glossary
■ Answers to Quizzes

302 Pages, 7 x 9, Softbound
ISBN: 0-672-27064-6
No. 27064, $17.95

Understanding Communications Systems, Second Edition
Cannon and Luecke

In an easy-to-understand, self-paced learning format, this book presents a fascinating look at the world of electronic communications and its impact on our everyday lives. The book explores many of the systems that are used every day—AM/FM radio, telephone, TV, data communications by computer, facsimile, and satellite. It explains how information is converted into electrical signals, transmitted to distant locations, and converted back to the original information.

Topics covered include:

■ The World of Communications
■ Using Electrical Signals for Communications
■ Basic System Functions and Conversions
■ The Communications Spectrum
■ Telegraph and Telephone System
■ Radio and Television Systems
■ Computer Networks and Systems
■ Facsimile
■ Satellite Communications Systems

288 Pages, 7 x 9, Softbound
ISBN: 0-672-27016-1
No. 27016, $17.95

Understanding CAD/CAM
Bowman and Bowman

For the newcomer to CAD/CAM, here's an in-depth look at this marriage between engineering design and manufacturing. From multi-color graphs and charts to 3-D depictions of machine parts, you will get the basic concepts and fundamentals underlying applications and future considerations.

Each description of this state-of-the-art communications tool is in everyday language that makes the book ideally suited for self-paced, individualized learning. Chapter quizzes and marginal notes allow for fast learning and increased retention.

The book discusses points to consider when buying a CAD/CAM system, including initial cost justification, purchase, and implementation. Training, system maintenance, and security are also discussed.

Topics covered include:

■ CAD/CAM Overview
■ Anatomy of a Graphics Workstation
■ Input/Output
■ Data Highways
■ Artificial Intelligence
■ The Engineer's Dialogue with the CRT
■ CAD and the Personal Computer
■ Applications: New Directions for Engineering
■ The Third Wave in Engineering (Cost Justification)

304 Pages, 7 x 9, Softbound
ISBN: 0-672-27068-4
No. 27068, $17.95

Understanding Digital Electronics, Second Edition
Gene W. McWhorter

Learn why digital circuits are used. Discover how AND, OR, and NOT digital circuits make decisions, store information, and convert information into electronic language. Find out how digital integrated circuits are made and how they are used in microwave ovens, gasoline pumps, video games, cash registers, and other high-technology products.

Topics covered include:

■ Let's Look at a System
■ How Digital Circuits Make Decisions
■ Building Blocks that Make Decisions
■ Building Blocks with Memory
■ Why Digital?
■ Digital Integrated Circuits
■ Mass Storage and Digital Systems
■ How Digital Systems Function
■ Programmed Digital Systems
■ Digital Electronics Today and in the Future

264 Pages, 7 x 9, Softbound
ISBN: 0-672-27013-7
No. 27013, $17.95

Visit your local book retailer, use the order form provided, or call 800-428-SAMS.

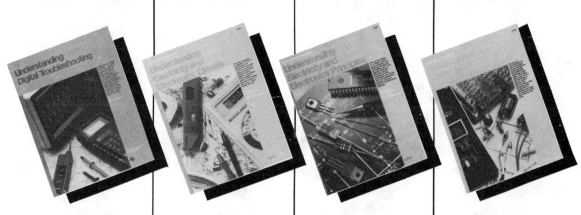

Understanding Digital Troubleshooting, Second Edition
Don L. Cannon

Digital electronic systems are more reliable than the systems they replace, yet, at some point, they will need repair and maintenance. This book provides an insight into this high technology world in a language that both technicians and non-engineers can understand. It presents the basic concepts and fundamental techniques needed to locate faults in digital systems and how to repair them.

- Digital Systems Fundamentals
- Digital Systems Functions
- Troubleshooting Fundamentals
- Combinational Logic Problems
- Sequential Logic Problems
- Memory Problems
- Input/Output Problems
- Basic Timing Problems
- Advanced Techniques

272 Pages, 7 x 9, Softbound
ISBN: 0-672-27015-3
No. 27015, $17.95

Understanding Electricity and Electronics Circuits
David Heiserman

Thorough, concise, and priced for the beginner or student, this self-instructional format of modern fundamental circuit principles of electricity and electronics gives complete information in a compact form.

It includes generous illustrations and key point notations in the margins as well as multiple choice, self-check questions with answers in the back. Theory is combined with practical examples and photographs. Learning can be easy!

Topics covered include:

- Understanding Basic Principles
- Sources of Electrical Energy
- The Simple Electrical Circuit
- DC Series Circuits
- DC Parallel Circuits
- Combined Series and Parallel Circuits
- Electromagnetism
- What Is Alternating Current?
- Calculating Resistance
- Inductance
- RL Circuits
- The Effect of Capacitance
- RC Circuits
- RLC Circuits
- Transformer Action
- Some Applications of Electronic Circuits
- Appendices: Glossary of Terms, Index, and Quiz Answers

328 Pages, 7 x 9, Softbound
ISBN: 0-672-27062-5
No. 27062, $17.95

Understanding Electricity and Electronics Principles
David Heiserman

A self-instructional format of modern fundamental principles of electricity and electronics, this book includes generous illustrations and keypoint notations in the margins as well as multiple choice, self-check questions and answers.

For the electronic or electrical hobbyist or student with no prior experience with either topic, this book combines theory with practical examples and illustrations for easy learning and increased retention.

Topics covered include:

- The World of Electricity and Electronics
- Basic Electrical Circuits
- How to Use Meters
- The Basic Telephone System
- Reading Diagrams
- Understanding Resistors
- How to Solder
- Understanding Transformers
- Understanding Capacitors
- Understanding Diodes and Transistors
- Understanding Integrated Circuits
- How Cathode Ray Tubes Work
- Basic Circuit Actions
- Audio Amplifiers
- Radio Transmitters and Receivers
- Television Transmitters and Receivers
- Digital Circuits and Computers
- Appendices: Glossary of Terms, Index, and Quiz Answers

256 Pages, 7 x 9, Softbound
ISBN: 0-672-27061-7
No. 27061, $17.95

Understanding Fiber Optics
Jeff Hecht

Fiber optics—an inexpensive medium for moving masses of data without electromagnetic interference—has revolutionized the telephone industry.

Anyone interested in fiber optic technology—technicians, engineers, or hobbyists—will find this an easy-to-comprehend tutorial. Components, concepts, systems, and principles are explained in a way that is easy to understand and use.

The latest communications applications are highlighted, including telephone, computers, LAN, video, and automotive. Transmitters, receivers, and call couplers are also discussed.

Topics covered include:

- Fundamentals and Applications of Fiber Optics
- Types of Fiber
- Cabling
- Transmitters and Receivers
- Connectors, Splicers, and Couplers
- Integrated Optics
- Instrumentation
- Long- and Short-Haul Applications
- Cable TV and Video
- Computers and LANs
- Optical Interconnection
- Auto and Aircraft Systems
- Non-Communication Applications

456 Pages, 7 x 9, Softbound
ISBN: 0-672-27066-8
No. 27066, $17.95

Visit your local book retailer, use the order form provided, or call 800-428-SAMS.

The Waite Group's Understanding MS-DOS®
O'Day and Angermeyer, The Waite Group

MS-DOS is a very powerful and intricate operating system with millions of users. This operating system can be explored by beginning programmers in a hands-on approach at the keyboard.

Understanding MS-DOS introduces the use and operation of this popular operating system for those with little previous experience in computer hardware or software. The fundamentals of the operating system such as EDLIN, tree-structured directories and pathnames, and such advanced features as redirection and filtering are presented in a way that is easy-to-understand and use.

Topics covered include:

- Organizing Data and Files
- Redirecting Input and Output
- Using the Text Editor EDLIN to Create and Edit Files
- Special Function Keys and Key Combinations
- Creating Batch Files of Often Repeated Commands
- Create and Use Tree Structured Directories

240 Pages, 7 x 9, Softbound
ISBN: 0-672-27067-6
No. 27067, $17.95

Understanding Security Electronics
Joseph J. Carr

This book details how to select, install, and maintain a security system. A self-instructional format is used to describe the theory of operation, design, and applications of electronic security devices and systems.

With this information homeowners, business professionals, and security personnel will be able to safeguard property on a do-it-yourself basis.

Electronics technicians and engineers will be able to apply their knowledge and experience to the field of security. Circuit designs and theory are provided for various control elements of security systems, and the advantages and disadvantages of various systems are discussed.

Topics covered include:

- Electronic Intrusion Alarms
- Electromechanical Detectors
- Photoelectric and Infrared Detectors
- Ultrasonic and Microwave Intrusion Detectors
- Proximity Detectors
- Audio and Visual Monitoring
- Alarm and Signaling Systems
- Access Control
- Holdup and Assault Alarms
- Custom Integrated Circuits
- Computers in Security Systems
- Detection of Objects
- Automobile Protection
- Computer Crime
- Electrical Eavesdropping and Secure Communications
- Personnel Identification

304 Pages, 7 x 9, Softbound
ISBN: 0-672-27069-2
No. 27069, $17.95

Understanding Solid State Electronics, Fourth Edition
Hafford and McWhorter

This book explains complex concepts such as electricity, semiconductor theory, how electronic circuits make decisions, how integrated circuits are made. It helps you develop a basic knowledge of semiconductors and solid-state electronics. A glossary simplifies technical terms.

- What Electricity Does in Every Every Electrical System
- Basic Circuit Functions in the Systems
- How Circuits Make Decisions
- Relating Semiconductors to Systems
- Diodes: What They Do and How They Work
- Diode Performance and Specifications
- Transistors: How They Are Made
- PNP Transistor and Transistor-Specifications
- Thyristors and Optoelectronics
- Introduction to Integrated Circuits
- Digital Integrated Circuits
- MOS and Large Scale Integrated Circuits
- Linear Integrated Circuits

286 Pages, 7 x 9, Softbound
ISBN: 0-672-27012-9
No. 27012, $17.95

Understanding Telephone Electronics, Second Edition
Fike and Friend

Bringing lower costs and enhanced capabilities to telephone communications, digital electronics, semi-conductor integrated circuits, microprocessors and microcomputers are rapidly changing today's analog systems to tomorrow's digital systems. This book explains how the conventional telephone system works and how parts of the system are gradually being replaced by state-of-the-art electronics. Written in an easy-to-understand format, fully-illustrated, and ideal for self-study, the book will explain the concepts and principles being applied to one of your vital communications links.

Topics covered include:

- The Telephone System
- The Conventional Telephone Set
- Electronic Speech Circuits
- A Microcomputer in the Telephone
- Digital Transmission Techniques
- Electronics in the Central Office
- Network Transmission
- Modems—Telephone Service for Computers
- Wireless Telephones

288 Pages, 7 x 9, Softbound
ISBN: 0-672-27018-8
No. 27018, $17.95

Visit your local book retailer, use the order form provided, or call 800-428-SAMS.